MW01536736

The People's Bible Teachings

CHRISTIAN WORSHIP

God Gives His Gospel Gifts

Johnold J. Strey

Johnold J. Strey

NORTHWESTERN PUBLISHING HOUSE
Milwaukee, Wisconsin

Northwestern Publishing House
N16W23379 Stone Ridge Drive, Waukesha WI 53188-1108
www.nph.net
© 2021 Northwestern Publishing House
Published 2021
Printed in the United States of America
ISBN 978-0-8100-2943-9
ISBN 978-0-8100-294-6 (e-book)

21 22 23 24 25 26 27 28 29 30   10 9 8 7 6 5 4 3 2 1

Table of Contents

Editor's Preface

The People's Bible Teachings is a series of books on all of the main doctrinal teachings of the Bible.

Following the pattern set by the People's Bible series, these books are written especially for laypeople. Theological terms, when used, are explained in everyday language so that people can understand them. The authors show how Christian doctrine is drawn directly from clear passages of Scripture and then how those doctrines apply to people's faith and lives. Most important, these books show how every teaching of Scripture points to Christ, our only Savior.

The authors of the People's Bible Teachings are parish pastors and professors who have had years of experience teaching the Bible. They are men of scholarship and practical insight.

We take this opportunity to express our gratitude to Rev. Bryan Gerlach, Director of the WELS Commission on Worship, and Rev. Michael Schultz, currently serving as the WELS Hymnal Project Director, for serving as consultants for this volume of the series. Their insights and assistance have been invaluable.

We pray that the Lord will use these volumes to help his people grow in their faith, knowledge, and understanding of his saving teachings, which he has revealed to us in the Bible. To God alone be the glory.

Curtis A. Jahn
Series Editor

Introduction

Few topics generate as much debate and discussion among Christians as public worship. A church that wants to promote itself in its community typically advertises its worship times more than anything else in its ministry. Christians often identify or describe other churches by the style and content of their services, perhaps even more than a careful examination of official confessions of faith. And there is certainly no shortage of opinions about best practices in Christian worship!

This book is humbly offered to the overall discussion of Christian worship, especially among Lutherans. The author makes no pretenses that reading this book will end all debates and discussion about worship! But this final volume published in the People's Bible Teachings series of books will help us to approach the subject of worship from biblical, historical, and practical perspectives.

In the pages that follow, we will explore the wisdom of God's Word, the experience of the church's history, and practical matters facing the church in its worship life today. We will consider several biblical principles that guide what we do in worship. We will learn about time-tested worship practices and patterns that have come down to us today. Finally, we will examine an assortment of practical matters that relate to Christian worship in the 21st century.

The title of this book may raise an honest question among its primary audience—members of churches that belong to the Wisconsin Evangelical Lutheran Synod (WELS). The first two words in the title of this book are also the first two words in the previous and current hymnals of the WELS—*Christian Worship: A Lutheran Hymnal* (1993) and *Christian Worship: Hymnal* (2021). Although the titles are similar, this volume is not written as a commentary on either hymnal but as an overall study of public worship. This volume will frequently cite *Christian Worship: Hymnal* (2021), but the biblical principles and practical lessons in this book are useful regardless of the specific hymnal or worship resources used in a congregation.

The subject of Christian worship is a wide and diverse study. We can hardly begin to plumb its depths, but let's begin where any Christian discussion should begin: with the truths in God's Word. May the Holy Spirit fill us with greater faith and insight as we take up this study of Christian worship!

1

The Purpose of Worship[1]

Imagine for a moment that you have just moved to a new community. Besides unpacking all your possessions and arranging your home, you need to make a number of personal choices. Who will be your new family doctor? What activities do your children want to become involved in? Are there community clubs or groups you would like to join? Where will you make your new church home?

Many readers of this book would answer the last question by finding a church that belongs to the same denomination as their previous church. Their intent is to join a church that shares the same confession of faith that they have. They want to find a church that is committed to preaching the forgiveness of sins through the saving work of Jesus Christ. They want a church that teaches the gospel faithfully and properly administers the Sacraments of Holy Baptism and Holy Communion.

Others looking for a church may use different criteria. They might look for a church with particular programs. They might look for a church that caters to a certain age group or to people in similar life situations as theirs. They might look for a church that offers a worship experience to their liking.

A simple internet search for "churches near me" is enough to discover how worship differs greatly from church to church. Even the names that churches use for their weekly services can indicate something significant. Many Lutheran congregations call their weekly gathering *worship* or *service*. The term *Mass* is used primarily by Roman Catholic congregations and implies a particular order of worship. Some churches use the word *Eucharist*, which refers to a celebration of Holy Communion.

The names worship, service, Mass, and Eucharist are traditional titles for Christian worship. But as you peruse your internet search results, other nontraditional terms stand out. One church calls its Saturday evening service "Saturday Night Live," a reference to the television show by the same name and an implication that this service will be informal and entertaining. Another church advertises a *blue jeans service*, implying that worshipers will be dressed casually and will experience a casual environment. A third congregation offers a *Sunday celebration* that suggests a happy and festive ambiance. Still another congregation gives different names to its three weekend gatherings, such as *blended worship*, *praise and worship service*, and *alternative and edgy service*. Each of those titles suggests something about that particular worship experience.[2]

One thing is clear from the wide variety of titles for churches' weekly worship gatherings. Across churches at large, there is not a consensus about worship. There are churches that follow a prescribed order of worship and there are churches that have very simple structure in worship. There are churches with long-standing worship traditions and churches with innovative worship. This leads us to ask: What is Christian worship supposed to be about? What is the purpose of worship?

Defining the purpose: two problems

Any time we have a question about Christian teaching or practice, we turn to the Bible for guidance. When we turn to the Bible to discover the purpose of worship, we find that the answer is not as simple as we might expect. The Bible does call on Christians to gather regularly as a body of believers. "Let us not neglect meeting together, as some have the habit of doing. Rather, let us encourage each other, and all the more as you see the Day approaching" (Hebrews 10:25 EHV). Yet the Bible does not give Christians an explicit set of instructions to follow when they gather together. Although God prescribed the rituals of worship in the Old Testament era, the New Testament clearly states that those commands no longer apply in the new era. The apostle Paul wrote, "Do not let anyone judge you by what you eat or drink, or with regard to a religious festival, a New Moon celebration or a Sabbath day. These are a shadow of the things that were to come; the reality, however, is found in Christ" (Colossians 2:16,17). When we look to Scripture for wisdom about our congregational gatherings, we see a *description* of what believers have done but not an exact *prescription* of what we must do.

As we try to discover a biblical purpose of worship, another complication confronts us. As strange as it may seem to us today, the words commonly translated "worship" in the New Testament do not refer to the regular gathering of a congregation around the Word and sacraments. Several Greek words in the New Testament are translated "worship," but they all refer to something other than Christians gathered together to hear God's Word.

- The word most often translated "worship" is *proskuneo*. This term conveys the idea of bowing one's face toward the ground as an act of respect or worship. For example, this is the word used to describe the actions of the Magi who came to visit the boy Jesus in Matthew 2:1-12.

- The second most common word translated "worship" is *latreuo* and refers to religious rites carried out as an act of worship. Although forms we use in today worship are properly called rites, the term *latreuo* does not necessarily imply actions performed by a group of people. The word is used in Luke 2:37 to refer to the widow Anna who regularly worshiped God in the temple in Jerusalem.

- A third term translated "worship" is *sebo*. This word carries the idea of someone who expresses allegiance to their god in their attitudes or by their actions. In Mark 7:5,6, Jesus cites Isaiah 29:13 as a verse that predicted the empty worship of the religious leaders of his day: The actions of the Pharisees appeared to express allegiance to God, but Jesus knew that their hearts did not reflect their outward actions.

- The word *leitorgeo* is the basis for our English word "liturgy." The secular meaning of the word referred to a public service project that benefited others or to someone who served in public office for the benefit of the community. In the New Testament, the word is affected by its context, referring to the service of Old Testament priests (Hebrews 10:11), church leaders who worshiped together (Acts 13:2), and sharing material blessings as a way to serve others in need (Romans 15:27).

- Finally, the word *threskia* is used a few times in the New Testament as an expression of religious beliefs and practices. For example, this word is used in Acts 26:5 by the apostle Paul to refer to the religion of Judaism, of which he was once a strict follower.

As we define the purpose of our public worship gatherings, we realize that the Bible doesn't always use the word worship the same way that we commonly use the word today. We also recognize that the descriptions of worship gatherings in the Bible are just that—descriptions. We will not find specifically prescribed patterns for us to follow today. Nevertheless, the descriptions of public worship found in Scripture are still instructive because they show us what God's people, guided by his Word, deemed to be the most appropriate words and actions for their regular assemblies.

Guidance from the Old Testament

The first mention of a public worship assembly in Scripture comes in Genesis 4:26, "At that time people began to *call on the name of the LORD*." Prior to this verse, believers in the newly created world worshiped God in a personal and informal way. For example, Abel, the second son born to Adam and Eve, sacrificed animals from his flocks as an act of worship to God (Genesis 4:1-5). But at the time of Enosh, the grandson of Adam and Eve, believers began to publicly worship the Lord.

The English translation of Genesis 4:26 might not capture the intended meaning of the original Hebrew words. In English, the expression "call on the name of the LORD" sounds like a description of prayer. But the original Hebrew expression also refers to public proclamation. In Exodus 34:5, this expression is used to describe God addressing Moses on Mount Sinai: "The LORD descended in the cloud and stood with him there, and *proclaimed the name of the LORD*" (ESV). When Genesis 4:26 tells us that "people began to call on the name of the LORD," it would be more accurate to say that people began to *proclaim* the name of the Lord. The phrase "proclaim the name of the Lord" refers to the act of proclaiming who God is and what he has done—his characteristics and his actions. The first public worship gatherings of God's people involved a proclamation of the Lord's words and works.[3]

The account of the Israelites crossing the Red Sea and escaping from the Egyptian armies is recorded in Exodus 14. After God miraculously delivered them, Moses and the Israelites burst out with a public song of praise to God. Their song praises God for his mighty deeds by proclaiming them:

> "I will sing to the LORD,
>   for he is highly exalted.
> Both horse and driver
>   he has hurled into the sea.

"The LORD is my strength and my defense;
    he has become my salvation.
He is my God, and I will praise him,
    my father's God, and I will exalt him.
The LORD is a warrior;
    the LORD is his name.
Pharaoh's chariots and his army
    he has hurled into the sea.
The best of Pharaoh's officers
    are drowned in the Red Sea.
The deep waters have covered them;
    they sank to the depths like a stone." (Exodus 15:1-5)

Public worship among the people of Israel was codified as they traveled from Egypt to the Promised Land. While the Israelites were camped at Mount Sinai, God mapped out very specific details for their public worship life. The Lord established three annual religious holidays (Exodus 23:14-17) and detailed specifications for the tabernacle (Exodus 25-27,30,35-38,40), vestments as sacred garments for the high priest and the other priests (Exodus 28), an ordination ceremony (Exodus 29; Leviticus 8), the weekly observance of the Sabbath as a day for rest and worship (Exodus 31:12-18; Leviticus 23:3), and the types of sacrifices and offerings they were to present to him (Leviticus 1-7).

The New Testament book of Hebrews provides further explanations about Old Testament worship practices. For example, the sacrifices repeated day after day and year after year were not just acts of worship. These sacrifices testified that the rebellious nature of sin required everyone to die as punishment. The writer says, "Without the shedding of blood there is no forgiveness" (Hebrews 9:22). At the same time, these sacrifices pointed forward to the gospel truth that the coming Savior's sacrifice would provide God's people with forgiveness of their sins.

"[Christ] has appeared once for all at the culmination of the ages to do away with sin by the sacrifice of himself. Just as people are destined to die once, and after that to face judgment, so Christ was sacrificed once to take away the sins of many; and he will appear a second time, not to bear sin, but to bring salvation to those who are waiting for him" (Hebrews 9:26-28). So the sacrifices God prescribed in the Old Testament also communicated God's great work of salvation that would be completed by his Son's future sacrifice.

The psalms of the Old Testament played a major component in worship among the Israelites. The heading, "For the director of music," appears at the beginning of many psalms and suggests that they would have been used in public worship. These Old Testament songs of prayer and praise also proclaim the same truths taught throughout Scripture. Martin Luther observed,

> The Psalter ought to be a precious and beloved book, if for no other reason than this: it promises Christ's death and resurrection so clearly—and pictures his kingdom and the condition and nature of all Christendom—that it might well be called a little Bible. In it is comprehended most beautifully and briefly everything that is in the entire Bible. It is really a fine enchiridion or handbook. In fact, I have a notion that the Holy Spirit wanted to take the trouble himself to compile a short Bible and book of examples of all Christendom or all saints, so that anyone who could not read the whole Bible would here have anyway almost an entire summary of it, comprised in one little book.[4]

Among the psalms are confessions of sin, prayers for God's mercy and deliverance, thanksgiving for God's blessings, acknowledgement of the importance of God's Word, and prophecies of the saving work of the coming Messiah,

Jesus Christ. The book of Psalms continues the pattern we have observed to this point—God's people praise him by proclaiming the things that he has done for them. Consider these verses of Psalm 103 as one of many examples from the psalms:

> Praise the LORD, my soul;
>   all my inmost being, praise his holy name.
> Praise the LORD, my soul,
>   and forget not all his benefits—
> who forgives all your sins
>   and heals all your diseases,
> who redeems your life from the pit
>   and crowns you with love and compassion,
> who satisfies your desires with good things
>   so that your youth is renewed like the eagle's.
>
> The LORD works righteousness
>   and justice for all the oppressed.
>
> He made known his ways to Moses,
>   his deeds to the people of Israel:
> The LORD is compassionate and gracious,
>   slow to anger, abounding in love.
> He will not always accuse,
>   nor will he harbor his anger forever;
> he does not treat us as our sins deserve
>   or repay us according to our iniquities.
> For as high as the heavens are above the earth,
>   so great is his love for those who fear him;
> as far as the east is from the west,
>   so far has he removed our transgressions from us.
>   (Psalm 103:1-12)

Guidance from the New Testament

Acts 2:42 provides us with a little glimpse into the early life of the Christian church. Luke tells us that the first

Christians "devoted themselves to the apostles' teaching and to fellowship, to the breaking of bread and to prayer." Luke lists four specific things to which the early church regularly and deliberately committed itself.

- "The apostles' teaching" reflects the spiritual and eternal truths that Jesus passed on to his disciples, which are now recorded for us in Scripture.
- "Fellowship" implies a relationship between people who share a common interest or activity. The early Christians shared a confession of faith in Jesus. They joined together in worship and witness. Their common faith and common work in God's kingdom reflected the fellowship they enjoyed together as God's people.
- "Breaking of bread" may refer to the fellowship meal Christians often shared when they gathered together, often called the *agape* meal. (*Agape* is one of the Greek words for "love.") It may also refer to the celebration of the Lord's Supper, or Holy Communion. Since the Christian *agape* meal was an expression of fellowship and could have been encompassed by the previous item in the list, it seems plausible that Luke is specifically referring to the Lord's Supper when he refers to the "breaking of bread."
- The final item in the list is "prayer"—or literally "the prayers." Christians gathered together, perhaps at regularly established times, and jointly brought their requests, intercessions, and thanksgiving to God.

In this little verse, we see a summary of the elements of public worship that have remained important to Christians

throughout the ages: proclaiming the Word of God, receiving the Lord's Supper, expressing our fellowship by our
common confession of faith, and offering prayers on behalf
of one another and for a wide range of concerns.

Acts 2:42 describes the activity of the first Christian
believers. Another key verse that guides Christian worship
is Colossians 3:16. In the middle of a section with several
encouragements for Christian living, Paul says, "Let the
message of Christ dwell among you richly as you teach and
admonish one another with all wisdom through psalms,
hymns, and songs from the Spirit, singing to God with
gratitude in your hearts." The "message of Christ" is Paul's
expression for the gospel—the good news that Jesus Christ
entered our world, fulfilled God's law perfectly in our
place, suffered on the cross to pay the penalty for our sin,
and rose from the dead to demonstrate his victory over sin
and death. Notice how Paul urged the Colossians to let the
gospel be present among them as they taught and admonished one another through the "psalms, hymns, and songs
from the Spirit" that they sang as a congregation. Their
music in public worship was not merely a personal expression of praise. Rather their songs had a teaching purpose
for the entire assembly.[5]

Paul's letters to the Colossians and the Ephesians are
very similar. There is a statement in Ephesians that closely
parallels Paul's thoughts in Colossians 3:16. Ephesians
5:19,20 says, "[Speak] to one another with psalms, hymns,
and songs from the Spirit. Sing and make music from your
heart to the Lord, always giving thanks to God the Father
for everything, in the name of our Lord Jesus Christ."
Notice the first words from Paul's statement in Ephesians:
"[Speak] to one another with psalms, hymns, and songs."
Paul indicates that Christians' singing is not only directed

to God but also to each another. We praise God for the gospel, the message that brings us to faith and brings us his forgiveness. As we praise God, we proclaim the very same gospel message that strengthens us and our brothers and sisters in faith.

Paul's words in Colossians and Ephesians underscore an observable pattern and encouragement in Scripture: We praise God when we proclaim the gospel.

Another New Testament letter written by Saint Paul offers us further guidance as we study the purpose of worship. In 1 Corinthians, Paul discusses the matter of speaking in tongues. The miraculous ability to speak in another language was a special gift that the Holy Spirit gave to the infant Christian church, presumably to aid the rapid spread of the gospel in the church's initial years. Unfortunately, some of the Corinthians who had received this unique spiritual gift took pride in themselves simply because they had this gift. Paul corrects their thinking with these words:

> A person who speaks in a tongue should pray that he may interpret. For if I pray in a tongue, my spirit prays, but my understanding is unfruitful. So what is to be done? I will pray using my spirit, and I will pray also using my understanding. I will sing using my spirit, and I will sing also using my understanding. Otherwise, how will an uninformed person say the "Amen" after you give thanks, since he does not know what you are saying? To be sure, you are giving thanks well enough, but the other person is not being built up. (1 Corinthians 14:13-17 EHV)

Notice Paul's concern that the words spoken in public worship should edify everyone who has gathered. Praising God in a language unknown to others in the assembly may have seemed outwardly impressive. Unfortunately, a message that could not be understood was a message that would not edify the gathered congregation. Paul went on to say, "I thank God that I speak in tongues more than all of you. But in the church I would rather speak five intelligible words to instruct others than ten thousand words in a tongue" (1 Corinthians 14:18,19). Paul's encouragement directed the Corinthians to ensure that the words they spoke in their worship gatherings built each other up in faith. This encouragement applied not only to their proclamation of God's Word but also to their statements of praise for God's grace.

There are several fine examples of praise that proclaims God's grace surrounding the story of Jesus' birth in the Gospel of Luke. An angel appeared to Zechariah in Luke 1:5-25 to tell him that he and his wife, Elizabeth, would have a son in their old age, and their son would be the forerunner of the Messiah. Zechariah did not believe the angel's message. As punishment for failing to believe God's messenger, Zechariah's ability to speak was taken from him until the birth of his son, John the Baptist. Once his speech was restored, some of his first words were a statement of praise to God for the salvation he was about to bring to his people. "Praise be to the Lord, the God of Israel, because he has come to his people and redeemed them. He has raised up a horn of salvation for us in the house of his servant David" (Luke 1:68,69). Zechariah's song, sometimes called by its Latin title, "Benedictus," has been adapted by Christians for use in the historic prayer service called *Matins* or Morning Prayer (*Christian Worship: Hymnal*, pages 207-214).

Mary, the mother of Jesus, is also visited by the angel Gabriel in the same chapter. The angel informs her that she will be the mother of Jesus, the Son of God and promised Savior. Mary travels to visit her relative Elizabeth. During her visit, she also sang a song of praise to God. Like

Zechariah's song, Mary's song also praises God for his specific acts of grace and goodness.

> "My soul glorifies the Lord
>   and my spirit rejoices in God my Savior,
> for he has been mindful
>   of the humble state of his servant.
> From now on all generations will call me blessed,
>   for the Mighty One has done great things for me—
>   holy is his name.
> His mercy extends to those who fear him,
>   from generation to generation. . . .
> He has helped his servant Israel,
>   remembering to be merciful
> to Abraham and his descendants forever,
>   just as he promised our ancestors."
>   (Luke 1:46-50,54,55)

The song of Mary, like the song of Zechariah, has also
been used in Christian worship for centuries. Mary's song,
known by its Latin title, "Magnificat," has been associated
with the service called *Vespers* or Evening Prayer (*Christian
Worship: Hymnal*, pages 215-224). In these songs, we see
further New Testament examples of praise that proclaims
the gracious works of God.

The last book of the Bible provides another example of
the connection between praise and proclamation. In Revelation, the apostle John sees a vision of the church and
all creation praising God. They praise the Lamb of God,
who is about to take a scroll in John's vision and open it
to reveal what will occur in the future. They sing, "You are
worthy to take the scroll and to open its seals, because you
were slain, and with your blood you purchased for God persons from every tribe and language and people and nation.
You have made them to be a kingdom and priests to serve
our God, and they will reign on the earth" (Revelation

5:9,10). Jesus, the Lamb of God, receives praise from the church and from all creation because he shed his blood on the cross to redeem the world from sin and bring us into the family of God.

Praise and proclamation

One of the difficulties with the English word *worship* is that it does not adequately describe what happens when Christians gather together. The verb *worship* implies an activity that we direct toward God. It is true that believers direct their praises to God when they gather together publicly. But we have seen from Scripture that worship, in the narrow sense of simply praising God, is not all that occurs when believers are gathered. Believers proclaimed the saving acts of God through the ceremonies of the Old Testament and the apostles' teachings in the New Testament. Even as believers worshiped God in response to his saving work, their worship echoed back to him the very things he has done to save them from sin.

Imagine that you have just received a birthday or Christmas gift from a relative. If you wrote a thank-you note to the giver, what words would you use to express your gratitude? "Thank you very much. I just love the gift. I feel so appreciated when I think about it. I really want you to know how grateful I feel." Even though these words show your appreciation, they say nothing about the gift that was given. The giver cannot even tell that you received the gift from these words. How about this: "Thank you very much. Your gift was wonderful, thoughtful, considerate, and heartfelt. When I received it, I could tell just how much sincerity was behind your gift. Thank you for your kindness." These words focus more on the giver than the recipient, but they still say nothing about the gift. We can still do better than that. "Thank you very much. I truly appreciated the gift certificate to the department store that you gave me. I plan to buy the kids some new clothes since they grow out of their old ones so quickly! I appreciate your thoughtfulness." That's better! When you express appreciation to someone for a gift, your words of thanks would seem empty if you did not thank him or her for *the specific gift* that was given.

In worship, we receive the gift of God's forgiveness. His grace is proclaimed to us. We naturally respond to God's gift and express our thanks. Just as it is natural to thank others for the specific gifts they have given us, so it is also natural to praise God by specifically citing his grace and forgiveness toward us. When we do that, we not only praise and thank God, but the gospel message we proclaim edifies our own souls and the souls of our gathered Christian brothers and sisters. We continue the same pattern of praise that proclaims the saving deeds of Christ that we see repeatedly in the Scriptures. Simply stated, praise is proclamation.

Consider another illustration. Your daughter has just participated in a piano recital. After countless hours of drilling and practicing, she flawlessly performs her piece before the audience. The next day, a friend calls you on the telephone, and you catch up on one another's family activities. During the conversation, you describe your daughter's performance: "She was the third-to-last student to perform in the program. She sat down confidently and played her piece perfectly. You should have heard the way she brought the emotion out of the music. She made us very proud!" Your description of your daughter's performance proclaimed what she had done, but in the process of describing her playing, you also praised her for the good performance she gave.

This anecdote from everyday life is also true in our worship. Proclaiming what God has done for us is the starting point of public worship, but we can hardly separate our proclamation of God's deeds from our praise. When the minister preaches the gospel in his sermon, he is not only proclaiming God's Word to us, but his words also praise God for forgiving us through Jesus Christ. When worshipers recite the Creed together, their words of proclamation also praise God for sending his Son to be our Savior. Just as praise is proclamation, so proclamation is praise.

Our observation of Scripture leads us to this conclusion about Christian worship. When believers gather for worship, their purpose is to proclaim the good news about forgiveness and salvation through Jesus Christ. As believers proclaim the saving work of Jesus, they are also praising him for what he has done for them. When believers respond to the gospel's good news of forgiveness by praising God, they naturally praise him by proclaiming the very same good news that fills their hearts with gratitude.

When Christians proclaim the gospel in public worship, they are praising God; and when Christians praise God in public worship, they do so by proclaiming the gospel.

2

The Gospel in Worship[6]

Two friends, Christians from different churches, discuss and compare their experiences each week when they go to church. The first person says, "The highlight of our Sunday worship is hearing the Word of God in the Bible readings and the sermon." The second person asks, "Isn't the most important part of worship the fact that we come together to praise God? After all, that's what the word *worship* means in the dictionary."

The second friend's question in this scenario is a common thought. English dictionaries list the word *worship* as both a noun and a verb. As a noun, worship refers to religious practices with creeds and rituals. As a verb, worship describes the respect, honor, and praise that people direct toward God. Notice that the English verb to worship does not necessarily imply the same gospel-proclaiming emphasis discovered from our study of Scripture in chapter 1. We learned that believers' primary purpose is to proclaim the gospel when they gather for worship. Just as the Greek words commonly translated as "worship" do not fully capture the purpose of Christian worship gatherings, so the English word *worship* does not adequately define the purpose of worship described in the Bible.

In chapter 1, we learned that believers gather together to proclaim the gospel and to respond to the gospel with praise and thanks. Even in their response, Christians proclaim the gospel. The main purpose of worship is to proclaim the gospel. In this chapter we will explore the way that Christians proclaim the gospel in public worship. In order to do that, we must begin with a basic understanding of law and gospel, the two central teachings in Scripture. We must also understand how God applies the gospel to our hearts through the means of grace. Once this groundwork is laid, we can appreciate how and why the gospel is proclaimed in public worship.

Law and gospel

A person feels sick. The symptoms remain for some time. He decides to schedule an appointment with his doctor to determine the cause of his illness. The doctor examines the patient. The tests reveal a serious ailment. Fortunately, there is medication to fight off the illness. Although the patient did not enjoy hearing the doctor's diagnosis, he is relieved to have an antidote for his medical problem.

This scenario illustrates the relationship between law and gospel, the two main teachings of Scripture. The law is like the illness; the gospel is like the medication. No one likes to hear the full extent of the law's diagnosis, for it reveals a serious spiritual disease within us. But a proper diagnosis of the law will help us understand that the gospel is the perfect and only medicine for our ailment. In order for us to understand the proper use of the gospel in Christian worship, we must first understand the relationship between law and gospel in Scripture.

The law explains what God expects from all people. The Ten Commandments, first given to the people of Israel in Exodus 20, describe the standards God has set for humankind. Jesus succinctly summarized the Commandments when he said, "Love the Lord your God with all your heart and with all your soul and with all your mind. . . . Love your neighbor as yourself" (Matthew 22:37,39). God commands that nothing become more important to us than him. He further commands that we show love and respect to everyone just as we love ourselves and expect respect from others. This command from God is not merely a suggestion for daily living; it is a demand that God requires us to fulfill perfectly. Jesus said in the Sermon on the Mount, "Be perfect, therefore, as your heavenly Father is perfect" (Matthew 5:48). God told the ancient Israelites through Moses, "Be holy because I, the LORD your God, am holy" (Leviticus 19:2).

Even a passing glance at your life's story shows how far short you have come from meeting the perfect demands of a holy God. Like the doctor's diagnosis for an ill patient, the law reveals our diagnosis: We are sinners who fail to love God and our neighbors perfectly. Saint Paul wrote, "No one will be declared righteous in God's sight by the works of the law; rather, through the law we become conscious of our sin" (Romans 3:20). God's law reveals the sobering truth that our sinful behavior is the symptom of sin's disease within our hearts from our first moment of existence. King David lamented in Psalm 51:5, "Surely I was sinful at birth, sinful from the time my mother conceived me." Just as a serious illness left untreated may result in death, the disease of sin brings its own set of deadly consequences. "The wages of sin is death," Saint Paul informs us (Romans 6:23). The death Paul has in mind is not only physical death, but also eternal death— permanent separation from the love and blessings of God in hell, where souls suffer the eternal wrath of God because of their sin.

The diagnosis we hear from the law leaves nothing to celebrate. When we see the standards of God's law and recognize our inability to achieve them even with our best efforts, we are left to despair. Like the apostle Paul, our souls cry out, "What a wretched man I am! Who will rescue me from this body that is subject to death?" (Romans 7:24). But this is the point God wants us to reach! God wants us to reach the point of despair over our sin, because then the gospel will be able to do its healing work in our souls.

The word *gospel* comes from a combination of the old English words *god* and *spell*, which mean "good news." With souls crushed by the law, the gospel message God brings to us in his Word is truly good news! The apostle Paul summarizes the gospel at the beginning of the resurrection chapter of the Bible:

> Brothers and sisters, I want to remind you of the gospel I preached to you, which you received and on which you have taken your stand. By this gospel you are saved, if you hold firmly to the word I preached to you. Otherwise, you have believed in vain. For what I received I passed on to you as of first importance: that Christ died for our sins

according to the Scriptures, that he was buried, that he
was raised on the third day according to the Scriptures.
(1 Corinthians 15:1-4)

The gospel is a historical fact. Jesus Christ, the sinless
Son of God, entered our world to be our Savior from
sin's eternal consequences. Just as the Old Testament
Scriptures had predicted, Jesus sacrificed his life on the
cross where he endured the punishment that God has prescribed for our sin. Hundreds of years before Jesus' birth,
the prophet Isaiah previewed Jesus' death and revealed
its purpose: "He was pierced for our transgressions, he was
crushed for our iniquities; the punishment that brought
us peace was on him, and by his wounds we are healed"
(Isaiah 53:5). With the penalty for our sin completely
satisfied, God the Father raised his Son from the dead on
Easter morning as definitive proof that Jesus had accom-
plished the world's salvation.

The demands and punishments of God's law would
have left us in despair over our sin. The gospel reveals the
wonderful truth that Jesus obeyed the law perfectly in our
place, paid the penalty for our sins by his death, and promises forgiveness and eternal life to all who believe in him as
their Savior. What a wonderful gift Christ has given us in
the gospel!

The means of grace

A grandmother knits a sweater for her granddaughter as
a Christmas present. Because she lives hundreds of miles
away from her granddaughter, she cannot present the gift
to her in person. So she carefully wraps the sweater, packs
it in a box, and ships it to her granddaughter's address. Her
heartfelt and handmade gift wouldn't do much good if her
granddaughter didn't receive it. The shipping company is

the means that delivers the grandmother's Christmas gift to her granddaughter.

Jesus' death has paid for the sins of the world. He won forgiveness for all mankind and proved his victory over death by his resurrection. But the gift of Christ's forgiveness cannot benefit our souls if we do not receive it. Just as the shipping company was the means that the grandmother used to deliver her gift, so God also uses means to deliver the gospel's forgiveness to individual souls. God uses the means of grace to present us with his gospel gifts. The means of grace is the gospel delivered to us in God's Word and in the Sacraments of Holy Baptism and Holy Communion.

The Word

God's Word proclaims the gospel message about Jesus Christ, our Savior. Jesus left no doubt about the purpose of the Old Testament Scriptures when he said, "These are the very Scriptures that testify about me" (John 5:39). The apostle John spoke just as clearly about the purpose of his Gospel record of Jesus' life: "These [words] are written that you may believe that Jesus is the Messiah, the Son of God, and that by believing you may have life in his name" (John 20:31). The Bible's gospel facts also contain the gospel's power to bring people to faith in Christ and to deliver them his forgiveness and salvation. The apostle Paul boldly proclaimed, "I am not ashamed of the gospel, because it is the power of God that brings salvation to everyone who believes" (Romans 1:16). In the most well-known verse in the Bible, Jesus shows us that the gospel message is the means God uses to create faith and deliver his eternal blessings to us. "God so loved the world that he gave his one and only

Son, that whoever believes in him shall not perish but have eternal life" (John 3:16).

The gospel message in God's Word is proclaimed in a wide variety of ways:[7]

- The gospel is proclaimed when we read the Scriptures: "That which was from the beginning, which we have heard, which we have seen with our eyes, which we have looked at and our hands have touched—this we proclaim concerning the Word of life. . . . We write this to make our joy complete" (1 John 1:1,4).

- The gospel is proclaimed in preaching. The risen Jesus said to his disciples, "Go into all the world and preach the gospel to all creation" (Mark 16:15).

- The gospel is proclaimed when we teach and explain the Word of God to others. In Acts 8, the Ethiopian official's question about a section in Isaiah's book provided Philip with an opportunity to explain the gospel. "The eunuch asked Philip, 'Tell me, please, who is the prophet talking about, himself or someone else?' Then Philip began with that very passage of Scripture and told him the good news about Jesus" (Acts 8:34,35).

- The gospel is proclaimed when a believer forgives the sins of another. On the evening of Easter Sunday, Jesus announced to his disciples, "If you forgive anyone's sins, their sins are forgiven; if you do not forgive them, they are not forgiven" (John 20:23).

- The gospel is proclaimed personally when a believer ponders its message in his heart: "The word is near you; it is in your mouth and in your heart" (Romans 10:8).

- The gospel can even be proclaimed through pictures and symbols. Just before Jesus' famous statement in John 3:16, he used an Old Testament incident to picture his coming sacrifice: "Just as Moses lifted up the snake in the wilderness, so the Son of Man must be lifted up, that everyone who believes may have eternal life in him" (John 3:14,15).

Although the gospel is proclaimed in many different ways, its power and purpose remain the same in all circumstances. The gospel brings people to faith in Jesus, sustains them in faith, and delivers the forgiveness of sins and promise of eternal life to all who believe it.

The Word of God contains the gospel, and so we recognize that the Word of God is a means of grace. We need to remember, however, that the Word of God contains law as well. A Christian may explain a point of moral teaching from the Bible to someone else, but if he does not explain how Jesus kept God's law perfectly and offered his life as payment for our sins, then the conversation does not present the gospel. A pastor may preach a sermon based on the Word of God, but if his sermon has not taken people to the cross and empty tomb of Jesus, then his sermon has not used the means of grace. Scripture contains both law and gospel. Both are essential, but only one can deliver God's grace into our hearts. The law condemns, but the gospel consoles. The law shows our need for Christ's forgiveness, but the gospel actually brings us Christ's forgiveness.

The sacraments

A married couple expresses their love for each other in multiple ways. They say to each other, "I love you." On the day of their wedding, they exchange rings as a symbol of their commitment to love each other throughout their lives. A kiss and a hug, a birthday present, flowers on their anniversary, dinner at their favorite restaurant for a special occasion—these are all ways that the couple expresses their love for each other.

God also expresses his love and grace to us in multiple ways. The gospel in the Word of God is not the only way God delivers his grace to us. The means of grace also include the sacraments. The common Lutheran definition of a sacrament includes three aspects: A sacrament is (1) an act instituted by Christ, which (2) uses an earthly element and (3) offers and gives us the forgiveness of sins. By this definition, there are two sacraments: Holy Baptism and Holy Communion. In the sacraments, God brings the very same forgiveness that he presents to us in his Word. The grace is the same; only the means are different.

Jesus instituted Baptism shortly before his ascension into heaven. In the Great Commission, Jesus told his disciples that the Word and Baptism were two means to bring people into the holy Christian church. Jesus said to his disciples, "Go and make disciples of all nations, *baptizing* them in the name of the Father and of the Son and of the Holy Spirit, and teaching them to obey everything I have commanded you" (Matthew 28:19,20). As the words of Jesus are spoken and the waters of Baptism are applied to a person, God miraculously adopts that person into his family of believers and personally applies his gifts of forgiveness and eternal life to him or her. On Pentecost, the birthday of the Christian church, Peter declared to the crowds, "Repent and be baptized, every one of you, in the name of Jesus Christ for the forgiveness of your sins. And you will receive the gift of the Holy Spirit" (Acts 2:38). Luther summarizes Baptism's power as a means of grace in the Small Catechism: "Baptism works forgiveness of sin, delivers from death and the devil, and gives eternal salvation to all who believe this, as the words and promises of God declare."[8]

Baptism is much like a wedding ring: It is a one-time gift from God, but it points us to God's ongoing love and commitment to us every day of our lives. Luther encouraged believers to view their baptism as their status before God and not merely as a past incident in their lives. Luther wrote in his Large Catechism, "When our sins and conscience oppress us, we strengthen ourselves and take comfort and say, 'Nevertheless, I am baptized. And if I am baptized, it is promised to me that I shall be saved and have eternal life, both in soul and body.'"[9]

Baptism makes us holy in God's sight, clothing us in the perfect righteousness of Jesus. Through faith created in our hearts by the Holy Spirit in Baptism, we are God's forgiven and redeemed children. But this wonderful truth does not negate the reality that we continue to struggle against sin. We return to our baptism to find strength to fight against our sinful nature and the sinful temptations all around us. Saint Paul notes that Baptism connects us to Jesus' death and resurrection. This connection enables us to fight against sin's temptations. Paul wrote:

> What shall we say, then? Shall we go on sinning so that grace may increase? By no means! We are those who have died to sin; how can we live in it any longer? Or don't you know that all of us who were baptized into Christ Jesus were baptized into his death? We were therefore buried

with him through baptism into death in order that, just as Christ was raised from the dead through the glory of the Father, we too may live a new life (Romans 6:1-4).

One of the ways we revisit the blessings of Baptism is through confession and absolution. In the previous section, we saw that God's Word delivers his grace in a variety of ways. One of those ways is when a pastor or another Christian announces Christ's forgiveness to us. The formal term for this announcement is called absolution. When Christian believers confess their sin, whether privately to another person or corporately in worship, and when the absolution is proclaimed, they have essentially revisited their baptism. Absolution takes us back to the promise of God's forgiveness that we first received in our baptism. Luther writes,

> When we rise from our sins or repent, we are merely returning to the power and the faith of baptism from which we fell, and finding our way back to the promise then made to us, which we deserted when we sinned. For the truth of the promise once made remains steadfast, always ready to receive us back with open arms when we return.[10]

In the Apology of the Augsburg Confession (1530), an official doctrinal statement of the Lutheran church, absolution is described as a sacrament: "Baptism, the Lord's Supper, and Absolution (which is the Sacrament of Repentance) are truly Sacraments. For these rites have God's command and the promise of grace."[11] Some prefer to work with a slightly broader definition of a sacrament, omitting the idea of an earthly element. Since the definition of the term is not prescribed in the Bible, there is nothing wrong with using a narrower or broader definition, although it is wise for us to agree to a common definition.

Luther used a broader definition earlier in his ministry but later preferred the narrow definition. What matters most is not our working definition of a sacrament, or whether we view absolution as a sacrament or simply as an extension of the Word of God. What matters most is that we view Baptism and absolution as means of grace through which God applies his grace to our souls.

Holy Baptism is a special one-time gift of God's grace with ongoing meaning and significance for our faith. By contrast, Holy Communion, or the Lord's Supper, is a gift of God's grace that we receive again and again. Jesus' institution of Holy Communion is recorded in the first three gospels—Matthew, Mark, and Luke—and by the apostle Paul in 1 Corinthians. The following quotation synthesizes Jesus' words from these four New Testament books into the Words of Institution:

> Our Lord Jesus Christ, on the night he was betrayed, took bread; and when he had given thanks, he broke it and gave it to his disciples, saying, "Take and eat; this is my body, which is given for you. Do this in remembrance of me."
>
> Then he took the cup, gave thanks, and gave it to them, saying, "Drink from it, all of you; this is my blood of the new covenant, which is poured out for you for the forgiveness of sins. Do this, whenever you drink it, in remembrance of me."[12]

There are several important truths we can note from Jesus' words of institution. Jesus tells his disciples that the bread and wine in Holy Communion are more than ordinary bread and wine. They are also the very body and blood of Jesus, once given on the cross and now given to us again in a miraculous but real manner. Although many have tried to interpret Jesus' words to suggest that the bread and wine are not actually his body and blood, Luther reminds us that God's Word is more powerful than any human opinions.

> With this Word you can strengthen your conscience and say, "If a hundred thousand devils, together with all fanatics, should rush forward, crying, 'How can bread and wine be Christ's body and blood?' and such, I know that all spirits and scholars together are not as wise as is the Divine Majesty in His little finger." Now here stands Christ's Word, "Take, eat; this is My body. . . . Drink of it, all of you; this is My blood of the new testament," and so on. Here we stop to watch those who will call themselves His masters and make the matter different from what He has spoken. It is true, indeed, that if you take away the Word or regard the Sacrament without the words, you have nothing but mere bread and wine. But if the words remain with them, as they shall and must, then, by virtue of the words, it is truly Christ's body and blood. What Christ's lips say and speak, so it is. He can never lie or deceive.[13]

Not only does Holy Communion present us with Jesus' body and blood, but it also delivers his forgiveness to us in yet another way. On the night he instituted Holy Communion, Jesus distributed the cup to his disciples and said, "Drink from it, all of you. This is my blood of the covenant, which is poured out for many for the forgiveness of sins" (Matthew 26:27,28). The forgiveness Jesus brings in the Lord's Supper is the same grace and forgiveness we receive when we hear his Word and when we were baptized into his name; but in this sacred meal, his forgiveness comes to us in a unique and tangible way.

Like Baptism, Holy Communion is a sacrament. Unlike Baptism, Holy Communion is something that Jesus invites us to receive repeatedly. In Paul's account of the Words of Institution, Jesus invites us to "do this" repeatedly. "This is my body, which is for you; do this in remembrance of me. . . . This cup is the new covenant in my blood; do this, whenever you drink it, in remembrance of me" (1 Corinthians 11:24,25). Although the statement, "Do this, whenever you drink it," does not mandate a specific frequency for our participation, the blessings of this sacrament encourage us to receive it frequently. Luther reminds us why frequent reception of the Lord's Supper is such a valuable blessing:

> By Baptism we are first born anew. But, as we said before, there still remains the old vicious nature of flesh and blood in mankind. There are so many hindrances and temptations of the devil and of the world that we often become weary and faint, and sometimes we also stumble. Therefore, the Sacrament is given as a daily pasture and sustenance, that faith may refresh and strengthen itself so that it will not fall back in such a battle, but become ever stronger and stronger. . . . Now to this purpose the comfort of the Sacrament is given when the heart feels that the burden is becoming too heavy, so that it may gain here new power and refreshment.[14]

In the Word of God and the words of absolution, in Holy Baptism and Holy Communion, Jesus graciously comes to us and brings us the forgiveness of sins that he won for us on the cross 2,000 years ago. Apart from these means of grace, we do not receive Christ's blessings. Through these means of grace, the Holy Spirit works and sustains faith that receives the grace of God through Jesus' redeeming work.

The means of grace in worship

God's people use the gospel in a number of different settings. We explain law and gospel to others in our personal witness and our congregations' evangelism efforts. We apply the gospel to people personally in counseling. We build up and increase our knowledge of the gospel in Bible classes and other educational settings. The gospel is put to work in each one of these situations, even though our specific objective varies.

We also put the gospel to work in public worship. In two different letters to his coworker Timothy, the apostle Paul told him that the reading and preaching of God's Word should be a part of his ministry. Paul wrote, "Devote yourself to the public reading of Scripture, to preaching and to teaching," (1 Timothy 4:13) and, "Preach the word" (2 Timothy 4:2). In his letter to the Ephesians, Paul envisions Christians proclaiming the gospel to one another as they praise God for his grace: "[Speak] to one another with psalms, hymns, and songs from the Spirit" (Ephesians 5:19).

Holy Communion is also a natural element of public worship, because its very nature is a communal activity. Referring to the single loaf of bread that commonly was used by early Christian worship assemblies, Paul notes the communal nature of the sacrament: "Because there is one loaf, we, who are many, are one body, for we all share the one loaf" (1 Corinthians 10:17). Because the Lord's Supper expresses unity among those who participate in it together, it is naturally included in public worship.

Does this repeated use of the gospel seem redundant? We received forgiveness when we were baptized. We learn about the gospel in Sunday school, Catechism classes, and Bible study classes. In worship, the gospel is proclaimed in absolution, the Scripture readings, the sermon, the Creed, the Lord's Supper, and even the hymns and songs we sing. Do we really need to revisit the same gospel message through the same means of grace over and over again in worship?

If the gospel were only a fact that we learned and remembered, perhaps we would only need to hear it occasionally. But the gospel is so much more than a fact to remember; it is spiritual power. In Romans 1:16, Paul describes the gospel's powerful quality to bring Christ's salvation to all who believe its message: "I am not ashamed of the gospel, because it is the power of God that brings salvation to everyone who believes." The gospel message about Christ brings people to faith in him: "Faith comes from hearing the message, and the message is heard through the word about Christ" (Romans 10:17). This powerful message encompassed the apostle's ministry and preaching. Paul told the Corinthians, "I resolved to know nothing while I was with you except Jesus Christ and him crucified" (1 Corinthians 2:2). There was no doubt in Paul's mind that believers should encounter the gospel regularly to keep their faith strong and vibrant.

Our bodies need proper nutrition to function well. Most of us eat three meals a day so that we have the nutrients and energy we need for daily life. If someone suggested that people really don't need to eat because they already know how to eat and they have tasted food before, we would find that suggestion bizarre at best and dangerous at worst. Eating is not about head knowledge; it provides necessary nourishment for the body!

Our sinful nature tries to convince us that the gospel is just head knowledge instead of something we need to *consume* regularly for good spiritual health. But the new self inside our hearts sees the gospel as necessary food for the soul! Our new self delights to dine at the Savior's gospel banquet in Word and sacrament. Our new self loves to return to the simple gospel message and receive forgiveness and strength from Christ again and again. Our

new self never tires of receiving ongoing spiritual nourishment when we study, ponder, and learn about the grace of
God. As we proclaim the gospel and administer the Lord's
Supper in public worship, our new self rejoices to hear the
good news of Christ's saving and redeeming work. And
unlike a physical meal, we cannot consume too much gospel! We cannot overdose on the forgiveness of sins! What
a blessing Christ gives us as we encounter his means of
grace each week in worship!

Luke's gospel includes the familiar account of Jesus visiting the home of Mary and Martha. As Mary sat at Jesus'
feet and listened to his Word, her sister Martha criticized
her because she did not help to prepare the meal they
were about to eat. Although there was nothing wrong
with meal preparation, there was nothing more important
than hearing Jesus, the Word who became flesh, explain
the Word of God. Jesus said to Martha, "You are worried
and upset about many things, but few things are needed—
or indeed only one. Mary has chosen what is better, and it
will not be taken away from her" (Luke 10:41,42).

There is nothing more important than hearing the
gospel. There is nothing more important than receiving
Christ's grace through the means of grace. There is nothing
more important than the forgiveness of sins that Jesus delivers to our souls through his Word and sacraments. In public
worship, we proclaim the gospel that Christ has given to
us. Pastors will do well to make gospel proclamations the
heart of their preaching and worship planning. Parishioners
will do well to expect that their pastors present them with
Christ's precious forgiveness every week in worship and
preaching. Nothing else can give us the spiritual strength,
power, nourishment, and peace we need than the gospel!

3

Principles for Worship—Part 1

The Bible has one clear distinct message and theme. Referring to the Old Testament, Jesus said, "These are the very Scriptures that testify about me" (John 5:39). Saint John stated near the end of his gospel, "These [words] are written that you may believe that Jesus is the Messiah, the Son of God, and that by believing you may have life in his name" (John 20:31). Saint Paul wrote, "Faith comes from hearing the message, and the message is heard through the word about Christ" (Romans 10:17). The Word of God points us to Jesus Christ and calls us to faith in his work of salvation. This is the Bible's focus, purpose, and goal.

The Bible speaks to many different issues, but none of those issues are as important or significant as the gospel. Consider just one example. The Bible has much to say about finances. We hear God's warning against the love of money and pursuit of earthly blessings over faith. We read encouragements to handle our God-given wealth wisely. We are wise to take Scripture's encouragements about financial stewardship to heart, but we would miss the point if we viewed Scripture as a financial advice handbook. God-pleasing stewardship flows out of faith, but it is not the essence or foundation of our faith.

This point will be important to keep in mind throughout the next two chapters. We are about to survey Scripture for its wisdom and encouragements about Christian worship. The Bible has much to say about public worship, and we are wise to take these important encouragements to heart. But we must remember that everything that follows in these two chapters is secondary to the primary purpose of worship: to proclaim the gospel. If we let any other principle become more important than receiving Christ's forgiveness through the means of grace, we will miss the point of worship and will turn Scripture into a corporate worship handbook. Rather, the principles that follow will serve us best when they serve under the gospel and help us to point worshipers to Christ.

This chapter explores three biblical worship principles. In some way, each of these principles will examine worship from the perspective of people. We will consider the importance of people's participation, the value of respecting the practices of Christians who have preceded us in history, and the importance of expressing our unity with one another through public worship.

The participation of the people

For most readers, the word *priest* brings to mind the picture of a clergyman. Many people tend to think of the words *priest, pastor,* and *minister* as synonyms used by various Christian denominations to refer to clergy. But the New Testament's use of the word *priest* is different from our common definition. The New Testament equates the title of priest to all believers in Jesus Christ. Saint Peter said to the readers of his first letter, "You are a chosen people, a royal *priesthood,* a holy nation, God's special possession" (1 Peter 2:9). In a statement of praise to God at the start of Revelation, Saint John also refers to all believers in Christ as priests: "To him who loves us and has freed us from our sins by his blood, and has made us to be a kingdom and *priests* to serve his God and Father—to him be glory and power for ever and ever!" (Revelation 1:5,6).

In order for us to appreciate the significance of this title, we need to consider the role of priests in the Old Testament. Old Testament priests served as the public mediators between God and humankind. When someone presented a sacrifice in the tabernacle or the temple, the priests were the ones who took the animal and carried out the instructions God prescribed instructions for the sacrifice (Leviticus 1–7). On the Day of Atonement, an important annual festival in the Hebrew calendar, only the high priest could enter the temple's Most Holy Place and perform the actions that God had prescribed (Leviticus 16). The priests' work constantly reminded the Israelites that someone needed to be a mediator between sinful human beings and a holy, righteous God. The repeated sacrifices reminded God's people that "without the shedding of blood there is no forgiveness" (Hebrews 9:22). Old Testament worship practices pointed people forward to the sacrifice that would end all sacrifices.

Now enter the New Testament. Jesus' sacrifice on the cross has paid the penalty for the sins of the world! The

Mediator and High Priest we needed to make us one again with God has come and taken away our sin. The writer to the Hebrews says:

> Christ did not enter a sanctuary made with human hands that was only a copy of the true one; he entered heaven itself, now to appear for us in God's presence. Nor did he enter heaven to offer himself again and again, the way the high priest enters the Most Holy Place every year with blood that is not his own. . . . But he has appeared once for all at the culmination of the ages to do away with sin by the sacrifice of himself. (Hebrews 9:24-26)

Surely it was not a coincidence that at the moment of Jesus' death, the thick curtain that blocked off the Most Holy Place in the temple was torn in two (Matthew 27:50,51). Jesus' sacrifice for sin had removed the barrier between us and God! It is no coincidence that the New Testament now uses the word *priest* to refer to all believers and not only public ministers of the gospel. Jesus' sacrifice for sin means that we do not need a mediator between God and us, for Jesus is that Mediator, and has made us one again with God!

The concept described above is often called the *universal priesthood of all believers*. By calling us to faith in his Son, God has made us his priests. "You are a chosen people, a royal priesthood, a holy nation, God's special possession, that you may declare the praises of him who called you out of darkness into his wonderful light" (1 Peter 2:9).

So what does the universal priesthood of all believers have to do with worship? In the Old Testament, believers were much more passive in worship while the priests carried out the God-prescribed actions and sacrifices. But now we are all priests! As God's priests, we do not need someone else to act or intercede for us. That has already been done through the work of Christ. Now we have the privilege to approach God directly in worship and prayer. Instead of passively observing the gospel communicated through Old Testament symbolic actions, we have the privilege of actively proclaiming the gospel through our public praises and confessions of faith. The priesthood of all believers does not negate the need for public ministers of the gospel who proclaim God's Word and administer his sacraments on behalf of his people. But the universal priesthood of all believers does suggest that God's people will participate actively in public prayer and praise, even as God's called servants preside over the church's public worship.

The active participation of God's people in worship was an important outgrowth of the Lutheran Reformation. In his desire to bring the gospel message to worshipers, Luther's worship reforms replaced Latin with German, the language of the people, in regions where Latin was not understood. Luther encouraged the use of German hymns and even wrote several hymns which put the gospel message on the lips of choirs and congregations. Although research tells us that it took many generations before Lutheran congregations became as active in public worship as we know today, Luther's worship reforms and typical Lutheran services in our day encourage the active participation of the people, who demonstrate their priesthood when they approach God publicly in prayers, confessions of faith, and praise.

Respect for the church's past experience

The roots of the Christian church extend back two millennia, and even further when we recognize that Old Testament believers waited for the same Savior in whom we also believe. Over thousands of years of history, God preserved his people in the faith and gathered his elect into his kingdom. Through the common bond of faith in Jesus Christ, we have a connection to countless souls who have gone before us.

The writer of the New Testament book called Hebrews lists the names of many great Old Testament heroes of faith in chapter 11, sometimes called the "Hall of Faith" chapter. After describing many past heroes of faith, the writer encourages his readers, "*Since we are surrounded by such a great cloud of witnesses,* let us throw off everything that hinders and the sin that so easily entangles. And let us run with perseverance the race marked out for us" (Hebrews 12:1). The writer, inspired by the Holy Spirit, uses the examples of Old Testament believers to encourage us today. The very next chapter contains a similar encouragement: "Remember your leaders, who spoke the word of God to you. Consider the outcome of their way of life and *imitate their faith*" (Hebrews 13:7). This verse adds the thought that believers who lived and died before us provide us with a pattern to imitate in our lives of faith today.

Martin Luther and the other Lutheran reformers recognized the value of a connection to the saints who came before us. When Lutherans first published their official confessions of faith in the *Book of Concord* in 1580, they were sure to include the three historic creeds of Christianity—the Apostles' Creed, the Nicene Creed, and the Athanasian Creed. The ecumenical creeds, as they are called, connected the Lutherans' confessions of faith to the very first centuries of the ancient church. The message was clear: Our Lutheran forefathers confessed the very same faith that believers have confessed throughout church history—the faith taught in the Scriptures and accurately reflected in Christianity's ancient creeds.

Martin Luther applied the same principle to the worship. Luther did not reconstruct the church's worship life from the ground up. Rather he retained whatever he could from the historic church while eliminating practices that had crept into worship which clouded, confused, or contradicted the gospel. When Luther introduced his Latin order of worship in 1523, he wrote, "The service now in common use everywhere goes back to genuine Christian beginnings, as does the office of preaching. . . . It is not our intention to do away with the service, but to restore it again to its rightful use."[15] Seven years later, Luther's colleague, Phillip Melanchthon, wrote in the Augsburg Confession that the Lutheran reformers had no desire or intention to divorce themselves from valuable and historic church practices. Speaking about the customary Communion services in the church, the Augsburg Confession states, "Our churches are falsely accused of abolishing the Mass. The Mass is held among us and celebrated with the highest reverence. Nearly all the usual ceremonies are also preserved. . . . It does not appear that the Mass is more devoutly celebrated among our adversaries than among us."[16]

Many elements of Christian worship help us to experience a connection to the church of ages past. Hymns from the Lutheran Reformation era connect us to our Lutheran forefathers who confessed the truth of the gospel at great personal risk. Some of the most common vestments worn by clergy find their origins in the first centuries of Christianity. The words of familiar canticles such as the "Gloria in Excelsis" (Latin for "Glory [to God] in the highest") have been sung for centuries. The following responsive dialogue at the beginning of the celebration of Holy Communion can be traced back as early as the second century, and serves as a subtle reminder of our connection to our brothers and sisters in Christ from the church's infant years.

> *Minister:*   The Lord be with you.
> *Congregation:* And also with you.
>
> *Minister:*   Lift up your hearts.
> *Congregation:* We lift them up to the Lord.
>
> *Minister:*   Let us give thanks to the Lord our God.
> *Congregation:* It is right to give him thanks and praise.

Professional sports teams with a long history occasionally have their players wear throwback jerseys for games. Throwback jerseys are designed to look like the uniforms that players wore decades earlier. Throwback jerseys are one way that teams recall their history and tradition in professional sports. Fans that see the players competing in their throwback jerseys are reminded of the storied franchise that they support.

When the church's public worship respects and experiences worship practices from the church's history, the message is the same. Ancient songs, historic customs, and even the pastor's throwback vestments imitate the faith of those who have gone before us and remind us that we are a part of the church that spans back to centuries before our time. Believers who preceded us confessed the same faith we confess. They faced the same struggles and temptations we face. They found peace and forgiveness in the same Savior who absolves us today. What a beautiful reminder of the great cloud of witnesses who have gone before us and whose examples of faith inspire us today!

Unity in the body of Christ

Many people belong to an organization that encourages an activity that they are interested in. Someone who likes to sing may join a community choir. Children who enjoy playing baseball often join a Little League baseball team in their city. College students who are interested in acting could join the drama club in their school. In each case, these people share a common interest that unites them together in a larger organization. The common activity that the group engages in strengthens the common bond that they share with one another.

Christians also have a common bond that unites them. Our common bond is not music, sports, or drama. Our common bond is our faith in Jesus Christ. In Ephesians 4, the apostle Paul explains that the preaching and teaching of God's Word unites God's people together through the common bond of faith in Jesus: "So Christ himself gave the apostles, the prophets, the evangelists, the pastors and teachers, to equip his people for works of service, so that the body of Christ may be built up *until we all reach unity in the faith and in the knowledge of the Son of God* and become mature, attaining to the whole measure of the fullness of Christ" (Ephesians 4:11-13). Earlier in the same chapter, Paul encourages his readers to live honorably and act lovingly toward their fellow Christians. Such behavior reflected the unity that the Holy Spirit gave them by bringing them to faith in Jesus. Paul said, "Make every effort to keep the unity of the Spirit through the bond of peace. There is one body and one Spirit, just as you were called to one hope when you were called; one Lord, one faith, one baptism; one God and Father of all, who is over all and through all and in all" (Ephesians 4:3-6).

The "one body" word picture in the previous quote is also found in other New Testament letters that Paul wrote. Paul wrote in Romans 12:4,5, "Just as each of us has one body with many members, and these members do not all have the same function, so in Christ we, though many, form one body, and each member belongs to all the others." Paul's words remind us that Christians who are united by faith are not clones of one another. Rather they are brought together by their common bond of faith in Jesus Christ and have been blessed with different talents to contribute to the church. Paul expands that point in 1 Corinthians 12:12,13 to note the unity we share despite differences in our backgrounds and life circumstances: "Just as a body, though one, has many parts, but all its many parts form one body, so it is with Christ. For we were all baptized by one Spirit so as to form one body—whether Jews or Gentiles, slave or free—and we were all given the one Spirit to drink."

Not only does the New Testament emphasize the unity that believers share, but it also warns against anything that could threaten our unity. One of the greatest threats to Christian unity is false teaching. Scripture repeatedly emphasizes the importance of holding on to all its teachings. Before ascending into heaven, Jesus commanded his apostles to make disciples by "teaching them to obey *everything* [he had] commanded [them]" (Matthew 28:20). The apostle Paul warned Titus, "As for a person who stirs up division, after warning him once and then twice, have nothing more to do with him" (Titus 3:10 ESV). Our modern religious climate prefers to ignore differences in doctrine and imagine that unity exists even when it does not. Therefore, as we strive to emphasize our unity in worship, we dare not give an impression that our unity is connected to something other than our fully united confession of faith, our fully united commitment to the Scriptures, and our fully united confidence in the gospel's power.

Self-centered attitudes and loveless actions are also threats to our Christian unity. Paul's first letter to the Corinthians contains pointed warnings against such actions and attitudes. One problem that threatened the Corinthians' unity was the factions that developed within their congregation. Instead of finding unity in their common confession of faith in Jesus, they formed cliques based on their favorite pastor. In 1 Corinthians 1:10-12, Paul urges his readers:

> I appeal to you, brothers and sisters, in the name of our Lord Jesus Christ, that all of you agree with one another in what you say and that there be no divisions among you, but that you be perfectly united in mind and thought. My brothers and sisters, some from Chloe's household have informed me that there are quarrels among you. What I mean is this: One of you says, "I follow Paul"; another, "I follow Apollos"; another, "I follow Cephas"; still another, "I follow Christ."

At this end of this rebuke, Paul asks them, "Is Christ divided? Was Paul crucified for you? Were you baptized in the name of Paul?" (1 Corinthians 1:13). The answer to each of these rhetorical questions is an obvious "No!" Personal preferences were not reasons for divisions within their congregation.

Later in the same letter, Paul addresses divisions that had developed in their celebration of the Lord's Supper. The Corinthians had a fellowship meal prior to the celebration of the Lord's Supper; this meal is often called the *agape* meal (*agape* is a Greek word for "love"). Believers would gather as a congregation and share a meal together, with the wealthier members of the congregation often providing the food for those who were less fortunate. Unfortunately, the wealthier members in Corinth started to show little regard for their less fortunate brothers and sisters.

> I hear that when you come together as a church, there are divisions among you, and to some extent I believe it. . . . So then, when you come together, it is not the Lord's Supper you eat, for when you are eating, some of you go ahead with your own private suppers. As a result, one person remains hungry and another gets drunk. Don't you have homes to eat and drink in? Or do you despise the church of God by humiliating those who have nothing? What shall I say to you? Shall I praise you? Certainly not in this matter! (1 Corinthians 11:18,20-22)

The kinds of divisions resulting from this loveless behavior hardly reflected the unity that believers should share when they jointly participate in the Lord's Supper. One chapter earlier, Paul reminded his readers about that unity: "Is not the cup of thanksgiving for which we give thanks a participation in the blood of Christ? And is not the bread that we break a participation in the body of Christ? Because there is one loaf, *we, who are many, are one body*, for we all share the one loaf" (1 Corinthians 10:16,17).

The illustrations at the start of this section reminded us that people who share a common interest strengthen their bond with each other by joining together in that common activity. In a similar way, believers who worship together strengthen the bonds of fellowship that exist because of our common confession of faith. Hebrews 10:25 reminds us, "Let us not neglect meeting together, as some have the habit of doing. Rather, let us encourage each other, and all the more as you see the Day approaching" (EHV). Gathering together as a Christian congregation around the

Word and sacraments strengthens us in faith and mutually encourages one another, building up the bonds of fellowship we share.

The unity that faith in Christ gives us and the Scriptures express have implications for the way we carry out public worship in our congregations. Paul's repeated picture of the church as a body reminds us that the members of the body are all different from one another. Christians are not clones, and Christianity does not create clones. But our faith and our worship gatherings bring us together as one body, despite—and even with appreciation for— our differences, "so that with one mind and one voice you may glorify the God and Father of our Lord Jesus Christ" (Romans 15:6). The gospel proclaimed in public worship unites people across generations, ethnicities, and other demographic distinctions. We are all equally sinners, and through our Spirit-given faith we are equally forgiven and adopted children of God.

Imagine this setting. A congregation gathers for worship on Sunday morning. In the assembly are a wide range of ages. People have gathered, representing several different ethnic backgrounds. The opening hymn is a German Lutheran hymn with roots dating back to the Lutheran Reformation. The main songs of the service are set to new music composed within the last decade. The words of the psalm are set to music arranged in an African-American Gospel style. The choir sings an anthem that uses an early American folk tune. Later in the service, the congregation sings a hymn to a melody from Hispanic culture. The music in a service such as this reflects the different members of the body of Christ gathered for worship, but it also helps those different members to appreciate and cherish one another's unique contributions.

It is not always practically possible to unite everyone together. A church that serves a community where
some do not speak English may choose to offer services
in different languages. The church's intent in that case
is not to divide people by demographics but to make sure
that worshipers understand the gospel message. A church
may offer services at times other than Sunday morning
to accommodate those who work on Sundays. A pastor
visits the shut-in members of his congregation, sharing
a devotion and the Lord's Supper with them because
their health prevents them from gathering together with
their fellow believers at church. The biblical encouragement that believers be a unified body does not prevent us
from addressing circumstances that necessitate gathering
together at different times for different reasons. But it does
encourage us to think and act in a way that unites the
body of Christ.

The unity we enjoy with fellow Christians who share
a common confession of faith is something we dare not
take for granted. On Thursday of Holy Week, Jesus prayed
to his Father in heaven for unity among his believers: "I
pray also for those who will believe in me through [the
apostles'] message, that all of them may be one, Father, just
as you are in me and I am in you. . . . I have given them
the glory that you gave me, that they may be one as we
are one—I in them and you in me—so that they may be
brought to complete unity. Then the world will know that
you sent me and have loved them even as you have loved
me" (John 17:20-23). The psalm writer cherishes that
unity: "How good and pleasant it is when God's people
live together in unity!" (Psalm 133:1).

The three worship principles we considered in this
chapter have looked at worship through the perspective of

people. We recognize that those who have gathered are a part of God's universal priesthood. We honor and respect the worship practices of believers who have preceded us into heaven and whose examples of faith inspire us today. We strive to express our unity with one another as we gather for worship.

In the next chapter, we will consider three additional principles for worship that focus especially on the *content* in Christian worship.

4

Principles for Worship—Part 2

Anyone who has been involved with a wedding ceremony knows that there are many details to be concerned about. Some of those details have to do with *people*: Who is invited to the ceremony? Which friends and family members will be members of the wedding party? How will the parents of the bride and groom be ushered forward when the ceremony is ready to begin? Then there are details that have to do with the *content* of the wedding service: What song will the organist play as the bride processes down the aisle? What hymns or solo anthems will be sung in the service? What Scripture readings will be a part of the ceremony? Some details fit into both categories, and not every detail necessarily fits neatly into a precise category. But it is important that the details about people and

and the details about content are both considered before the day of the ceremony. The likelihood of a problem-free ceremony is much higher when both sets of details are addressed in preparation for the wedding service.

What is true of a wedding service in particular is true of public worship in general. Scripture guides us with wisdom that addresses the *people* gathered for worship, and Scripture guides us with wisdom that addresses the *content* of worship. Some of the things that the Bible says about public worship may overlap into both categories, and not everything the Bible tells us can be placed neatly into a precise category. But Scripture does guide us with principles that address the people gathered in worship, and Scripture also guides us with principles that speak to the content of worship. The principles about people discussed in the last chapter and the principles about worship content in this chapter do not exhaust everything Scripture has to say about public worship, but these principles will guide us well as we plan and carry out public worship.

Christian freedom

An important biblical concept that guides what we do in public worship is called *adiaphora*. The word *adiaphora* is a Greek term that has been taken into English. The term literally means "indifferent things" (*Adiaphoron* is the singular form). Adiaphora refers to everything that God has neither commanded nor forbidden us to do.

God has called us to preach his Word of forgiveness, baptize, and receive the Lord's Supper. These means of grace are not adiaphora, because God directs us to use these to spread and strengthen his kingdom. God's Word forbids us from worshiping other gods and preaching anything in his name that is not found in Scripture. Idolatry and false doctrine are not adiaphora because God forbids both. Between the things that God commands and forbids is the area of adiaphora, or Christian freedom. For example, God has not directed us to follow a specific order of service each Sunday. He has not dictated what hymns we should sing each week in public worship. Our hymns and orders of service are adiaphora, for they are aspects of worship that he has not commanded or forbidden.

There is a great deal in public worship that God has not commanded or forbidden. This statement alone might leave someone with the impression that we then have the freedom to do whatever we please in public worship. However, Scripture teaches us that in matters of adiaphora, our goal ought not be simply to do as we please. In cases of adiaphora, we have a God-given opportunity to show our love for our fellow believers by considering what action would best serve them and demonstrate Christian care and concern.

There are two main sections in the Bible where the concept of adiaphora is taught: Romans 14,15 and 1 Corinthians 8–10. In both sections, the main issue Paul discusses is eating meat. Modern American Christians may find that to be an odd topic for a discussion about Christian freedom, but this would not have seemed odd at all to our Christian ancestors in the first century. With no refrigeration to preserve meat, a person who wanted meat for a meal would have purchased it in the local marketplace on the same day that the animal had been slaughtered. The simple reality was that most of the meat sold in the marketplace came from animals that had been sacrificed to false gods in pagan worship rituals earlier that same day. Some Christians felt that eating such meat would be wrong. Other Christians knew that they were not worshiping a false god by eating meat, even if it had come from a pagan sacrifice, and so they did not have a problem eating meat. The apostle Paul explained that there was no problem eating meat, even if it came to the marketplace after it had been sacrificed in a pagan ritual. He wrote to the Corinthians,

> So then, about eating food sacrificed to idols: We know that "An idol is nothing at all in the world" and that "There is no God but one." For even if there are so-called gods, whether in heaven or on earth (as indeed there are many "gods" and many "lords"), yet for us there is but one God, the Father, from whom all things came and for whom we live; and there is but one Lord, Jesus Christ, through whom all things came and through whom we live. (1 Corinthians 8:4-6)

If Paul had concluded the discussion there, every individual Christian would be free to do what he or she preferred in this matter of adiaphora. But the Holy Spirit led Paul to issue a caution about the exercise of Christian freedom: "Not everyone possesses this knowledge. Some people are still so accustomed to idols that when they eat sacrificial food they think of it as having been sacrificed to a god, and since their conscience is weak, it is defiled" (1 Corinthians 8:7). Even though any Christian had the freedom to eat meat if he wanted to, Paul wanted Christians who recognized this freedom to be considerate of their fellow believers who had a difficult time distinguishing between eating meat and partaking in a pagan sacrifice. With concern for those with a sensitive conscience, Paul wrote:

> Be careful, however, that the exercise of your rights does not become a stumbling block to the weak. For if someone with a weak conscience sees you, with all your knowledge, eating in an idol's temple, won't that person be embold-

ened to eat what is sacrificed to idols? So this weak brother or sister, for whom Christ died, is destroyed by your knowledge. When you sin against them in this way and wound their weak conscience, you sin against Christ. Therefore, if what I eat causes my brother or sister to fall into sin, I will never eat meat again, so that I will not cause them to fall. (1 Corinthians 8:9-13)

Freedom to carry out a specific action does not mean that the action is wise. Speaking to the same issue, Paul urged his readers to consider the effects of their actions on others. " 'I have the right to do anything,' you say—but not everything is beneficial. 'I have the right to do anything'— but not everything is constructive. No one should seek their own good, but the good of others" (1 Corinthians 10:23,24). Christians united as the body of Christ need to take the other parts of the body into consideration when they deal with adiaphora. In love for our brothers and sisters in faith, and with a desire to give a clear confession of faith in all that we do, we may choose to restrain the use of our freedom. Paul's words to the Romans underscore this point: "Make up your mind not to put any stumbling block or obstacle in the way of a brother or sister. If your brother or sister is distressed because of what you eat, you are no longer acting in love. Do not by your eating destroy someone for whom Christ died" (Romans 14:13,15).

So how do Paul's instructions about adiaphora apply to Christian worship? The exact form that public worship takes is an adiaphoron. Apart from the directives to preach, teach, absolve, baptize, and commune, the Bible does not give explicit instructions about public worship. In fact, the New Testament specifically states that there are no commands from God about special days or customs for worship: "Do not let anyone judge you by what you eat or drink, or with regard to a religious festival, a New Moon celebration or a Sabbath day" (Colossians 2:16). But as we have seen, our freedom needs to be tempered by wisdom that seeks to give a clear confession and avoids unnecessary confusion. In addition to Paul's previously quoted statement from 1 Corinthians 10:23,24, his additional comments in Romans guide us with a spirit of Christian love for one another. "Let us therefore make every effort to do what leads to peace and to mutual edification. . . . Each of us should please our neighbors for their good, to build them up" (Romans 14:19; 15:2). The decisions we make about public worship are done with complete freedom, but are made with a desire to best serve and edify all the members of the body of Christ.

In everyday life, we realize that there are decisions we can make that are not wrong but are also not wise. There is nothing necessarily sinful about skipping breakfast and drinking coffee while commuting to work in the morning, but we also realize that such a choice is not the healthiest decision we could make. It is wiser and healthier if we enjoy a more balanced meal to start the day. We will not break any traffic laws if we regularly drive our cars with the gas gauge just hovering above empty, but we also realize that failing to fill our car's tank may cause us to be stranded in an inopportune time and place. Decisions we make in daily life are not always based on whether something is absolutely right or wrong but on whether something may be wise or unwise.

What is true in everyday life is true in public worship. We may have the freedom to sing a particular Christian song in public worship, but if that song contains a message that is potentially unclear or misleading, wisdom suggests that we make a different choice. We may have the freedom to use a specific historic ceremony in our services, but if that ceremony fails to communicate clearly to today's worshipers as well as it did in the past, wisdom suggests that we forgo an unclear custom. We may have the freedom to use vastly different forms of worship in every congregation, but if greatly varying practices causes confusion among Christians within the same denomination, wisdom suggests that we restrain our freedom out of love for others.

In a letter written in 1525, Luther reflected similar wisdom:

> Now even though external rites and orders . . . add nothing to salvation, yet it is un-Christian to quarrel over such things and thereby to confuse the common people. We should consider the edification of the lay folk more important than our own ideas and opinions. Therefore, I pray all of you, my dear sirs, let each one surrender his own opinions and get together in a friendly way and come to a common decision about these external matters, so that there will be one uniform practice throughout your district instead of disorder—one thing being done here and another there—lest the common people get confused and discouraged.

> For even though from the viewpoint of faith, the external orders are free and can without scruples be changed by anyone at any time, yet from the viewpoint of love, you are not free to use this liberty, but bound to consider the edification of the common people. . . .

> Now when your people are confused and offended by your lack of uniform order, you cannot plead, "Externals are free. Here in my own place I am going to do as I please." But you are bound to consider the effect of your attitude on others. By faith be free in your conscience toward God, but by love be bound to serve your neighbor's edification.[17]

When decisions are made about the specific content or forms in public worship, our freedom must be exercised with brotherly Christian wisdom that is driven by love for our fellow believers and for our larger fellowship. Saint Paul's words are a good reminder for us in matters of adiaphora: "Be completely humble and gentle; be patient, bearing with one another in love. Make every effort to keep the unity of the Spirit through the bond of peace" (Ephesians 4:2,3).

The best of God's gifts in music and the arts

Beauty was a mark of God's original, perfect creation. Genesis 2:9 notes, "The LORD God made all kinds of trees grow out of the ground—trees that were *pleasing to the eye* and good for food." God could have created an entirely pragmatic world—a world with one kind of tree and one kind of fruit. But God's kindness and love for the crown of his creation could be seen in the beautiful world that God made for Adam and Eve and all their descendants to enjoy. Whether we look at the world around us, the universe above us, or the way that God created us, the evidence of his kindness and love in his beautiful creation inspires our praise. King David wrote, "I praise you because I am fearfully and wonderfully made; your works are wonderful, I know that full well" (Psalm 139:14).

The gifts of God that we see in his created world are sometimes called *First Article gifts*. In the First Article of the Apostles' and Nicene Creeds, we confess that God is the creator of heaven and earth. His creation inspires our praise. Just as God's First Article gifts inspire our thanksgiving, his *Second Article gifts* also fill our hearts with gratitude and praise. The Second Article of the Apostles' and Nicene Creeds discusses the saving work of Jesus on our behalf. In Philippians 2:6-11, a section that many believe is a quotation from an ancient Christian hymn, the apostle Paul shows how the humiliation and exaltation of Jesus, truths we consider in the Second Article of the Creeds, inspire our praise:

> [Jesus Christ], being in very nature God,
>> did not consider equality with God something to be
>>> used to his own advantage;
> rather, he made himself nothing
>> by taking the very nature of a servant,
>> being made in human likeness.
> And being found in appearance as a man,
>> he humbled himself
>> by becoming obedient to death—
>>> even death on a cross!
>
> Therefore God exalted him to the highest place
>> and gave him the name that is above every name,
> that at the name of Jesus every knee should bow,
>> in heaven and on earth and under the earth,
> and every tongue acknowledge that Jesus Christ is Lord,
>> to the glory of God the Father.

There is no doubt that God has given us his best gifts in his creation and our salvation. And there is no doubt that souls who personally have received Christ's forgiveness through faith in Jesus and whom the Spirit has brought to appreciate all of God's gifts will want to give their best back to God in thanksgiving.

Abel, the son of Adam and Eve, responded to the blessings of God by offering a sacrifice from the best animals in his flocks (Genesis 4:4). When the Israelites offered sacrifices to God as an expression of their total devotion to him, the animals used for those sacrifices were to be the best of that person's flocks—an animal without any flaws or defects (Leviticus 1:3). When the great temple in Jerusalem was built under King Solomon's reign, only the finest materials were used in its construction: dressed stones, bronze pillars, stands, and basins, and cedar wood overlaid with gold (1 Kings 6,7).

God's people respond to God's gifts by giving their best back to him. Anything less would be unthinkable! Centuries after King Solomon, the Israelites had fallen into the sinful pattern of giving God less than their best in their offerings. Malachi echoed the Lord's displeasure for their subpar offerings:

> "When you offer blind animals for sacrifice, is that not wrong? When you sacrifice lame or diseased animals, is that not wrong? Try offering them to your governor! Would he be pleased with you? Would he accept you?" says the LORD Almighty. . . . "Oh, that one of you would shut the temple doors, so that you would not light useless fires on my altar! I am not pleased with you," says the LORD Almighty, "and I will accept no offering from your hands. My name will be great among the nations, from where the sun rises to where it sets. In every place incense and pure offerings will be brought to me, because my name will be great among the nations," says the LORD Almighty. (Malachi 1:8,10,11)

The God who gave us a beautiful world and who continues to shower us with beautiful gifts of his kindness inspires us to respond to his goodness with our best as we proclaim his grace in public worship. One of the ways that Christians throughout the ages have given their best gifts back to God in worship is by proclaiming the gospel message through music and other arts. Arts and music have been used by the church to portray and proclaim the very same biblical message of law and gospel in a way that engages all our senses and touches our hearts. Using the arts to honor Christ by proclaiming his forgiveness also honors a concept we learned in chapter 1: Praise is proclamation.

Psalm 150, the final entry in the book of Psalms, serves as a doxology—a short statement of praise—to conclude the Old Testament's hymnal. Notice how the psalm writer encourages a generous use of the musical arts and of all creation in praise of the Lord:

> Praise the LORD.
>
> Praise God in his sanctuary;
>   praise him in his mighty heavens.
> Praise him for his acts of power;
>   praise him for his surpassing greatness.
> Praise him with the sounding of the trumpet,
>   praise him with the harp and lyre,
> praise him with timbrel and dancing,
>   praise him with the strings and pipe,
> praise him with the clash of cymbals,
>   praise him with resounding cymbals.
>
> Let everything that has breath praise the LORD.
>
> Praise the LORD.

Martin Luther also recognized the great potential that music and the arts have in public worship. While some more radical reformers in Luther's day wanted to ban altars, music, ceremony, and the arts, Luther himself saw these as blessings from God with the ability to proclaim the gospel.[18] In his commentary on Psalm 101, Luther said, "God's Word is presented so powerfully, lucidly, and clearly in preaching, singing, speaking, writing, and painting that they must concede it is the true Word of God."[19] Luther did not throw out the proverbial baby with the bathwater; he did not dismiss music and the arts as a mere external addition to worship. Rather he saw the arts as a vehicle to proclaim the gospel in a beautiful way, responding to God's grace by putting our best efforts forward in gospel proclamation. In the preface to a volume of church music published in 1538, Luther said, "The gift of language combined with the gift of song was only given to man to let him know that he should praise God with both word and music, namely, by proclaiming [the Word of God] through music and by providing sweet melodies with words."[20] Several years earlier, in the preface to the first Lutheran hymnal published in 1524, Luther stated his appreciation for music and the arts as good gifts of God to be placed into his service:

> That it is good and God pleasing to sing hymns is, I think, known to every Christian; for everyone is aware not only of the example of the prophets and kings in the Old Testament who praised God with song and sound, with poetry and psaltery, but also of the common and ancient custom of the Christian church to sing Psalms. St. Paul himself instituted this in 1 Corinthians 14:15 and exhorted the Colossians 3:16 to sing spiritual songs and Psalms heartily unto the Lord so that God's Word and Christian teaching might be instilled and implanted in many ways. . . . Nor am I of the opinion that the gospel should destroy and blight all the arts, as some of the pseudo-religious claim. But I would like to see all the arts, especially music, used in the service of Him who gave and made them. I therefore pray that every pious Christian would be pleased with this [the use of music in the service of the gospel] and lend his help if God has given him like or greater gifts.[21]

Countless examples of the way that art and music teach the faith and honor God with our best could be cited. Here are two brief examples. Lucas Cranach was a painter in the Reformation era who painted a famous portrait of Luther as well as other paintings that depicted Lutheran theology through art. In one of his paintings,

Cranach pictured Luther preaching to a congregation while pointing to an image of Christ on the cross. Cranach's portrait visualized the central message of Lutheran preaching—"Jesus Christ and him crucified" (1 Corinthians 2:2)—through the medium of painting. The great Lutheran musical composer, Johann Sebastian Bach, wrote many works for choir and organ that portrayed biblical truths through music. Bach wrote a short piece for organ based on the hymn, "If You But Trust in God to Guide You" (*Christian Worship: A Lutheran Hymnal* 444). As the title suggests, the hymn is a statement of trust in the Lord. In Bach's arrangement, the bass line, played by the feet in the pedal division of the organ, features several small and large leaps over other notes. This feature is Bach's way to musically depict the leaps of faith that are a part of our Christian lives as we trust our God and follow him in faith into each new day.

Art and music are gifts of God. Like anything else we have in this world, sinful human beings are prone to take God's good gifts and abuse them. Genesis 3 records the fall into sin; in the very next chapter, the gift of art is abused as Lamech uses poetry to boast about a murder he committed (Genesis 4:23,24). Readers will not need to think long to recall modern-day examples of art and music that mock biblical values or ridicule Christian beliefs. We must acknowledge with sadness that God's good gifts, including art and music, can be easily used for a sinful purpose, but the potential misuse of the arts does not negate their proper and beneficial use in public worship.

Our use of the arts in worship is just another aspect of our Christian stewardship. Stewardship is the way we manage the blessings God gives us. When it comes to stewardship, we want to respond to God's grace with our best. This is not only true with our monetary gifts or the time and talents we give to our local congregation. This is also true with the way we use God's best gifts as we proclaim the gospel and praise him in public worship. May every pastor, parishioner, musician, and church member strive to give their best gifts in the service of the Lord, who gave his best and greatest gift to us—his one and only Son!

Guided by form

Most business meetings follow an agenda. The agenda indicates what items of business will be discussed and the order in which those items will be considered. A formal meeting procedure, such as *Robert's Rules of Order*, may be used to maintain good decorum during the meeting and prevent chaotic discussion. A meeting agenda and procedure helps to ensure that the meeting will take place smoothly and the necessary business receives proper time for discussion.

In this sense, public worship is much the same. Lutherans typically have a set form for worship that they use—an order that is either found in a hymnal or reprinted in a service booklet for the congregation to follow. The order indicates the Scripture readings they will hear, the hymns they will sing, and the times when the pastor or congregation will speak.

The apostle Paul described the benefits of an orderly service in 1 Corinthians. Worship in ancient Corinth had been marked by disorderly instances of many people speaking in tongues. Although this was a gift from God for the benefit of the early Christian church, the Corinthians abused this gift by failing to interpret the miraculous message that some had received so that the message could edify the entire congregation. Paul's solution provided order to what was otherwise a chaotic worship gathering:

What then shall we say, brothers and sisters? When you come together, each of you has a hymn, or a word of instruction, a revelation, a tongue or an interpretation. Everything must be done so that the church may be built up. If anyone speaks in a tongue, two—or at the most three—should speak, one at a time, and someone must interpret. If there is no interpreter, the speaker should keep quiet in the church and speak to himself and to God.

Two or three prophets should speak, and the others should weigh carefully what is said. And if a revelation comes to someone who is sitting down, the first speaker should stop. For you can all prophesy in turn so that everyone may be instructed and encouraged. The spirits of prophets are subject to the control of prophets. For God is not a God of disorder but of peace. . . . Everything should be done in a fitting and orderly way. (1 Corinthians 14:26-33,40)

Paul's words demonstrate one reason why a form for worship can be a great blessing to God's people. A well-planned form for worship will be arranged for the strengthening of the church. Paul's proposal ended the chaotic approach to speaking in tongues that the Corinthians had tolerated and introduced an orderly way of worship that could serve as a vehicle for proclaiming God's Word.

The benefit of a form for worship does not eliminate all problems that may occur in a set order of worship. Jesus himself had harsh criticism for the religious leaders of his day who observed outward forms of worship without inward hearts of faith. Jesus said to the Pharisees, "Isaiah was right when he prophesied about you hypocrites; as it is written: 'These people honor me with their lips, but their hearts are far from me'" (Mark 7:6).

Someone might hear Jesus' statement and wonder if he wasn't giving a broader condemnation against forms used in worship. Jesus condemned the Pharisees for observing outward rituals without inward faith, but he did not condemn forms and rituals themselves. In fact, Jesus honored the form of worship that had been established for the synagogue. Luke 4:16-21 records the occasion when Jesus served as the guest preacher for Sabbath Day worship in his hometown's synagogue. According to the synagogue's worship form and customs, Jesus stood to read, he read from the scroll that was handed to him (and may have read a Scripture lesson that had been appointed for that specific day), he returned the scroll, and then he sat down to preach. Jesus' use of the synagogue form for worship demonstrates that forms can be used to provide an orderly service that benefits the souls of those who have gathered for worship.

The Bible's encouragement for orderly worship is not an end to itself. The orders of worship that we use also reflect what we believe. An incident in the Bible that took place outside the realm of worship will help us understand this concept inside the realm of worship.

In Galatians 2:11-16, Saint Paul describes an unfortunate confrontation that took place between Saint Peter and himself. Peter was visiting the Christian congregation in Antioch, located over three hundred miles north of Jerusalem on the Orontes River. In Acts 11:19-26, we see how this congregation, made up of both Jews and Gentiles, was established by the witness of Christians fleeing persecution and later assisted by Paul and Barnabas. Sometime later, Peter came to visit the congregation. While Peter was there, additional visitors came from Jerusalem. At their arrival, Peter began to change his behavior. Previously he was happy to sit down and eat meals with the gentile believers in Antioch. Once the visitors from Jerusalem arrived, Peter reverted to an Old Testament ceremonial way of operating: He withdrew from eating with Gentiles because he feared the reaction that might come from a segment of Jewish believers who wanted to hold on to certain Old Testament customs and laws, including the practice of not eating with *unclean*, uncircumcised people and eating *unclean* food. Paul describes the incident in Galatians 2:11-14:

> When [Peter] came to Antioch, I opposed him to his face, because he stood condemned. For before certain men came from James, he used to eat with the Gentiles. But when they arrived, he began to draw back and separate himself from the Gentiles because he was afraid of those who belonged to the circumcision group. The other Jews joined him in his hypocrisy, so that by their hypocrisy even Barnabas was led astray.
>
> When I saw that they were not acting in line with the truth of the gospel, I said to [Peter] in front of them all, "You are a Jew, yet you live like a Gentile and not like a Jew. How is it, then, that you force Gentiles to follow Jewish customs?"

God had clearly revealed to Peter that those customs were no longer required and no longer served a purpose after Jesus fulfilled the law and won our redemption (Acts 10). Unfortunately, Peter's misleading behavior also led other Jewish Christians to withdraw from their gentile counterparts, even though such behavior was contrary to the unity that faith in Jesus brought to these believers. Paul responded with harsh criticism because Peter's actions did not reflect the oneness that Jewish and gentile Christians now shared.

Just as Peter's actions during fellowship meals in Antioch communicated a message—and in that case, the wrong message—so our actions, customs, and forms in public worship communicate a message about what we believe and teach. Because worship forms can also teach truths about our faith, especially when people repeatedly experience them over several years, we want to ensure that our actions and forms in worship communicate the right message.

Some Baptist congregations conclude their services with the sinner's prayer, a prayer that people who recently came to faith in Christ would use to accept Jesus Christ into their heart. However, Scripture teaches that human beings cannot accept Jesus as their Savior on their own (1 Corinthians 12:3), because they are born into this world spiritually dead (Ephesians 2:1-3). The sinner's prayer is really a reflection of decision theology, the false teaching that we can choose to accept Jesus Christ by our own power. If a Lutheran congregation included the sinner's prayer in worship, they would be communicating a message that conflicts with their beliefs.

Just as we must be cautious that our worship forms do not send the wrong message, so we should be aware that our worship forms can reinforce a proper understanding of what Scripture teaches. For example, whenever we see an infant baptism at the start of worship, several different biblical teachings are reinforced by the words and customs used in the baptismal service. The teaching of original sin is reinforced, that all people, including infants, are sinful from conception and birth and need God's forgiveness (Psalm 51:5). We are reminded of Jesus' Great Commission, which teaches us that Baptism is a means of grace for all nations, without exclusions or exceptions (Matthew 28:19). An infant baptism puts before our eyes the truth that the Holy Spirit is at work in this means of grace, washing away sin and bringing another soul to faith (Titus 3:5).

Many more examples, both positive and negative, could be given, but these two examples help us see that worship forms reflect and reinforce what we believe. Worship scholars often use the Latin phrase *lex orandi, lex credendi* to express this concept. *Lex orandi, lex credendi* means "the form of praying [is] the form of believing." In other words, the way we pray reflects what we believe. This point can be expanded to apply to everything that occurs in our worship forms: The way we worship reflects what we believe. The reverse is also true: What we believe directs the way we worship. Our faith directs how we worship, and our forms of worship can reinforce the truths we believe by repeated use over many months, years, and decades.

This final principle for worship leads into the next section of our study. Now that we have surveyed Scripture for its guidance and direction in public worship, we will look at specific forms and patterns that believers have used throughout the church's history that proclaim the gospel faithfully and honor the other principles we have gleaned from God's Word.

5

The Liturgy—An Overview

Sunday morning worship is about to begin. The organist completes her preservice music. The pastor enters the front of the church and introduces the service before it starts. He welcomes the congregation and says a few words about the focus of the day's service. His final statement is, "After our opening hymn, we will follow the liturgy that begins on page 40 in front of the hymnal."

The term *liturgy* might not be familiar to all Christians, but it is familiar among many Lutherans. We sometimes use the term to describe the order of service that is used during worship as in the example above. While the term can refer generally to an order of service, it can also refer to a specific pattern for worship that has been passed down throughout the church's history. The word is sometimes capitalized to distinguish between a *liturgy* as an order of service and the *Liturgy* as a particular form of worship.

With the biblical guidance for worship from the previous chapters in mind, we will now look at the Liturgy, one of the most common patterns of worship used among Lutherans. As noted in chapter 1, this term comes from the Greek verb *leitourgeo* and noun *leitourgia*. The words initially referred to public service that benefited the greater population; Christians later adopted the term to refer to the service of the people that took place in public worship. This pattern for worship finds its roots in the early years of the Christian church, and continues to find a home in many Christian churches in the 21st century. It also has been shaped throughout 2,000 years of Christian history. The Liturgy finds a natural place in Lutheran worship today because it provides an excellent framework for the gospel to be proclaimed and the Lord's Supper to be celebrated.

It is not within the scope of this basic volume on worship to provide a detailed historical development of the Liturgy. Several other professional volumes are available to meet this need. However, our overview of the Liturgy will make several connections to its development in Christian history. We will refer to texts and patterns of the Liturgy as found in the services of *Christian Worship: Hymnal*.

Perhaps you have heard someone make the statement, "You can't see the forest because the trees are in the way." That statement means that others are so concerned with the individual details of a project that they cannot see the bigger picture. As we learn about the Liturgy in the next four chapters, we will look at the larger picture of the *forest* in this chapter before we take a closer look at the individual *trees* that make up the Liturgy.

Ordinary and Proper

A basic description of the Liturgy is that it is an order of worship with two components: the Ordinary and the Proper. The Ordinary refers to parts of the service whose words generally remain the same from week to week; they are *ordinarily* present in the service. The Proper refers to parts of the service that change from week to week; they are present in the service, but their texts are *proper* or unique to each individual service.

The Ordinary, by definition, consisted of five songs that are usually referred to by their Latin (or Greek) titles. Those songs include the "Kyrie," the "Gloria," the "Credo," the "Sanctus," and the "Agnus Dei."

Kyrie is the Greek word for "Lord." It is the first word in the Greek sentence, *Kyrie eleison,* translated, "Lord, have mercy." Sometimes the "Kyrie" has been used as an extension of the confession of sins. In *Christian Worship: Hymnal,* the "Kyrie" is its own element in the service following the confession of sins, where God's forgiven people plead for his mercy in all aspects of their lives.

The second major song of the Ordinary is known by the Latin word *Gloria,* the first word of the first phrase of the song "Glory to God in the Highest." The song's first phrase quotes the song of the angels on the night of Jesus' birth in Luke 2:14. After our pleas for God's forgiveness and his mercy, believers praise Jesus Christ as the One who has taken away our sin and now rules and reigns from heaven above. Notice how praise from God's people also proclaims the saving work of Jesus, the gospel:

> Glory to God in the highest, and peace to his people
> on earth.

> Lord God, heavenly King, almighty God and Father,
>   we worship you, we give you thanks, we praise you
>   for your glory!
> Lord Jesus Christ, only Son of the Father, Lord God,
>   Lamb of God,
>   you take away the sin of the world; have mercy on us.
> You are seated at the right hand of the Father;
>   receive our prayer.
> For you alone are the Holy One, you alone are the Lord,
>   you alone are the Most High, Jesus Christ,
>   with the Holy Spirit in the glory of God the Father.[22]

The third song that comprises the Ordinary is the Nicene Creed, known by the Latin word *Credo*, "I believe." The Nicene Creed is a fourth-century confession of faith that was first developed at the Council of Nicaea in A.D. 325 and later clarified at the Council of Constantinople in A.D. 381. The Creed and the two church councils that developed it were the church's response to false teachings about Jesus Christ promoted by Arius, who denied that Jesus was true God. The early church's Scripture-based confession of faith in Jesus Christ and the triune God is another strong gospel-proclaiming element of the Liturgy. The Creed is generally spoken after the sermon. We are accustomed to speaking the Creed today, but throughout the church's history the Creed was often chanted by a choir. Martin Luther's hymn "We All Believe in One True God" (*Christian Worship: Hymnal* 941) is a paraphrase of the Nicene Creed that allowed the Liturgy's confession of faith to be sung by the entire assembly rather than just the choir.

The final two songs of the Ordinary occur within the portion of the Liturgy that immediately precedes the distribution of Holy Communion. The "Sanctus," Latin for "holy," recalls Isaiah's vision of the angels and his call to be the Lord's prophet in Isaiah 6:1-8. The angels in Isaiah's vision called out to one another: "Holy, holy, holy is the LORD Almighty; the whole earth is full of his glory." These words are attached to the words of the Palm Sunday crowd in Matthew 21:9: "Blessed is he who comes in the name of the Lord! Hosanna in the highest!" (ESV). As we are about to receive Jesus' body and blood in the sacrament, believers acclaim the holy Lord whose presence they are about to enter, and they praise Christ who once came into Jerusalem to win our salvation and now comes to us in the sacrament to bring us the blessings of salvation that he won for us.

One more song completes the five songs of the Ordinary. *Agnus Dei* is the Latin phrase for "Lamb of God." The words of this song echo the words that John the Baptist spoke to point people to Jesus at the start of Jesus' ministry in John 1:29: "Look, the Lamb of God, who takes away the sin of the world!" Immediately before God's people come forward to receive Jesus' body and blood, we sing these simple words three times: "Lamb of God, you take away the sin of the world." We add the plea "Have mercy on us" to the first two statements and "Grant us your peace" to the final statement. There could hardly be a more fitting song for God's people to sing just before they approach the altar! We come to the Lord's Supper to receive the forgiveness that Christ won for us by giving his body and shedding his blood on the cross, and so we cry for his mercy and acknowledge his saving work in the words that we sing just before our reception of the sacrament.

These five parts of the service—the "Kyrie," "Gloria," "Credo," "Sanctus," and "Agnus Dei"—make up the Ordinary. However, they are not the only parts of the service that ordinarily appear with the same texts each week in worship. The Liturgy typically begins with the same invocation of the triune God: "In the name of the Father and of the Son and of the Holy Spirit." The pastor and assembly recite the nearly two-millennia-old dialogue called the Preface at the beginning of the Holy Communion portion of the service. Following a suggestion from Luther, Lutheran services regularly end with the threefold blessing that God first prescribed to be spoken over his Old Testament people in Numbers 6:24-26.[23]

In contrast to the Ordinary and the other features of the Liturgy whose texts remain the same from week to week, the Proper encompasses the features of the Liturgy whose texts change from week to week. Several elements of the Liturgy belong to the Proper. The Prayer of the Day is a short prayer that follows the "Gloria." Its words often indicate the general focus that is woven through that day's service. Three Bible readings follow the Prayer of the Day, which are often connected by a common emphasis. The Psalm of the Day is sung between the first two readings. The Gospel Acclamation, a sung Bible verse or statement framed with alleluias, leads into the Gospel. The Hymn of the Day follows the Scripture readings and precedes the sermon and frequently echoes thoughts from the Scripture readings in its poetry. The other hymns in the service also change from week to week and further reflect the focus of the day, the theme of the current church season, or other thoughts appropriate to the specific day, time, or occasion. The most obvious feature of the service that changes from week to week is the sermon. Each week the pastor chooses a portion of Scripture that will be the basis for his sermon. His selection is often one of the readings in the service. The sermon provides the pastor with an opportunity to teach and apply the message of law and gospel in that particular Scripture selection (called the *sermon text*) to his particular congregation on that particular day. While the Ordinary proclaims the gospel each week in a similar fashion, the Proper proclaims the gospel each week in a way that is unique to the season, Sunday, and circumstances in each individual congregation.

The structure of the Liturgy, with the Ordinary and the Proper, provides a way for congregations to proclaim the gospel in worship with familiarity and variety every week. The message of sin and grace is woven throughout the words of the Ordinary and the Scripture readings, songs, and sermon of the Proper. The structure encourages the assembly's participation in songs repeated each week and hymns that are unique to each day. The structure also connects us together with our Christian and Lutheran forefathers who worshiped with similar forms in their own times, places, and languages. The Liturgy provides an opportunity for a generous use of the arts and music, a form of worship that guides our gospel proclamation, and a context where we can wisely put our Christian freedom into practice with a worship format that connects us to each other and still allows for variety and flexibility from church to church. In short, the Liturgy's structure puts the biblical principles for worship that we learned earlier into practice for God's people who have gathered for public worship.

Sacramental and sacrificial

Another useful way to understand the Liturgy is to view it as a conversation between God and his people: God speaks, and we respond. With that perspective in mind, the Liturgy can be divided into another pair of categories: *sacramental* and *sacrificial*.

The term *sacramental* refers to the parts of the Liturgy in which God speaks to us. The term itself may be misleading if we assume that the sacramental parts of the service are only the parts that have to do with the sacraments. Our Lutheran understanding of the sacraments will be helpful for properly defining this term. In Baptism and the Lord's Supper, we recognize that God is coming to us, forgiving us, assuring us of his grace and mercy, and nourishing faith within our souls. God comes to us in the sacraments. In the same way, the sacramental parts of worship are the parts of the service where God speaks to us. He absolves us. He speaks to us through the Scripture readings. His gospel message to us is explained in the sermon. He comes to us in Holy Communion. He blesses us before we leave his house and return to our daily lives.

The term *sacrificial* refers to the parts of the Liturgy in which we respond to God. Just as the sacrifices of Old Testament believers were acts of worship and devotion toward God, so the sacrificial parts of the service are the aspects of worship where we speak to God and respond to his grace. We confess our sins. We praise him for his forgiveness. We sing songs and confess our faith in response to his Word. We plead for his mercy before we come to Holy Communion and bring our prayers to him throughout the service.

The minister's posture as he presides at the Liturgy can be helpful to recognize whether a part of the service is sacramental or sacrificial. Depending on the space and arrangements in the front of a church building, the pastor may take his place in front of the altar for one or more portions of the service. When he faces the congregation and his back is to the altar, his posture indicates that this is a part of the service directed toward us—a sacramental part of the Liturgy. When he faces the altar and his back is to the congregation, his posture indicates that this is a part of the service directed toward God—a sacrificial part of the Liturgy.

The distinction between sacramental and sacrificial portions of the service is helpful, but it is also important that we do not rigidly view each part of the service as belonging only to one category or the other. We noted in chapter 1 that when believers praise God (sacrificial), they proclaim what he has done (sacramental). Our prayers and hymns often thank God for the saving acts of his Son. Our response to God's Word in the Nicene Creed restates what he has done to save us. Likewise, we learned that proclaiming what God has done for us in Christ (sacramental) brings praise to him (sacrificial). The pastor who preaches the death and resurrection of Jesus Christ to his hearers not only proclaims the gospel to God's people, but he also brings praise to God for his great acts of grace. We may view individual parts of the service as sacramental or sacrificial, but because praising and proclaiming the gospel are so closely connected, we realize that these two categories are not mutually exclusive from each other.

Pattern of the Liturgy

The meeting of a church council is typically divided into several sections. An opening devotion, approving the previous meeting's minutes, reports from various boards and committees, discussion of old and new business, voting on resolutions, a closing prayer—these are all typical elements of a church council meeting. There may be several different ways to categorize these segments of the meeting, but the overall content and flow of a church council meeting will generally follow a common pattern.

The same could be said about the Liturgy. There are several individual parts that make up the Liturgy, and there are several different ways we could categorize these parts. The three settings of The Service in *Christian Worship: Hymnal* use two simple headings—The Word and The Sacrament—to divide the service into distinct sections. Some have suggested a four-fold approach: Gathering (the opening part of the service before the Scripture readings), Word, Sacrament, and Sending (the concluding part of the service after Holy Communion). Other ways to categorize the parts of the service are possible. In whatever way we choose to group the individual parts together, we will still see the prevalence of Christ's Word and sacrament as the gospel-foundation for worship.

We will now move from a general overview of the Liturgy (the forest) to a specific look at the individual parts of the service (the trees). As we look at the specific parts of the Liturgy from beginning to end, we will see once again that the gospel message that strengthens our faith is the same gospel message that is uniquely and carefully woven throughout the entire service.

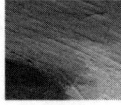

6

The Liturgy—Opening of the Service

This chapter begins a three-chapter look at the individual parts of the Liturgy. In this chapter, we will consider the opening portion of the service. The two main parts of the Liturgy—sometimes called the Service of the Word and the Service of the Sacrament—will be considered respectively in chapters 7 and 8.

Opening hymn

Psalm 100:4 encourages us, "Enter [the LORD's] gates with thanksgiving and his courts with praise." As God's people gather each week for worship, we follow the psalm writer's encouragement by joining our voices in thanksgiving and praise with the opening hymn.

The concept of an opening hymn can be traced back to early Christian worship. Celestine I (d. A.D. 432), bishop in Rome, decreed that worship should begin with a psalm sung as the ministers approached the altar.[24] This entrance psalm, which was later shortened to just a few key verses, was called the *Introit*, a Latin word that means "entrance." A document from the late seventh century in Rome indicates that the entrance, or procession, that accompanied the Introit had become quite elaborate, borrowing from the customs of the Roman imperial court and attaching Christian meaning to them.[25]

At the time of the Lutheran Reformation, the Introit, which was sung in Latin, began to be replaced with an opening hymn sung in the language of the assembly. This was particularly the case when a congregation did not have a choir and the people were not familiar with Latin.[26] Readers who remember worshiping with *The Lutheran Hymnal* (1941) may recall that worship began with an opening hymn but also included the Introit early in the service, either sung by the choir or, more commonly, spoken by the minister. Those who prepared the services in *Christian Worship: A Lutheran Hymnal* (1993) and *Christian Worship: Hymnal* (2021) recognized that the opening hymn has replaced the purpose of the Introit, and so an Introit is not found in the services in these books.

At different times throughout church history, the Introit was used either simply or with accompanying ritual and ceremony. The same kind of variety can be experienced today during the opening hymn. Congregations may sing the hymn with little ceremony, or they might include an accompanying procession. A procession is much like the parades we experience in our communities on the Fourth of July. This parade typically begins with someone carrying the national flag, a symbol of our country's history and our freedoms. A procession during the opening hymn may be led by symbols that call to mind the important truths of our faith. A processional cross reminds us that "we preach Christ crucified" (1 Corinthians 1:23). Candles recall the biblical imagery of Jesus Christ as the "light" who came into our sin-darkened world (John 1:9). A large Bible carried in procession visually underscores the importance of God's Word in worship and for our faith.

When we gather together for worship, we set aside our individual identities and are united as the redeemed people of God. The opening hymn helps us to emphasize our unity rather than our individuality. We unite our voices together in words and melody. While the opening hymn may reflect the emphasis of the day's service, there is also wisdom in selecting a more general hymn of praise. Many pastors prefer to choose relatively familiar hymns at this point in the service, which help to increase the sense of unity among the gathered worshipers as they unite their voices together.

Invocation

Before he ascended into heaven, Jesus gave his disciples the Great Commission. A significant aspect of the Great Commission includes the Sacrament of Holy Baptism: "Go and make disciples of all nations, baptizing them in the name of the Father and of the Son and of the Holy Spirit" (Matthew 28:19). Through the miracle of "the washing with water through the word" (Ephesians 5:26), the Holy Spirit brings people to faith as the name of the triune God is spoken.

The Liturgy begins with a regular reminder of our baptism as the minister speaks the words of the invocation:

"In the name of the Father and of the Son and of the Holy Spirit." There is both a sacramental, God-to-us aspect to these words and also a sacrificial, us-to-God aspect. These are the very words that were spoken when we were baptized and God adopted us. These are now the words we use to call on the triune God as his own children. There is no ambiguity in these words: We do not call on God with a generic term or phrase but with words that reveal him as the one true triune God.

Prior to the Reformation, the invocation was a part of a private preparation ritual for priests before the Mass began.[27] In his Small Catechism, Luther envisioned the invocation as the first statement in a Christian's private devotional time in the morning and evening. For example, he wrote, "In the morning, when you rise, you shall bless yourself with the holy cross and say, 'In the name of God the Father, Son, and Holy Spirit. Amen.' "[28] Lutherans later took this private devotional practice and made it part of congregational worship at the start of the service.[29]

A little cross is included within the words of the invocation in *Christian Worship: Hymnal* in connection with the reference to Jesus Christ, the Son of God. This cross within the text indicates that the minister will make the sign of the cross toward the congregation if he is facing the people. Some worshipers may choose to make the sign of the cross on themselves as that moment, from head to heart and shoulder to shoulder. This practice is intended to help worshipers remember the connection between their baptism, reflected in the words of the invocation, and the death of Jesus Christ, represented by the sign of the cross. The apostle Paul says in Romans 6:3,4, "Don't you know that all of us who were baptized into Christ Jesus were baptized into his death? We were therefore buried with him through baptism into death in order that, just as Christ was raised from the dead through the glory of the Father, we too may live a new life." As the invocation is spoken and the sign of the cross is made, worshipers receive a visual and tangible reminder that their baptism connects them to the death of Jesus and all its blessings to us in this life and for eternity.

Confession and Absolution

Psalm 24:3 asks, "Who may ascend the mountain of the LORD? Who may stand in his holy place?" The next verse answers, "The one who has clean hands and a pure heart." King David, the writer of Psalm 24, understood that a sinful person has no right to come into the presence of the Almighty God. Only through the forgiveness that David's descendant Jesus obtained for us can we stand in God's presence. For this reason, it is a fitting practice to begin worship by confessing our sins and hearing absolution, the declaration of God's gracious forgiveness to us.

Readers who are accustomed to confession and absolution in worship may be surprised to learn that, historically speaking, this is a relatively recent addition to the Liturgy. A late first-century Christian document called the *Didache*, or *The Teaching of the Twelve Apostles*, speaks about confessing one's sins before receiving Holy Communion, but no form for confession and absolution is given, and there is no indication that this would be a public rite rather than a private, personal practice. The *Didache* says, "On the day which is the Day of the Lord gather together for the breaking of the loaf and giving thanks. However, you should first confess your sins so that your sacrifice may be a pure one."[30] In the medieval church, the priest said private prayers of confession as he put on his vestments before the Mass began, but there was not a formal congregational rite for confession and absolution in the service itself.[31] Neither of the two orders of service that Martin Luther prepared—his 1523 Latin service or his 1526 German service—included confession and absolution as a formal part of the service. Lutherans encouraged the practice of private confession and absolution at the start of the Reformation; as worship and Communion attendance increased and the amount of time a pastor would spend privately absolving members proportionately increased, a general rite for confession and absolution in public worship eventually became more common among Reformation era Lutherans.[32]

One of the blessings of a formal rite for confession and absolution in worship is that it begins the service with a clear and personal proclamation of the two key teachings of the Bible—law and gospel. In *Christian Worship: Hymnal*, The Service includes two possible texts for the confession of sins after the invocation. The first text says:

> Holy God, gracious Father,
>   I am sinful by nature
>   and have sinned against you in my thoughts,
>   words, and actions.
>   I have not loved you with my whole heart;
> I have not loved others as I should.
>   I deserve your punishment both now and forever.
> But Jesus, my Savior, paid for my sins
>   with his innocent suffering and death.
> Trusting in him, I pray: God, have mercy on me, a sinner.

Notice how these words accurately and honestly confess what Scripture teaches about sin. We begin by confessing original sin, our inherited sinful condition. We acknowledge that this sinful condition manifests itself not only in outward sinful actions but even in the words we say and the thoughts we think. We confess sins of commission—doing, saying, and thinking what is evil—and sins of omission—failing to love God and our neighbor as we ought. Finally, without false excuses and explanations, we acknowledge that our sins and our sinful condition merit God's condemnation now and forever. But our knowledge and trust in Jesus' sacrifice for sin on the cross gives us confidence in God's forgiveness. We join our voices to the words of the tax collector in Jesus' parable, who prayed, "God, have mercy on me, a sinner" (Luke 18:13).

One of the most joyous moments a pastor experiences in worship is to turn to his congregation and personally apply the good news of Christ's forgiveness to the souls who have just confessed their guilt to God. The first absolution text in The Service in *Christian Worship: Hymnal* states:

> Our gracious Father in heaven has been merciful to us. He sent his only Son, Jesus Christ, who gave his life as the atoning sacrifice for the sins of the whole world. Therefore, as a called servant of Christ and by his authority, I forgive you all your sins in the name of the Father and of the Son and of the Holy Spirit.[33]

Notice the unconditional nature of this declaration. There are no strings attached, as if God will forgive us partly because of Jesus' sacrifice and partly because of our improved lives. Sinners weighed down with guilt are lifted up to hear an unambiguous and authoritative statement from the pastor that their sins are washed away in the blood that Jesus shed for them on the cross. The risen Lord Jesus placed divine authority into the words of absolution when he said to his disciples on Easter evening, "If you forgive anyone's sins, their sins are forgiven; if you do not forgive them, they are not forgiven" (John 20:23). In other

words, the pastor is not simply reminding us about Jesus'
forgiveness, but he actually applies Jesus' forgiveness to us
at that very moment!

Notice that the final words in this form of absolution
echo the words of the invocation and the words of our
baptism. The minister customarily makes the sign of the
cross again, giving worshipers another audible and visual
reminder of their baptism. As noted in chapter 2, confessing our sins and receiving absolution is essentially reliving
our baptisms, where Jesus first washed us from the guilt of
our sins and adopted us into his heavenly kingdom.

Confession and absolution make a fitting beginning
to worship because they are the essence of Christian
preaching and teaching. Jesus told his disciples before his
Ascension into heaven, "Repentance for the forgiveness
of sins will be preached in [my] name to all nations" (Luke
24:47). Confession and absolution also make a fitting
beginning to worship because they are the essence of the
Christian life. Luther correctly noted in the first of his
Ninety-Five Theses, "When our Lord and Master Jesus
Christ said, 'Repent,' he willed the entire life of believers
to be one of repentance."[34] Although confession and absolution are relatively new additions to the 2,000-year-old
story of the Liturgy, they are certainly fine additions that
direct our focus at the start of worship to the essence of
Christian worship and to the essential teachings of the
Christian faith: law and gospel.

Lord, Have Mercy

In Mark 10:46-52, Jesus and his disciples entered the
city of Jericho. As they did, they encountered a blind
man named Bartimaeus who was begging along the side
of the road. When he heard that Jesus was walking by,

he cried out, "Jesus, Son of David, have mercy on me!" Bartimaeus pleaded for the Lord's mercy and received it as Jesus heard his plea and restored his sight. In a similar way, we cry out to Jesus for his mercy in the next part of the Liturgy, known as "Lord, Have Mercy," or simply as *Kyrie*, a Greek word that means "Lord" in a form used to address someone. As noted in the previous chapter, the "Kyrie" is the first of the five parts that comprise the Ordinary of the Liturgy.

Congregational participation in the earliest centuries of Christianity often consisted in simple responses from the people. In a day and age with high illiteracy and no printing presses, this was a practical way for believers to participate in public worship. *Kyrie eleison*, "Lord, have mercy," was one of those simple, repeated phrases spoken in response to each petition of a longer prayer.[35] Over time, a nine-fold "Kyrie" developed, the middle responses changed to *Christie eleison* (Christ, have mercy), and the prayer petitions were dropped leaving just the bare statements for the Lord's mercy. Luther suggested a "Kyrie" with a simple three-fold form: "Lord, have mercy. Christ, have mercy. Lord, have mercy."[36]

The phrase, "Lord, have mercy," alone sounds like a prayer of repentance. Worshipers might assume that the "Kyrie" is an extension of the confession of sins if there are no petitions preceding the repeated phrase. This is how the "Kyrie" was treated in one of the services in *Christian Worship: A Lutheran Hymnal* (1993). In *Christian Worship: Hymnal* (2021), each setting of The Service reflects the original design of the "Kyrie" as a response to petitions of a prayer. When the "Kyrie" is used in this way, independent from the Confession of Sins, it underscores this important truth: Even after we receive Christ's forgiveness, we still

need God's mercy and protection in every other aspect of
our lives.

Glory to God

On the night of Jesus' birth, the angels broke out into
a song of praise to God for the newborn Savior: "Glory to
God in the highest heaven, and on earth peace to those on
whom his favor rests" (Luke 2:14). As recipients of the forgiveness and mercy of God, we break out in a song of praise
to God for his grace and mercy to us. This song, "Glory
to God," or "Gloria in Excelsis," is the second part of the
Ordinary of the Liturgy.

The opening words of the "Gloria" quote the song of
the angels in Luke's Christmas account. The source of
the rest of the text is unknown, but it was written within
the first few centuries of the church's history. The earliest
known written version of the "Gloria" is found in a late
fourth-century document commonly called the *Apostolic
Constitutions*.[37] Scholars agree that the origins of the "Gloria" are from Eastern Christianity, where it was first sung
not in the Liturgy but in a version of the service we know
as *Morning Prayer* or *Matins*.[38] The "Gloria" came into the
Liturgy gradually, first in Christmas services, then in Easter
services when led by a regular priest or in Sunday services
led by a bishop, and then finally in all celebrations of the
Liturgy from the 11th century forward.[39] Luther thought
so highly of the words of this song that he said it "did not
grow, nor was it made on earth, but it came down from
heaven."[40] He suggested its inclusion in his Latin order of
service, although he made no mention of it in his German
service.[41] Despite its absence from Luther's German service, Lutheran churches in the Reformation era frequently
included a version of the "Gloria" in the Liturgy.

The opening chapter of this book demonstrated the biblical pattern that to praise God is to proclaim what he has done. In this song, the first major song of praise in the Liturgy, the gathered congregation follows that principle: We praise God by proclaiming what he has done for us.

A translation of the "Gloria" is found on pages 83,84 of chapter 5. Consider how many biblical truths and allusions are found in these words! We thank God for bringing us peace through his Son, repeating the words of the Christmas angels. We praise Jesus as the Lamb of God who takes away the sin of the world, echoing the words of John the Baptist in John 1:29. We acknowledge the risen Christ who sits in exalted glory at the right hand of God, reflecting the words of Saint Paul in Colossians 3:1. Common terms for God from the Old Testament, such as "Holy One" (Psalm 22:3), "LORD" (Exodus 34:6), and "Most High" (Psalm 47:2) are applied to Jesus, subtly emphasizing Jesus' unity with the God of the Old Testament. We conclude with a confession of the triune God—Father, Son, and Holy Spirit. When we realize the rich, gospel-proclaiming content of these words, it comes as no surprise that Luther spoke so highly of the "Gloria" and that these words are still sung regularly in Christian worship today.

The "Gloria" has become the inspiration for many hymn paraphrases. A hymn paraphrase takes a prose text (a text that does not rhyme or follow a pattern of syllables) and creates a poem closely based on the original words that can be sung to a melody. *Christian Worship: Hymnal* contains two hymns that are paraphrases of the "Gloria"—hymns 935 and 936. Additional paraphrases of the "Gloria" are available through the electronic resources that support the hymnal.

When we sing the "Gloria" in worship, we experience another connection with generations of Christians who have gone before us. At the same time, we are not legalistically bound to use these words every time we celebrate the Liturgy. In his Latin service, Luther suggested that the pastor could omit the "Gloria" at his discretion. A common custom is to omit the *Gloria* during the contemplative season of Advent and especially during the penitential season of Lent. A common substitute for the "Gloria" during the Easter season is the song "This Is the Feast" (*Christian Worship: Hymnal* 938). Kurt Eggert (1923–1993), the pastor and church musician who oversaw the production of *Christian Worship: A Lutheran Hymnal*, wrote the canticle "O Lord, Our Lord" as an alternate song of praise, which now appears as hymn 939 in *Christian Worship: Hymnal*. From time to time or on special occasions, worship planners might select another hymn or song to use at this point in the service. In any case, our goal will be to praise God by proclaiming what he has done for us in Jesus Christ. When our songs proclaim the gospel, then we not only sing praise to God, but the gospel message benefits the faith of those who have gathered for worship.

7

The Liturgy—Service of the Word

Now that we have learned about the opening portion of the Liturgy, we turn our attention to its first major section—the Service of the Word. The message of law and gospel is proclaimed in the Scripture readings, Scripture-based responses, and Scripture-proclaiming sermon. Since the gospel is the most important part of worship, and since the gospel is proclaimed in the Word of God, it comes as no surprise that the Word of God plays such a prominent role in the Liturgy.

Many of the first Christians were Jews who came to realize that Jesus was the Savior God had promised in the Old Testament. With such a strong Jewish influence in early Christianity, it would only be natural for those influences to play a part in the formation of Christian worship. The synagogue service that was common in Jesus' day parallels portions of the Word section of the Liturgy. We cannot say to what degree the Jewish synagogue service influenced the early formation of the Liturgy, but we can see some clear parallels between the two forms.

The Jewish synagogue service began with several statements of invocation, confession of faith, blessing, and prayer. The final statement in this sequence was the blessing of Aaron, the high priest, from Numbers 6:24-26. Two readings followed: One was from the section of the Old Testament called the *Torah*, translated "law." The Torah consists of the first five books of the Old Testament, written by Moses. The second reading came from one of the Old Testament prophets. A psalm was sung between these two readings. Then a homily was preached by either the local rabbi or a visiting rabbi.[42] In Luke 4:14-30, we see how Jesus was a guest preacher in his hometown's synagogue and based his message on words from the prophet Isaiah.

We can notice some general similarities between this outline of the Jewish synagogue service and the Liturgy's Service of the Word. A prayer was included near the beginning of the synagogue service, just as the Prayer of the Day introduces the Word of God portion of the Liturgy. Today the Liturgy typically includes three Scripture readings. The first reading generally comes from the Old Testament, and the second from one of the epistles, or letters, of the New Testament. Between the First and Second Readings we sing a psalm—a pattern duplicated from the synagogue service. Shortly after the Scripture readings comes the sermon. Finally, the blessing of Aaron that preceded the readings in the Jewish synagogue service comes at the conclusion of the Lutheran Liturgy.

The way that the Word section is structured in the Liturgy may reflect ancient Jewish influence, but an even stronger reason for its structure is to place emphasis on the Word as the means of grace that proclaims Jesus Christ to the worshipers. The selection of readings and even some of the customs in this part of the service point worshipers to Jesus Christ as the predominant message in the Scriptures. That is not to suggest that any change in this pattern is inappropriate. Rather we will simply see that careful thought has contributed to the structure of the Service of the Word.

Prayer of the Day

Prayer is a natural part of the Christian life. In one of the shortest verses of the Bible, Saint Paul encouraged his readers, "Pray continually" (1 Thessalonians 5:17). Prayer naturally accompanies our study of Scripture. The psalm writer prayed for insight into God's Word when he wrote, "Open my eyes that I may see wonderful things in your law" (Psalm 119:18). As the gathered congregation prepares to hear the Word of God in worship, we naturally turn to the Lord in prayer.

The Prayer of the Day is a short prayer that follows the "Gloria" and precedes the Scripture readings. The Prayer of the Day serves as a transition from the beginning portion of the Liturgy into the Service of the Word. In one sense, it concludes the introductory section of the service, which includes confession, praise, and prayer. In another sense, this prayer introduces the Word portion of the service, which includes Scripture readings, Scripture-based songs, and a Scripture-based sermon. The Prayer of the Day often reflects the common emphasis in the readings for each service.

The Prayer of the Day was historically introduced by the minister's greeting to the congregation, "The Lord be with you," and the congregation's response, "And also with you." We find traces of this kind of greeting in the apostle Paul's greetings at the end of some of his letters. "The Lord be with all of you" (2 Thessalonians 3:16) and "the Lord be with your spirit" (2 Timothy 4:22) conclude two of Paul's New Testament letters. This greeting between pastor and people in the Liturgy marks the beginning of both the Word and the sacrament portions of the Liturgy. At the beginning of these important parts of worship, where the means of grace will be applied to God's people, pastor and parishioners ask that God be with one another and bless us through the gospel.

Historically, this prayer was called the *Collect*. The idea behind the term may be that the Prayer of the Day *collects* the gathered prayers of the congregation. After the greeting, the minister says, "Let us pray." A brief moment of silence may be offered so that everyone can pray a silent prayer before all the individual prayers are collected together into one prayer.[43] Although this custom may not be common in congregations today, it offers a possible explanation for the original term for the Prayer of the Day. A short time for silent, individual prayer is worth consideration.

The prayers prepared for this part of the Liturgy are from both ancient and modern sources. Some can be traced to collections of prayers that are 15 centuries old. At the time of the Lutheran Reformation, some of these ancient prayers were retained, others were edited and revised, and new prayers were composed by our Lutheran forefathers.[44] A similar process occurred in connection with the publication of *Christian Worship: Hymnal*. Prayers of the Day from the ancient church and the Lutheran Reformation were retained, sometimes with updated translations, and new prayers were prepared. We see the principles of Christian freedom and respect for our history honored with the Prayer of the Day.

The Prayer of the Day typically fits into a five-part pattern: (1) an address to God, (2) the basis for our prayer, (3) the prayer's request, (4) the purpose or desired benefit for which we pray, and (5) a closing doxology. Every prayer will not necessarily have all five parts of this pattern, but this pattern describes the basic flow in ancient and modern Prayers of the Day.[45] Consider the Prayer of the Day for Ash Wednesday as one example:

> Almighty and merciful God, you never despise what you have made and always forgive those who turn to you. Create in us such new and contrite hearts that we may truly repent of our sins and obtain your full and gracious pardon; through your Son, Jesus Christ our Lord, who lives and reigns with you and the Holy Spirit, one God, now and forever.

The prayer begins with an address to our "almighty and merciful God." The basis for our prayer is his unconditional forgiveness for those who turn to him in repentance. On that basis, we ask God to "create in us such new and contrite hearts"—an echo of Psalm 51, which is appointed for Ash Wednesday. The result of this petition is that the Holy Spirit will lead us to repentance, and our gracious God will bless us with pardon and forgiveness. The prayer concludes with a doxology, a short statement of praise to God. Notice how the traditional conclusion for the Prayer of the Day proclaims gospel truths: We confess the risen Jesus "who lives," and we confess the Trinity as we acknowledge that "Jesus Christ our Lord . . . reigns with [the Father] and the Holy Spirit, one God, now and for-ever." This Ash Wednesday prayer from 1529 is not only a fine example of the structure of the Prayer of the Day, but its content and spirit serve as a model prayer for every day of Lent and every day in life![46]

First Reading

The first Scripture reading we hear in the Liturgy nor-mally comes from the Old Testament. Readings from the Old Testament are a relatively new feature—and really, a restored feature—to the Liturgy. Early Christian worship, borrowing from synagogue patterns, initially included a reading from the Law and the Prophets. In time, readings from the Epistles and then the Gospels were added. Selec-tions from the Old Testament were reduced to one reading and then dropped altogether.[47] In more recent times, the Second Vatican Council (1962–1965) of the Roman Cath-olic Church revised the pattern of Scripture readings used in their churches and added an Old Testament selection back into their services. Other liturgical churches (includ-ing Lutherans) followed this custom, resulting in the com-mon practice today of three readings: an Old Testament selection called the First Reading, an Epistle selection called the Second Reading, and finally a reading from one of the four Gospels. We will talk more about the pattern of Scripture readings in chapter 10 when we discuss the Church Year in greater detail.

In the Gospel of John, Jesus said to his critics, "You study the Scriptures diligently because you think that in them you have eternal life. These are the very Scriptures that testify about me" (John 5:39). Jesus was referring to the Old Tes-tament when he spoke about "the Scriptures." Throughout the Old Testament, law and gospel were proclaimed to lead

God's people to see their need for the promised Savior and learn more about the Savior to come. Even with New Testament hindsight, we can still learn much about Jesus from the Old Testament's prophecies about him. It is only fitting then that we regularly hear from the Old Testament in worship. This reading takes us back in time and points forward to the Savior God promised. There is frequently a close connection and common theme between the First Reading from the Old Testament and the Gospel that is read later. This connection underscores Jesus' words: "These are the very Scriptures that testify about me."

One regular exception to the practice of using an Old Testament excerpt for the First Reading comes in the Easter season, when it is common to read selections from the New Testament book of Acts. Acts records the history of the infant Christian Church in the first years after Jesus' ascension. The apostles' preaching in Acts frequently presents us with an emphasis on Jesus' resurrection—a fitting emphasis for Easter as we celebrate Christ's resurrection.

Psalm of the Day

The book of Psalms was the hymnal of the Old Testament. Just as a psalm was sung after the first reading in the Jewish synagogue service, so the Liturgy today includes the Psalm of the Day as a sung response after the First Reading. We sing an entire psalm or several selected verses from a psalm. Some of the psalm verses reflect thoughts in one or more of the readings for that day.

Modern hymnals arrange hymns by different seasons and topics. Although the book of Psalms is not arranged in a topical way, these inspired songs of the Old Testament cover a wide range of matters that are as diverse as a hymnal's topical index. The Psalms teach biblical doctrine, encourage godly living, and especially reveal truths about the coming Christ. Luther thought so highly of the Psalms' rich and thorough content that he considered them to be a "little Bible." Luther wrote this in his preface to the book of Psalms:

> The Psalter ought to be a precious and beloved book, if for no other reason than this: it promises Christ's death and resurrection so clearly—and pictures his kingdom and the condition and nature of all Christendom—that it might well be called a little Bible. In it is comprehended most beautifully and briefly everything that is in the entire Bible. It is really a fine enchiridion or handbook. In fact, I have a notion that the Holy Spirit wanted to take the trouble himself to compile a short Bible and book of examples of all Christendom or all saints, so that anyone who could not read the whole Bible would here have anyway almost an entire summary of it, comprised in one little book.[48]

The poetry of the psalms is different from the poetry of modern hymns. Psalms do not rely on an established meter (number of syllables per line) or rhyme. Psalms, as well as the other books of Hebrew poetry in the Old Testament, rely on parallel thoughts. The writer makes a statement, and then he says the same thing in different words with a parallel phrase. Notice how Psalm 1 reflects this parallelism. The first verse expresses the same point three times, with each phrase building on the previous phrase. The second verse uses two parallel phrases to express the same idea.

> Blessed is the one
>   who does not walk in step with the wicked
> or stand in the way that sinners take
>   or sit in the company of mockers,
> but whose delight is in the law of the LORD,
>   and who meditates on his law day and night.

Because Hebrew poetry relies on parallel thoughts and not meter or rhyme, it translates well into other languages. It also works well to sing the psalms antiphonally. This reflects the way that we think the psalms were originally sung. Antiphonal singing between two groups can highlight the parallel nature of psalm verses: The first phrase is sung by one individual or group, and the second phrase by another. Psalms may alternate between minister or choir and congregation, two soloists or groups in the choir, men and women of the congregation, right and left sides of the congregation, or any other combination of singers that works well.

It is customary to end the psalms we sing in public worship with a short statement of praise to the triune God: "Glory be to the Father and to the Son and to the Holy Spirit. As it was in the beginning, is now, and will be forever. Amen." This phrase is sometimes called the little doxology or the "Gloria Patri," the first two words of the phrase in Latin. This conclusion to the psalms is a way to take these Old Testament songs and connect them to the New Testament. In early Christian history, the little doxology was seen as a confession of faith in the Trinity and as a statement against false teachings about Jesus Christ and the triune God that the early church had to combat. Bible passages with phrases similar to the little doxology include Romans 16:27, Ephesians 3:21, and Philippians 4:20.[49]

Second Reading

The First Reading from the Old Testament points forward from the time it was written to the promise of the coming Savior. The Second Reading from the epistles of the New Testament points back from the time it was written to the fulfillment of the Old Testament promises in Jesus Christ. The two Scripture readings that precede the Gospel point in different directions *chronologically*, but *theologically* they point to the same person: Jesus Christ.

Depending on the season of the church year and the system of readings that a congregation uses in worship, the Second Reading will either be a series of semicontinuous readings from one book over several weeks, or it may serve as a fitting complement to the Gospel reading that follows. A Gospel account that records a historical event from Jesus' life can be matched with an excerpt from an Epistle that teaches the same truth but in the context of a letter with instruction for the readers. A Gospel account that describes Jesus' preaching and teaching to the crowds of his day can be matched with an Epistle account that offers a similar instruction. The combination of these two readings, along with the First Reading, presents a fuller picture of the specific scriptural emphasis that is presented in each service.

God's people are grateful for the gift of God's Word. The first two readings conclude with a statement of our gratitude. At the end of the First and Second Readings, the minister says, "The Word of the Lord," and the assembly responds, "Thanks be to God."

Gospel Acclamation

The Gospel Acclamation, also called the Verse of the Day, is a sung Scripture verse or statement framed with alleluias. In earlier Christian history, before two readings became standard in the Liturgy, it was common for a psalm to be sung between the first two readings (just as it has been restored today) and for "Alleluia!" to be sung between the Second Reading and the Gospel. When three readings were reduced to two, the Psalm and Alle-

luia were merged together. This led to the current practice of singing a Scripture verse framed with alleluias prior
to the Gospel.[50]

Historically, this part of the service was called the
Gradual. The term comes from the Latin *gradus*, "step."
Saint Augustine describes the Gradual as an established
custom already in the fifth century.[51] Its name may come
from the practice of a choir singing it from the steps
surrounding the lectern.[52] The term might also refer to
another historic custom of speaking the Bible readings
from the steps below the altar; the minister would then
move from the steps to the lectern to read the Gospel
while the choir sang the Gradual.[53]

The word *Alleluia* and its variant spelling, *Hallelujah*,
come from a Hebrew word that means "praise the Lord."
Several psalms, including the very brief Psalm 117, include
this word. Some Bible translations, such as the New Inter-
national Version (NIV), the English Standard Version
(ESV), and the Evangelical Heritage Version (EHV),
translate the term into English. Other translations, includ-
ing the Christian Standard Bible (CSB) and the GOD'S
WORD (GW) translation, choose to retain it as a unique
Hebrew term. In the Liturgy, singing Alleluia before the
Gospel is meant to express the Christian's joy when we are
about to hear the words and works of Jesus in the Gospel.
The two previous Bible readings, one coming before the
time of Christ and the other after, have pointed us to the
One whose life and teaching will be proclaimed in the
Gospel. Our anticipation is about to end, and so in joy we
sing our alleluias that lead into the Gospel. An exception
to this practice occurs during Lent, when common custom
omits the word *Alleluia* not just in the Gospel Acclamation
but throughout the entire service. The omission of Alle-

luia in Lent strengthens its impact on Easter Sunday when Alleluia returns generously to the service that celebrates Christ's resurrection.

When a judge enters his courtroom during a trial, the assembly stands to show him respect. When the bride processes down the church aisle at the start of the wedding ceremony, the assembly stands to honor her on her special day. When the minister is about to read the Gospel of Jesus Christ, the assembly stands to honor Christ. Acclaiming the Gospel by action (standing) and song is our way to demonstrate respect and honor for Christ, who is among us just as he promised: "Where two or three gather in my name, *there am I with them*" (Matthew 18:20).

Like the Psalm of the Day, the Gospel Acclamation is meant to be sung. Just as the Prayer of the Day, Psalm of the Day, and Hymn of the Day change each week, so there is a specific Gospel Acclamation Bible verse intended to be sung by a choir or soloist for each Sunday and festival in the church year. The resources that support *Christian Worship: Hymnal* provide musical settings for these acclamations. The congregation begins and ends the acclamation by singing "Alleluia," and the choir or soloist sing the appointed verse between the congregation's alleluias. *Christian Worship: Hymnal* provides a general verse for each major season of the church year that the congregation may sing if there is no soloist or choir to sing the specific Bible verse for that day.

Gospel

The word *gospel* spelled with a lowercase g refers to the doctrine of the gospel, the teaching about Jesus Christ contained throughout Scripture. The doctrines of law and gospel were the emphasis in chapter 2, where we learned that proclaiming the gospel through Word and sacrament is the most important part of worship. In the context of the Liturgy, we also talk about the Gospel with an uppercase G as the third Scripture reading in the service, taken from Matthew, Mark, Luke, or John. The first four books of the New Testament are called Gospels because they record the life, ministry, work, and saving deeds of Jesus Christ. The previous Scripture readings have pointed us to Jesus Christ; now we hear about the events of Jesus' ministry, his preaching, and his saving work directly from eyewitnesses and close associates of those witnesses. Here is the historical account of the truths that the other readings teach us, the good news about "the Word [who] became flesh and made his dwelling among us" (John 1:14). The Gospel Reading presents us with the gospel of Jesus Christ.

Bursts of acclamation and praise bookend the reading: We sing "Alleluia" before the Gospel, and then we respond to the reading, "Praise be to you, O Christ!" With these words, we praise Christ as someone among us at that moment, just as he said: "Where two or three gather in my name, *there am I with them*" (Matthew 18:20).

Several customs have developed to highlight the reading of the Gospel. We stand and sing our acclamations before and at the end of the reading where we respond, "Praise be to you, O Christ!" Additional customs have been used at different times in Christian history. In the medieval church, an ornate book containing the Gospels was carried in procession into the assembly, and the Gospel was read from amid the people to picture the biblical truth that Jesus Christ is "God with us" (Matthew 1:23, Isaiah 7:14). Incense was used, perhaps to picture the truth that "Christ loved us and gave himself up for us as a *fragrant* offering and sacrifice to God" (Ephesians 5:2). Candles carried in procession with the Gospel book visualized Jesus' words: "I am the light of the world. Whoever follows me will never walk in darkness, but will have the light of life" (John 8:12).[54]

The number and type of customs we use in connection with the Gospel is a matter of Christian freedom. Standing and acclaiming Christ with short statements of praise are extremely common today. Some of the other customs from the church's past are not as common, though some congregations may choose to use those customs, especially on festive days. It is important to remember what these customs are designed to communicate—the centrality of the gospel of Jesus Christ. We are not elevating the value of this reading above the others, for "all Scripture is God-breathed" (2 Timothy 3:16), but we are expressing the truth that Scriptures testify about Jesus (John 5:39) and that there is no greater message to be found in the Scriptures than "Jesus Christ and him crucified" (1 Corinthians 2:2).

Hymn of the Day

Each Scripture reading in the service is followed by singing. The Gospel Reading is sometimes followed by a choir anthem that reflects the theme of the day or the content of the reading. Yet the primary musical response to the Gospel and to all the Scripture readings is the Hymn of the Day.

We can see the roots of the Hymn of the Day in our Lutheran musical heritage. As he reformed worship, Luther prepared hymns that enabled the congregation to sing the customary songs of the Liturgy. He also prepared hymns that proclaimed many truths about the life of Jesus and the teachings of Scripture. The first category of hymns would be used any time the Liturgy was celebrated; the second category of hymns would enhance the gospel message on specific days and seasons of the church year. Luther's hymn "From Heaven Above to Earth I Come" (*Christian Worship: Hymnal* 331) tells the Christmas gospel. "Christ Jesus Lay in Death's Strong Bands" (439,440) proclaims the Easter gospel after noting the death of Christ in the opening phrase of the hymn. "Dear Christians, One and All, Rejoice" (557) beautifully summarizes law and gospel and the plan of salvation throughout its ten stanzas. Luther's hymns enhanced the people's participation in worship and increased the opportunities the Liturgy provided to praise God by proclaiming the gospel in song. The hymns of Luther that proclaim specific gospel truths for specific occasions are one precursor to the modern practice of the Hymn of the Day.

The cantatas of Johann Sebastian Bach are another precursor to the Hymn of the Day. Bach's cantatas are longer musical works made up of multiple sections for choirs, soloists, and orchestra. Over two hundred of Bach's cantatas have survived to our day. Each cantata was intended to be sung in worship on a particular day in the church year. Bach's cantatas were musical commentaries on the Scripture readings for a specific Sunday or festival. Here we have a practical example of a musical work connected to a specific day.

Our modern practice of the Hymn of the Day builds on this Lutheran musical heritage. As we learned in chapter 5, each Sunday and festival of the church year has a Proper, a specific set of readings and responses used on that specific day. The Scripture readings, Prayer of the Day, Psalm of the Day, Gospel Acclamation, and Hymn of the Day are preselected to reflect the overall emphasis for that occasion. Pastors and congregations have every right to use a hymn other than the suggested Hymn of the Day, but it is also good to remember that the suggestions offered by those who prepare a church body's worship resources are given with a great deal of thought. A Hymn of the Day may be selected for its historical connection to a specific Sunday, the strength of its gospel message, its connection to the readings and thoughts for that day, its musical heritage in Lutheranism, or for other practical reasons—and often for several of these reasons.

As an example of the Hymn of the Day's use in a specific service, consider Luther's previously mentioned hymn "Dear Christians, One and All, Rejoice." This is the suggested Hymn of the Day for the Sixth Sunday of Easter, which is the Sunday prior to our celebration of Jesus' Ascension into heaven. The last two stanzas of Luther's hymn are poetic reflections of Jesus' words to his disciples in John 13–16. Jesus' words, spoken on Thursday of Holy Week, prepared them for his ascension and the coming of the Holy Spirit shortly thereafter on Pentecost.

> "Now to my Father I depart, the Holy Spirit sending
> and, heav'nly wisdom to impart, my help to you extending.
> He will a source of comfort be, teach you to know
>   and follow me,
> and in all truth will guide you.
>
> "What I on earth have lived and taught be all your life
>   and teaching;
> so shall my kingdom's work be wrought and honored
>   in your preaching.
> Take care that no one's man-made laws should e'er destroy
>   the gospel's cause;
> this final word I leave you."

At first glance, a worshiper might not realize the connection between this Hymn of the Day selection and the Sixth Sunday of Easter. A closer look at Luther's hymn, especially stanzas 9 and 10 above, helps us see why this is a wise choice for the Sunday before Ascension.

Because this hymn selection plays an important role in each service, worship planners and musicians may give extra attention to this hymn choice. Many church music publishers have produced special musical settings of hymns called *concertatos*. A concertato adds interest to a hymn by incorporating choirs, soloists, instruments, and interesting accompaniments into the hymn's performance. A longer Hymn of the Day could be sung antiphonally between different groups in the congregation—men and women or the right and left sides of the assembly. Soloists and choirs may introduce hymns with more challenging melodies by singing one or more of the opening stanzas. This enables the congregation to participate in the remaining stanzas with more confidence and encourages the use of a hymn that might otherwise not be sung. The way the Hymn of the Day is sung will vary from church to church depending on the musical resources available in each congregation. Whether the Hymn of the Day is sung simply or with a great deal of musical creativity, its purpose is to proclaim the unique gospel message of the day in praise to God who has given us the gospel to proclaim!

Sermon

Three of the letters written by the apostle Paul in the New Testament were written to young pastors whom he had trained to serve in the ministry. These letters, 1 and 2 Timothy and Titus, were written to the two men after whom the letters are named. They are called the *pastoral epistles* not only because they are written to pastors but also because they contain Paul's inspired directives for his young pastoral associates.

Since these three letters are written to pastors, it comes as no surprise that Paul encourages these men in their teaching and preaching. Paul encouraged Titus, "You . . . must *teach* what is appropriate to sound doctrine" (Titus 2:1). To Timothy, he wrote, "Devote yourself to the public reading of Scripture, to *preaching* and to *teaching*" (1 Timothy 4:13), and, "*Preach* the word; be prepared in season and out of season; correct, rebuke and encourage—with great patience and careful instruction" (2 Timothy 4:2).

The word *preach* sometimes carries a negative connotation among people today. Someone who doesn't like your advice might respond, "Don't preach at me!" The English sense of the word can carry a negative tone, but the biblical sense of the word is different. The basic sense of the Greek word *karusso*, "preach," means to announce an official message as a herald. A herald is a messenger who speaks for the king or another important person. A herald does not proclaim his own message. In fact, a herald isn't doing his job if he proclaims anything other than what the king has directed him to proclaim. But when the herald announces the message given to him, he does so with the authority of the king behind him. He is no longer presenting an opinion; he is now proclaiming an official message with official authority.

When Paul encouraged Timothy to "preach the word," he was directing him to preach the message given to him by God, not his own religious ideas or philosophies. Paul was also directing him to proclaim God's Word with the divine authority that comes from the Word. The same is true of pastors today. A pastor has no business stepping into the pulpit and preaching a sermon that consists of his own spiritual thoughts and musings. This is true in any situation, but especially if the message he is preaching contradicts the Word of God. The faithful pastor steps into the pulpit each week and *preaches*: He proclaims the message that God has given him to declare in the Scriptures, and he proclaims that divine message with divine authority.

So what makes a faithful sermon? What does faithfully preaching God's Word look like? Pastors have a variety of preaching styles and ways to structure a sermon, but the common thread through them all must be that they authoritatively proclaim both law and especially gospel. If the gospel is the most important part of worship, then proclaiming the gospel is the most important part of the sermon. The law of God, revealing our sin and need for salvation, must first be preached, preparing worshipers' hearts and minds so that they thirst for and rejoice to hear the good news that Christ has won their full salvation on their behalf.

When pastors faithfully preach the gospel, they are taking their cue from Paul's words to the Colossians: "Let the message of Christ"—that is, the gospel about Jesus Christ— "dwell among you richly as you teach and admonish one another with all wisdom" (Colossians 3:16). The word of Christ must be proclaimed, pondered, and appreciated for our faith to grow, as Saint Paul said elsewhere: "Faith comes from hearing the message, and the message is heard through the word about Christ" (Romans 10:17). The gospel message about Jesus' holy life lived for us, his innocent death on our behalf, and his triumphant Easter resurrection assures believers that the sins that plague their conscience have been fully and freely forgiven by Jesus' saving work. Our faith grows and our Christian nature rejoices to hear the good news of Jesus Christ, the Savior of sinners.

Practically speaking, how are the messages of law and gospel proclaimed in the Liturgy? Typically the pastor selects one of the three Scripture readings for the day as the basis for his sermon. The reading the pastor uses for his sermon is called the *sermon text*. The pastor will study the text by first studying it in its original language—Hebrew for the Old Testament or Greek for the New Testament. Our pastors learn to work in the Bible's languages as college and seminary students so that they can study and learn for themselves what the Scriptures say. Anyone who is comfortable communicating in more than one language understands that some of the original meaning or nuance behind a statement can be lost in the translation process. We have many fine and faithful Bible translations at our disposal, but the pastor's work in the original language will allow the sermon to present the full flavor of a text. The pastor's language study for his sermon could be compared to the difference between regular and high definition television. The former is perfectly fine, but the latter allows viewers to see their program even more clearly. Likewise, the pastor's language preparation for his sermon helps him bring the sermon text's message into the listener's spiritual view even more clearly.

As the pastor crafts his sermon, he keeps in mind the other parts of the service—especially the other Scripture readings, the Prayer of the Day, and the hymns. These individual parts of the service form a cohesive unit with a common focus. That focus becomes even clearer through the sermon. The pastor also strives to balance the explanation of the sermon text and its application. He wants to make sure his congregation understands what the Bible text says and how it applies to their daily lives as Christians. In all this work, the pastor strives to be a faithful herald who proclaims the Bible's messages of law and gospel with the divine authority of the risen Jesus behind him.

Confession of Faith

Nearly everything to this point in the Word portion of the Liturgy has been taken directly from the Word of God—the First Reading, Psalm of the Day, Second Reading, Gospel Acclamation, and Gospel Reading. Sung and spoken commentaries on the Word of God have been offered in the Hymn of the Day and the sermon. The final three segments of this portion of the Liturgy offer worshipers the opportunity to respond to the Word of God with their faith-filled confession, offerings, and prayers.

The pastor has preached his sermon as a herald of the King of heaven and earth. Law and gospel, sin and grace, repentance and forgiveness of sins have been proclaimed to God's gathered people in worship. It is appropriate that the people respond with a confession of faith that assents to the proclaimed Word! The apostle Paul wrote in Romans 10:9,10, "If you declare with your mouth, 'Jesus is Lord,' and believe in your heart that God raised him from the dead, you will be saved. For it is with your heart that you believe and are justified, and it is with your mouth that you profess your faith and are saved." A confession from our lips is a very appropriate response to the faith that has just been nourished from the gospel in the Scripture readings and sermon.

Two of the earliest official Christian statements of faith, the *Nicene Creed* and the *Apostles' Creed*, have become closely associated with the Liturgy, even though the creeds' association with the Liturgy took place hundreds of years after these creeds were first written. As noted in chapter 5, the Nicene Creed was originally prepared at the First Ecumenical Council (a meeting of important theologians throughout the Christian church) held at Nicaea in Bithynia (now in modern Turkey) in

A.D. 325. The council, and the Creed that came from it, were the church's response to the false teaching, promoted by a man named Arius, that Jesus was not fully God. At the Second Ecumenical Council held in Constantinople (modern Istanbul, Turkey) in A.D. 381, the Nicene Creed was further modified to better respond to these ongoing false teachings about Jesus Christ. The only additional modification of the Nicene Creed came in A.D. 589 at the Third Council of Toledo (in Spain), when the Latin word *filioque*, "and the Son," was added: "We believe in the Holy Spirit, the Lord and Giver of life, who proceeds from the Father *and the Son*."[55]

While the Nicene Creed originated as an official public confession of faith of the church, the origins of the Apostles' Creed are connected to the early church's baptismal practices. Theologians writing in the first few centuries of Christian history indicate that when new converts to Christianity were baptized, they spoke a confession of faith that expressed key Christian teachings. Because Christians are baptized into the name of the Father, Son, and Holy Spirit, this baptismal confession of faith focused on the three persons of the Trinity. The wording of this confession was not necessarily identical everywhere, although the practice of a baptismal confession appears to have been universal. Even though it is called the Apostles' Creed, it is likely not written by the apostles. Nevertheless, the Apostles' Creed is properly named because it faithfully reflects the apostles' teachings recorded in the Scriptures. The basic form of the Apostles' Creed that we have today can be traced to the late fifth century.[56]

The Apostles' and Nicene Creeds were incorporated into the Liturgy sometime after they had become the church's statements of faith. For example, the Nicene

Creed became a part of worship in Spain after the Third Council of Toledo in A.D. 589. This practice eventually spread to Germany,[57] but the Creed was not added to the Liturgy in Rome until the 11th century.[58]

The Creeds are common components of our Lutheran services today. In many of our congregations, the Nicene Creed is used on Sundays when Holy Communion is celebrated, and the Apostles' Creed is used in other Sunday services. A local congregation might have its own practice and pattern for using the Creeds in worship. For variety, a congregation could substitute an appropriate part of Luther's Small Catechism for the Creed on an appropriate day. For example, Luther's comments on the Third Article of the Creed, which confess what we believe and teach about the Holy Spirit, would be fitting on Pentecost Day, the festival of the coming of the Holy Spirit (Acts 2:1-41).

Prayer of the Church

We have responded to God's Word by confessing our faith. We also respond with prayer—the Prayer of the Church. Unlike the specific nature of the Prayer of the Day, the Prayer of the Church is very broad and general in its scope. The Prayer of the Church takes its cue from Ephesians 6:18: "Pray in the Spirit on all occasions with all kinds of prayers and requests."

The New Testament encourages us to pray for a wide variety of reasons. We are encouraged to pray for all of God's people (Ephesians 5:19), pray for the spread of the gospel (Colossians 4:3), pray for our enemies (Matthew 5:44), pray for leaders in the government (1 Timothy 2:2), pray for those who are sick (James 5:14), pray for help against temptation (Matthew 26:41), and pray for greater faith and spiritual understanding (Ephesians 1:18). These and many other biblical encouragements inform the Prayer of the Church. The Prayer of the Church may also express thoughts related to the theme of the day or the current church season, but its primary purpose is to pray for all sorts of people and all sorts of situations.

Congregations can arrange this prayer in a variety of ways. The Prayer of the Church may be entirely spoken by the pastor. The prayer may be spoken responsively by the pastor and congregation. Examples of responsive Prayers of the Church are found in all three settings of The Service in *Christian Worship: Hymnal*. Another way to arrange the Prayer of the Church is to end each petition with a common phrase. For example, at the end of each paragraph, the minister might say, "Lord, in your mercy," and the congregation adds, "Hear our prayer." A time for silent prayer may be included at some point so that worshipers may offer their individual petitions to this all-encompassing prayer.

Offering

Psalm 96:8 encourages us, "Ascribe to the LORD the glory due his name; bring an offering and come into his courts." With a specific offering in mind, Paul told the Corinthians, "On the first day of every week, each one of you should set aside a sum of money in keeping with your income" (1 Corinthians 16:2). Believers respond to the gospel not only by confessing their faith and turning to God in prayer but also by supporting the ministry of the church with their offerings.

In the early Christian church, believers brought gifts supporting the ministers and the needy at this point in worship. A prayer was offered, setting aside these gifts on the altar for the Lord's use. From these gifts, the bread and wine for celebrating the Lord's Supper were selected.[59] In our services today, ushers collect the monetary offerings of worshipers. The offerings we give support our called workers, our local church, our Lutheran schools, and other local ministries. WELS congregations also set aside a portion of their offerings to support the work of our synod. This work especially supports the schools that train our future pastors and teachers and the missionaries our church body supports in our own country and around the world.

Optional ending

The Liturgy is the church's historic order of worship that incorporates Word and sacrament. All three settings of The Service in *Christian Worship: Hymnal* include the celebration of Holy Communion. However, any setting of The Service can be used without the celebration of the sacrament. An optional ending for those situations is given on page 171 of the hymnal.

After the offering, a hymn is sung. Some pastors refer to this as the sermon hymn, since worshipers are more likely to see the connections between the sermon and a hymn chosen to reflect it if the hymn is sung shortly *after* the sermon.

After the hymn, The Service concludes with a prayer asking for God's blessing on his Word in our hearts and lives. The Lord's Prayer follows. The Lord's Prayer is found in two different places in the Gospels: Matthew 6:9-13 and Luke 11:2-4. Since Jesus taught this prayer on two different occasions, it doesn't surprise us to see some variations in wording between these two versions. Like the Prayer of the Church, the prayer that Jesus taught his disciples to pray brings a wide variety of petitions to God. Congregations may choose to speak the modern English translation of the Lord's Prayer or the traditional Elizabethan English text.

Finally, The Service concludes with the Blessing and an optional closing hymn or canticle. These items will be further explained at the end of the next chapter.

8

The Liturgy—Service of the Sacrament

After the natural pause in the service that the offering provides, the next major portion of the Liturgy begins as God's people celebrate Holy Communion. Just as Jesus Christ was proclaimed in the Word of God, so now he will be received in his Holy Supper. Just as the gospel in the Word delivered Christ's forgiveness to us and strengthened our faith, so the gospel in the Sacrament will do the same.

As noted in chapter 2, it may seem redundant to receive these same blessings of the gospel multiple times in the same service. One way to respond to that possible objection is to view the gospel as medicine for the soul. This perspective is reflected in the writings of Saint Ignatius, a student of the apostle John, who called Holy Communion "a medicine of immortality." But unlike the medication that a doctor may subscribe to a patient today, we cannot overdose on the gospel. When we realize the depths of our sinful condition and the very real spiritual enemies that surround us, we will see our need for God's gospel gifts that much more. Luther says it well in the Large Catechism:

> Those who are mindful of their weakness desire to be rid of it and long for help. They should regard and use the Sacrament just like a precious antidote against the poison that they have in them. Here in the Sacrament you are to receive from the lips of Christ forgiveness of sin. It contains and brings with it God's grace and the Spirit with all His gifts, protection, shelter, and power against death and the devil and all misfortune.[60]

As the church celebrates Holy Communion, it has in freedom developed various rites and ceremonies that help to communicate the truths about the real presence of Jesus' body and blood, the forgiveness Christ gives us in the sacrament, and the great and awesome miracle that we are about to receive. Let's look at the features in the Service of the Sacrament.

Preface

The Word portion of the service was introduced by a greeting between the pastor and people. The minister says, "The Lord be with you," and the assembly responds, "And also with you." This common worship greeting also marks the start of the Service of the Sacrament. Chapter 3 cited this opening greeting and the short responses that follow as an example of one of the most ancient elements of the Liturgy, found in nearly every ancient communion rite. The modern use of these ancient responses is one example of honoring the history of the church in the context of our worship today.

After the greeting, the minister invites the congregation, "Lift up your hearts," and the people respond, "We lift them up to the Lord." This exchange may have originally been an invitation to stand, since standing was viewed as the posture of prayer. Today we hear this exchange and the one that follows as an invitation to express thanksgiving to God in our hearts. The minister goes on to say, "Let us give thanks to the Lord, our God," and the people respond, "It is right to give him thanks and praise." This third exchange appears to come from the introduction of Jewish thanksgiving prayers. Since the promises of God to the Jews in the Old Testament find their fulfillment in Jesus Christ in the New Testament, we are not surprised to see these roots here and elsewhere in the Liturgy.[61]

The Preface responses, especially the second and third responses, invite us to have a spirit of thanksgiving as we participate in this holy meal. Paul refers to the cup of wine as the "cup of *thanksgiving* for which we *give thanks*" (1 Corinthians 10:16). Scripture tells us that our Lord gave thanks in connection with the institution of the sacrament: "While they were eating, Jesus took bread, and when he had *given thanks*, he broke it and gave it to his disciples, saying, 'Take and eat; this is my body.' Then he took a cup, and when he had *given thanks*, he gave it to them, saying, 'Drink from it, all of you. This is my blood of the covenant, which is poured out for many for the forgiveness of sins" (Matthew 26:26-28). The opening responses encourage us toward the same spirit of thanksgiving as we celebrate the Lord's Supper. In some circles it is common to refer to the Lord's Supper as the Eucharist, a term based on the Greek word *eucharisteo*, "to give thanks."

After this short opening dialogue, the minister continues speaking, echoing the congregation's final words by stating, "It is truly good and right that we should at all times and in all places give thanks [to God]." These words lead into the Proper Preface. The Proper Preface is a statement spoken by the minister that incorporates the thoughts of the specific part of the church year or festival into our Communion celebration. These words have a devotional tone to them: Rather than teaching the truths of the faith as we did in the Word portion of the Service, the minister's words are celebratory statements.

The Proper Preface is unique to the Communion services of Western Christianity. Its roots can be traced back as early as the fourth century, when ministers would have improvised their celebratory prayers. In time, many Proper Prefaces were written for specific festivals and occasions, and eventually they were reduced to a smaller group of selected statements that connect to specific seasons of the church year.[62]

Holy, Holy, Holy

The invitation to give thanks to God in the Preface's opening responses and the recollection of Jesus' saving work for us in the Proper Preface lead to this statement and prayer from the minister: "Therefore, with all the saints on earth and hosts of heaven, we praise your holy name and join their glorious song." These words introduce the main song of praise in the Communion rite, the *Sanctus* which is Latin for "holy."

The "Sanctus" has been a part of the celebration leading up to Holy Communion in worship since at least the fourth century.[63] The opening words of the song come from Isaiah 6:3. As Isaiah receives his divine call to serve as the Lord's prophet, he sees a vision of angels around the throne of God saying, "Holy, holy, holy is the LORD Almighty; the whole earth is full of his glory." To the angels' words are added the praises of the Palm Sunday crowds, who shouted in Matthew 21:9, "Blessed is he who comes in the name of the Lord! Hosanna in the highest!" (ESV). The holy and almighty Lord Jesus Christ has come among his gathered people in worship. He answers our cries of "Hosanna!"—a Hebrew word that means "save us, please!"—by coming to us substantially in the sacrament where he gives us his true body and blood that saved us from sin, death, and hell. Recognizing these truths, it is only fitting that we anticipate our reception of the Lord's Supper with this fitting song of praise that brings together the praises of heaven and earth and the words of the Old and New Testaments.

At this point, it is useful to note how thoughts of praise and thanksgiving have ascended through the beginning of the Service of the Sacrament. In the preface, the minister invited the assembly to give thanks to God, and the people agreed. The minister, in turn, agreed with the people in his response, which precedes the Proper Preface. Then, in the Proper Preface, the minister states specific reasons for our thanksgiving as he points us to the saving work and gracious promises of our Lord Jesus, especially as they pertain to the specific season of the church year. These invitations and reasons for giving thanks now ascend to the "Sanctus," a great hymn of praise uniting all creation that gives further reason for thanksgiving: The three-times-holy God who fills all creation is now coming to us in the sacrament! This ascending language of thanksgiving leads beautifully into the Prayer of Thanksgiving.

Prayer of Thanksgiving

The Prayer of Thanksgiving in *Christian Worship: Hymnal* reintroduces a historic feature of the Service of the

Sacrament. In order to better understand the Prayer of Thanksgiving, recall the institution of the Lord's Supper from Matthew 26:26-28.

> While they were eating, Jesus took bread, and when he had given thanks, he broke it and gave it to his disciples, saying, "Take and eat; this is my body."
>
> Then he took a cup, and when he had given thanks, he gave it to them, saying, "Drink from it, all of you. This is my blood of the covenant, which is poured out for many for the forgiveness of sins."

In the original Greek language of Matthew's and Mark's accounts of the institution of Holy Communion, there are two different words translated "give thanks." The word *eulogeo* is used in connection with the bread—a word that means "to bless." The word *eucharisteo* is used in connection with the cup—a word that means "to give thanks," from which we derive the term Eucharist as a name for the Lord's Supper. As we look at the other sections of Scripture that deal with Holy Communion, we see that these two terms are used interchangeably. In Luke 22:19,20 and 1 Corinthians 11:23-25, the word *eucharisteo* is used with the bread, and in 1 Corinthians 10:16, the word *eulogeo* is used in reference to the cup. From these words in Matthew, Mark, Luke, and 1 Corinthians, we understand that Jesus spoke a prayer of thanksgiving as he instituted the sacrament, in which he blessed or consecrated the bread and wine for the sacred purpose of giving us his true body and blood.

When we receive a gift, it is only natural to give thanks for the gift. It comes as no surprise, then, that from the earliest history of Christianity, believers regularly included a prayer of thanksgiving when they gathered to receive the

Lord's Supper. These prayers were initially spoken extemporaneously by the presiding minister, but later many of them were written. These Eucharistic Prayers, as they are often called, typically gave thanks to God for the blessings of creation, the blessings of salvation, and the blessings that worshipers were about to receive in the sacrament.

Over several centuries of Christian history, the Eucharistic Prayer became embedded with unclear language that led to an unclear understanding of the Lord's Supper. Instead of thanking God for the sacrifice of Jesus on the cross, the prayers began to speak of a sacrifice that Christians were offering God in the Lord's Supper. This shift in language ultimately changed the understanding of Holy Communion from a gift of God to us and into an act that we perform for God. This misunderstanding was so damaging that Luther described these prayers as "that abominable concoction drawn from everyone's sewer and cesspool." Why did Luther give such a harsh assessment? His reason was simple: "The mass became a *sacrifice*" through the false doctrine contained within these prayers.[64] Luther's solution was to eliminate these prayers from the service altogether. Instead, the simple Words of Institution stood alone without any misleading language altering their meaning.

In recent decades, Lutherans have reconsidered the value of a Prayer of Thanksgiving that clearly proclaims what the Bible teaches about the sacrament and eliminates any language or ideas that could be potentially misleading about the sacrament. Lutherans have acknowledged an implied prayer when the pastor speaks the Words of Institution. For example, C. F. W. Walther, the founder of the Lutheran Church—Missouri Synod (1811–1887), wrote that when the minister speaks these words, "he earnestly prays that Christ might be present in the sacramental action by virtue of his promise, and, by means of these external symbols, himself distribute his body and blood to the communicants."[65] Taking the next step and including a fitting Prayer of Thanksgiving is a natural addition to our worship.

As an example, note how the following Prayer of Thanksgiving, newly composed for *Christian Worship: Hymnal*, recalls Jesus' work of salvation and gives thanks to God for the blessings of salvation received in the sacrament:

> Blessed are you, Lord God, eternal King and gracious Father. In love you made us the crown of your creation. In mercy you planned our salvation. In grace you sent your Son to redeem us from sin.
>
> We remember and give you thanks that your eternal Son, Jesus Christ, became flesh and made his dwelling among us, that he willingly placed himself under law to redeem those under law, that he humbled himself by becoming obedient to death on a cross, that he has destroyed death and has brought life and immortality to light through the gospel.
>
> Bless us as we receive your Son's body and blood in this Sacrament. Forgive our sins, increase our faith, strengthen our fellowship, and deepen our longing for the day when Christ will welcome us to his eternal feast. Praise and thanks and honor and glory be to you, O God our Father, and to your Son and to the Holy Spirit, one God, now and forever.
>
> Amen.[66]

The Prayer of Thanksgiving traditionally concludes with the Lord's Prayer. As Jesus' model prayer concludes our prayer of thanksgiving for salvation and the sacrament, we experience a pattern of prayer similar to the pattern of thoughts expressed by Paul in Romans 8:32: "He who did not spare his own Son, but gave himself up for us all—how will he not also, along with him, graciously give us all things?" So also, in these two back-to-back prayers, we give thanks for the blessings of salvation given to us in Jesus in the Prayer of Thanksgiving, and then we pray that God would also provide "all things" we need in the Lord's Prayer.

Words of Institution

The language of ascending thanksgiving and celebration lead to this moment in the service: the Words of Institution. The Words of Institution are compiled from four sections of the New Testament: Matthew 26:26-28; Mark 14:22-24; Luke 22:19,20; and 1 Corinthians 11:23-25. These compiled accounts bring the New Testament's details about the institution of Holy Communion together in one text:

> Our Lord Jesus Christ, on the night he was betrayed, took bread; and when he had given thanks, he broke it and gave it to his disciples, saying, "Take and eat; this is my body, which is given for you. Do this in remembrance of me."
>
> Then he took the cup, gave thanks, and gave it to them, saying, "Drink from it, all of you; this is my blood of the new covenant, which is poured out for you for the forgiveness of sins. Do this, whenever you drink it, in remembrance of me."[67]

These words establish what we believe concerning the sacrament and guide our celebration of the Supper. As Luther said in the Small Catechism, "These words are the main thing in this sacrament, along with the eating and drinking."[68] As the minister speaks these words, the congregation understands that we are about to receive the very sacrament that Jesus gave to his church as a blessing for all times. The Words of Institution are not a magical formula, but a statement to the congregation that the elements on the altar are being consecrated for the Lord's use and that the assembly, following Christ's "Do this" command, is about to receive the Lord's Supper according to Christ's command and promise.

C. F. W. Walther listed five important reasons why the Words of Institution are so vital in our celebrations of the Lord's Supper. These words serve as:

1. **A testimony.** By means of the festive repetition of the words of institution, the public servant openly attests that he wishes to celebrate the most holy testament of Christ according to his institution, ordinance, and command, and therefore not according to his own devising, but as a caretaker of God's mysteries.

2. **A separation.** By this action, he separates the external symbols of bread and wine from their common use, so that they are no longer mere bread and wine but instruments, carriers, and means through which Christ's body and blood are to be distributed.

3. **An invocation.** [The minister] earnestly prays that Christ might be present in the sacramental action by virtue of his promise, and, by means of these external symbols, himself distribute his body and blood to the communicants.

4. **A witness.** [The minister] gives testimony that, by virtue of the ordinance and institution of the truthful and almighty Christ, the consecrated bread is the communion of his body and the consecrated wine is the communion of his blood.

5. **An admonition.** The minister admonishes all participants to come forward in true faith and repentance, true fear and reverence and with an earnest desire to amend their life.[69]

The minister often accompanies these words with gestures that emphasize the meaning and importance of the Words of Institution. Some pastors will make the sign of the cross over the elements as they quote the words of Jesus, "This is my body," and, "This is my blood." The sign of the cross reminds us of Christ's death and, like the Words of Institution, serves as a gesture of consecration, setting these specific elements aside for the Lord's purpose. Other pastors may choose to raise the Communion hosts (bread) and the chalice for the same reasons. Whatever customs we use in our congregations can be visual tools to underscore the meaning of what is taking place—these elements are being set aside for our celebration of the Lord's Supper, in which Christ gives us his true body and blood for our forgiveness and strength.

Peace of the Lord

Following the Words of Institution, the minister speaks a short blessing: "The peace of the Lord be with you always." The assembly simply responds, "Amen." This brief blessing is a remnant of the kiss of peace, a custom that was included in ancient Christian services. Justin Martyr (A.D. 100–165) wrote in his first *Apology*, "Having ended the prayers, we salute one another with a kiss."[70] The New Testament refers to this kiss of peace in a few places, including 1 Corinthians 16:20 and 1 Peter 5:14.

Martin Luther thought very highly of this little phrase and blessing. He called it "a public absolution of the sins of the communicants, the true voice of the gospel announcing remission of sins, and therefore one and most worthy preparation for the Lord's table, if faith holds to these words as coming from the mouth of Christ himself."[71]

Lamb of God

Just before worshipers come forward to receive Jesus' body and blood in the sacrament, we sing a short song known by its Latin title, "Agnus Dei" (ah'-nyoos day'-ee), which means "Lamb of God." The "Agnus Dei" was added to worship in the Western Church around A.D. 700.[72] The song echoes John the Baptist's words in John 1:29: "Look, the Lamb of God, who takes away the sin of the world." Worshipers sing, "Lamb of God, you take away the sin of the world; have mercy on us." This sentence is repeated three times; the final time the last phrase is changed to "grant us your peace." Luther added the words, "O Christ," to the start of each sentence, and many Lutheran orders of service follow his example to specify that Jesus is the Lamb of God to whom we sing this song.[73]

The song is a beautiful little confession of sins as we come forward to receive his forgiveness in the Supper. The text reminds us that Jesus is the sacrifice to which all the Old Testament sacrifices pointed. His death on the cross has won the forgiveness of sins for the entire world, and we come forward to the altar to personally receive his gift of forgiveness. The body he gave and the blood he shed as a sacrifice on the cross are now received in the sacrament. Luther wrote, "The Agnus Dei, above all songs, serves well for the sacrament, for it clearly sings about and praises Christ for having borne our sins and in beautiful, brief words powerfully and sweetly teaches the remembrance of Christ."[74]

Distribution

At the invitation and promise of our Savior, worshipers come forward to receive Christ's body and blood in the sacrament. In many Lutheran churches, people receive the

Lord's Supper in *tables*: groups of several people come for-ward together, receive the elements, and are dismissed as another group comes forward. Depending on the church's furnishings, communicants may stand or kneel in these groups. Standing was the ancient practice for receiving Communion, while kneeling became more common start-ing in the 12th century.[75] In larger settings, it is often useful to practice *continuous distribution*, when people come forward in a line to receive the elements from two minis-ters and then return to their seats.

It is typical Lutheran practice for the ministers to repeat a phrase or sentence as communicants receive the ele-ments of the Lord's Supper. If worshipers are communing in tables, the ministers may say to each group:

> Take and eat; this is the true body of our Lord and Savior Jesus Christ, given into death for your sins.

> Take and drink; this is the true blood of our Lord and Sav-ior Jesus Christ, poured out for the forgiveness of your sins.

The ministers may speak a specific phrase to each per-son instead. This form is especially useful when continuous distribution is used:

> The body of Christ, given for you.

> The blood of Christ, poured out for you.

As a dismissal blessing to each table, or to the entire congregation after communing in a continuous fashion, the minister may say:

> The true body and blood of our Lord Jesus Christ strengthen and preserve you to life everlasting. Go in peace.[76]

While there is not a single correct wording that pastors should use, it is important that these words clearly reflect the truth that we are receiving the body and blood of Christ in the sacrament. In the 19th century, following the union of Lutheran and Reformed churches in Germany, their service books directed ministers to say, " 'Take and eat,' Christ says, 'this is my body,' " etc. By adding the little phrase "Christ says" and by quoting Jesus instead of making a direct statement, each person could interpret Christ's words however he wanted—either as Christ giving us his very body in the Supper or as Christ saying that the bread is only a symbol of his body.[77] This incident from church history shows us why it is important that we carefully consider the words and phrases we include during the distribution of the sacrament so that we give a clear confession of Scripture's truths and teaching about Holy Communion.

During the distribution, it is a common custom that those in the congregation who are not at the altar sing a hymn. This custom has both ancient and Reformation era roots.[78] Hymns that reflect the message of the sermon, the celebration of Holy Communion, or the season of the church year are all appropriate during the distribution.

Verses, Prayer, Blessing

Many Lutherans use the words of Psalm 136:1 as a mealtime prayer of thanks. That same Bible verse is used as the pastor and people's statement of thanks after receiving Holy Communion. To that verse, we also add 1 Corinthians 11:26, which acknowledges that our participation in the Lord's Supper proclaims our faith in Jesus' death for us.

A short prayer follows these spoken Bible verses. Each setting of The Service in *Christian Worship: Hymnal* includes a different post-Communion prayer. The following prayer has been used frequently among Lutherans after Communion. It was prepared by Martin Luther, who may have taken an existing post-Communion prayer and updated it for use in his German order of service:[79]

> We give thanks, almighty God, that you have refreshed us with this saving gift. We pray that through it you will strengthen our faith in you and increase our love for one another. We ask this in the name of Jesus Christ our Lord, who lives and reigns with you and the Holy Spirit, one God, now and forever.[80]

Finally, we are sent with the Lord's blessing. The Lutheran liturgy concludes with the blessing that God directed Aaron to speak over the Old Testament people of Israel in Numbers 6:24-26. Once again, this feature of the service follows a suggestion from Martin Luther. In his Latin Mass (1523), Luther suggested that either Psalm 67:6,7 or Numbers 6:24-26 be used as the blessing to conclude the service. In his German mass (1526), Luther simply prescribed the blessing of Aaron from Numbers 6.

In the Aaronic blessing, we see that even the Old Testament alludes to the fact that we worship the triune God. The blessing's first phrase refers to the Father's work to keep us, that is, to preserve us. The second phrase refers to the grace of God, which we understand is most clearly revealed to us in the gracious saving work of our Redeemer, Jesus Christ. The final phrase of the Aaronic blessing speaks of the peace that God gives us; this is the work of the Holy Spirit, who brings us to faith in Christ, that results in a blessed peace between us and God. The Liturgy has Trinity bookends with the invocation at the beginning and the blessing of Aaron at the end.

Many congregations follow the blessing with a closing hymn. For practical reasons, it is usually ideal for a closing hymn to be familiar and brief. The final hymn may be a short hymn, a few well-selected stanzas of a hymn, or the final stanza of a hymn whose other stanzas were sung earlier in the service. Many hymns conclude with a stanza that is a *doxology*, a short statement of praise to the triune God. Doxology stanzas make very fitting conclusions to the service: From start to finish, we have received the blessings of our triune God, and now we conclude by praising him for his blessings one more time.

9

The Daily Office

Our personal schedules contain weekly events: A weekly meeting at work, children's sporting events, a weeknight education class, and watching a favorite television show are among many examples of weekly events. Our personal schedules also revolve around a daily routine: We wake up and prepare for the day, arrive at work in the morning, break for lunch at noon, return home in the evening, eat dinner, enjoy some time with our family, and finally go to bed.

The church's worship life has also developed weekly and daily patterns. The service we studied in the previous chapters, the *Liturgy*, is a service that developed especially with Christians' weekly worship gatherings in mind, but our Christian ancestors also developed patterns for daily worship. This daily pattern of services is called the *Daily Office*. (The word *office* as a worship term originates with the Latin word *officium*, which means "service.") As with the chapters on the Liturgy, our study of the Daily Office is not a thorough historical treatment but an overview of the development and use of these services as they have come down to us in the Lutheran church today, particularly in *Christian Worship: Hymnal*.

Development of the Daily Office

Several factors influenced the development of the Daily Office. The Jewish practices of morning and evening sacrifices and their accompanying rituals had already established the concept of specific times of day for gathering together as God's people.[81] Many faithful Jews had the custom of praying three times daily; for example, we learn from the Old Testament that Daniel prayed three times each day (Daniel 6:10). The New Testament describes Peter and John arriving at the temple at 3:00 P.M., "the time of prayer" (Acts 3:1), and how Peter prayed privately at noon (Acts 10:9). Saint Paul gave the general encouragement, "Pray continually," to his readers (1 Thessalonians 5:17). Several psalm verses also describe times and patterns of prayer. Psalm 55:17 says, "Evening, morning and noon I cry out in distress, and [God] hears my voice." Psalm 119:62 says, "At midnight I rise to give you thanks for your righteous laws." The Daily Office's pattern of several times for prayer may have been inspired by Psalm 119:164: "Seven times a day I praise you for your righteous laws."[82]

The *Didache*, a Christian writing from the late first or early second century, suggests that one pray the Lord's Prayer three times each day.[83] An early third century document called the *Apostolic Tradition* by Hippolytus of Rome, directs believers to set aside several specific times each day for personal prayer: upon waking in the morning, at 9:00 A.M., at noon, at 3:00 P.M., in the evening before going to bed, at midnight, and "at cockcrow" before sunrise.[84]

While we recognize that descriptive Bible verses and ancient customs are not prescriptive formulas for daily prayer, we also realize that these verses and customs encouraged the first Christians toward the development of frequent, daily times for prayer. These formal daily times for worship shifted from personal, private prayer to small or large gatherings for prayer. The legalization of Christianity by the Roman Empire in the fourth century provided circumstances in which daily gatherings of Christians for morning and evening prayer could develop without hindrance. At the same time, the monastic movement, in which some Christians chose to live life apart from regular society and devote themselves to prayer, led to the development of the complete set of Daily Office services.[85]

A document by Saint Benedict (c. A.D. 480–550) called the *Rule* (or *Canon*) *of St. Benedict* helped to define what has now come down to us as the services of the Daily Office. Variations and adaptations of the Daily Office occurred over the many centuries of the medieval church and the many locales in which the Western church was found, but this series of services became widely practiced, especially in monastic communities.

- *Matins* was originally an overnight service, held at midnight or later.
- *Lauds* was held at sunrise. (In some settings, Matins and Lauds were combined into one service to greet the new day.)

- *Prime* preceded the start of one's work.
- *Terce* was held at the third hour of the day, 9:00 A.M.
- *Sext* was held at the sixth hour of the day, noon.
- *None* was held at the ninth hour of the day, 3:00 P.M.
- *Vespers* marked the end of the day at sunset.
- *Compline* was held just before going to bed at night.[86]

In some settings, Lauds at sunrise and Vespers at sunset became public services for all to attend. When circumstances permitted, the laity and clergy attended these services together with those who had committed their lives to the monastery. These public daily prayer services were called the Cathedral Office. The full set of services observed in the monastery apart from the public were called, appropriately, the Monastic Office.[87]

The services of the Daily Office were distinguished by their generous use of the Psalms. The entire book of Psalms was prayed over a set period of time. The *Rule of St. Benedict* prescribed the Psalms to be prayed in a week throughout the course of Daily Office services. In other places, all 150 psalms were prayed in as little as a day or as much as two weeks.[88] Scripture readings, canticles and hymns, prayers, preaching, and other elements became standard features of these daily prayer services.[89] We will note some of the specific features of individual services when we look at them in detail later in this chapter.

The Daily Office remained in use throughout the medieval church. As time passed, the Daily Office was seldom observed outside monasteries. As was the case with the

Liturgy, the content of the Psalms and other Scripture selections gradually gave way to additional ceremonies and customs that clouded clear gospel content. The Daily Office slowly became more of an obligation to be performed by monks and clergy rather than a set of times throughout the day for spiritual respite in prayer and reflection on God's Word.[90]

When Luther sought to reform the Liturgy, he took a balanced approach—retaining content and customs that were good and beneficial while eliminating or replacing anything that contradicted the gospel message and the Scriptures. Luther took a similar approach with the Daily Office. In a document from 1523 in which Luther outlined his Latin service, he spoke very highly of the Daily Office, simply calling for the removal of practices that compromised the gospel: "As for the other days which are called weekdays, I see nothing that we cannot put up with, provided the [weekday] masses be discontinued. For Matins with its three lessons, the minor hours, Vespers, and Compline *de tempore* consist . . . of nothing but divine words of Scripture."[91] Three years later, in instructions for his German order of service, Luther describes the worship patterns in Wittenberg. Sundays included Matins in the early morning, the Liturgy later in the morning, and Vespers in the evening, each with a sermon. Weekdays included Matins and Vespers again, which were especially attended by students.[92] Many German Lutheran congregations at the time of the Reformation followed Luther's suggested patterns to a greater or lesser degree, though the Daily Office services were primarily observed in schools and were not seen as congregational services.[93]

In addition to its three Liturgy-based service settings, *Christian Worship: Hymnal* also includes services from the

Daily Office. Morning Prayer is based on Matins, which means "morning." Evening Prayer is based on Vespers, which means "evening." Prayer at the Close of Day is based on Compline, which means "complete"—the service prayed before one goes to sleep, when the day is completed. The hymnal also includes brief versions of all the Daily Office rites that can be used as short devotional services for school chapel services, church meetings, conferences, devotions in the home, and other similar settings.

Morning Prayer

After an optional opening hymn, the Service of Morning Prayer begins with two responsive verses from Scripture. The first verse comes from Psalm 51:15: "O Lord, open my lips, and my mouth will declare your praise."[94] This verse was deliberately chosen to be the first statement a believer would say at the start of a new day. The verse that follows, Psalm 70:1, was the first sentence in most other Daily Office services: "Hasten to save me, O God; O Lord, come quickly to help me." This sentence reflects the prayer of the believer who recognizes his need for God's mercy and assistance every moment of the day.[95] These two verses are followed by a sentence that relates to the current church season and gives us reason to praise and thank God.

The beginning of a new day of God's mercies calls for thanksgiving. As a modern adaptation of Matins, Morning Prayer appoints Psalm 95 to be sung by the congregation. The congregation sings the first seven verses of Psalm 95, which call on God's people to praise and thank him in song because he is the one true God who created and sustains the world and especially us, his believers, who are "the people of his pasture and the sheep of his hand" (Psalm 95:7). Another psalm that is often sung in modern versions of Morning Prayer is Psalm 63, which was associated with the service of Lauds at dawn.[96]

Services of the Daily Office historically included several psalms. After Psalm 95 is sung, one or more additional psalms are sung. These psalms tend to have a specific connection to the theme or focus of the overall service.

From the opening sentences through this point in the service, nearly everything has been direct quotations from the Psalms sung back to God as prayer and praise. Following the psalms, we turn to another portion of the Bible where God's Word is addressed to us. Morning Prayer envisions a single Scripture reading, but when this service is used on Sundays, the minister may read all three appointed readings for the day in succession. If he is preaching on one of the day's readings, he may omit that reading at this point and incorporate it into the introduction of his sermon later in the service. A hymn serves as a musical response to and commentary on the Scripture reading.

The Daily Office services are meant to be flexible in nature, because they are intended for a wide range of settings: weekday services in a congregation, occasional alternates for Sunday orders of worship, chapel services in high school and college settings, or worship at a short retreat or seminar. The flexibility of Morning Prayer is seen by the next item in the service: The rubric (printed directions) for the sermon state, "A sermon or brief address may follow." The word *may* indicates whenever the editors of the service intended something to be *optional*. In the weekly services of the congregation, it goes without saying that a sermon will be included. In a school chapel service, the leader may offer a shorter devotional message rather than a full-length sermon. In a setting where there is only time for a very brief service, there might not be a sermon or address at this point, but the Scripture readings and any introductory comments will suffice; in this case, the previous hymn might also be omitted. This rubric allows Morning Prayer to be adapted to different settings and to be flexible for different-length services.

A response of praise and faith follow the reading and sermon. Morning Prayer includes a canticle with origins dating back to at least A.D. 500.[97] "We Praise You, O God" is commonly known by its first few words in Latin, *Te Deum Laudamus*. Even though this is a song, it also has the characteristics of a confession of faith similar to the ecumenical creeds. In fact, Martin Luther thought so highly of the "Te Deum" that he spoke of it as being on the same par as the Apostles' and Athanasian Creeds.[98] The text of the "Te Deum" envisions all of God's creation, including the saints and angels, praising the triune God for the birth, death, resurrection, and future return of Jesus Christ. Scholars today acknowledge that the author of this text is unknown, although there was a long-standing legend that claimed that Saints Ambrose and Augustine sang this text antiphonally in the fourth century when Ambrose baptized Augustine.[99] *Christian Worship: Hymnal* includes the shorter (and probably original) version of the "Te Deum," but a phrase in the longer version indicates that this was a song for the start of a new day: "Vouchsafe, O Lord, to keep us this day without sin."[100]

The Song of Zechariah (Luke 1:68-79) is included as an alternate sung response to the Word. This canticle, known by its first word in Latin, *Benedictus*, has a long association with the sunrise service of Lauds. In this song, the father of John the Baptist praises God for fulfilling his promise to redeem his people, and he prophesies about the forthcoming ministry of his newborn son. The final two verses of the

song show the likely reason why this biblical song was chosen to be sung at sunrise during Lauds: "Because of the ten-
der mercy of our God, by which the *rising sun* will come to
us from heaven to *shine on those living in darkness* and in the
shadow of death, to guide our feet into the path of peace."
Christian Worship: Hymnal includes hymn paraphrases of
both the "Te Deum" (952,953) and the "Benedictus" (954).

After an optional offering, Morning Prayer concludes
with several short prayers: "Lord, Have Mercy" ("Kyrie"),
then one of two prayers for the start of a new day, and
finally the Lord's Prayer. Matins ends with a short response
called the *Benedicamus* ("Let us praise the Lord" in Latin)
that was the original ending of Daily Office services[101] and
finally the Blessing from 2 Corinthians 13:14.

Evening Prayer

The Service of Evening Prayer begins with a series of
responsive sentences, a translation of an ancient evening
hymn, and a prayer that together are called the Service of
Light. This rite is a modern adaptation of an evening ritual
called the Office of Lights, or *Lucernarium* in Latin. Candles
lit at sunset for practical purposes were also used to communicate a symbolic message about Jesus,[102] whom Saint
John describes as the "light of all mankind" that "shines in
the darkness" of our sinful world (John 1:4,5). Saint Hippolytus describes a *Lucernarium* service in his third-century
Apostolic Tradition. This service included the lighting of a
lamp, a short greeting and thanksgiving dialogue between
minister and assembly, and a prayer of thanks for light.[103]
The adaptation in *Christian Worship: Hymnal* begins with
responsively sung verses based on John 1:4,5; Luke 24:29;
and 2 Corinthians 4:6. The hymn that follows uses a new
melody and modern translation by Pastor Michael Schultz

of an ancient hymn known by its Greek title, *Phos Hilaron*, "Glad Light." The hymn is so ancient that already by the fourth century, Basil the Great of Caesarea said that he did not know who wrote the hymn.[104] One of two prayers is then spoken to conclude the opening Service of Light; both prayers reflect the imagery of Jesus and God's Word serving our souls as spiritual light.

Like Morning Prayer, the introduction of Evening Prayer leads into a time for singing and praying psalms. Like its morning counterpart, Evening Prayer has a long-standing association with a specific psalm—in this case, Psalm 141. Unlike Morning Prayer, this first psalm does not serve as the first major song in the service—the hymn *Phos Hilaron* does—but it marks the first in a series of psalms that are prayed by the gathered assembly. The version in *Christian Worship: Hymnal* contains the first two verses of Psalm 141. The choice of this psalm for the end of the day is clear from its text: "Let my prayer rise before you as incense, the lifting up of my hands as the *evening* sacrifice." One or more additional psalms follow Psalm 141. These additional psalms are selected with more specific connections to the church season or the occasion of the service in mind.

Another difference in the use of psalms between Morning and Evening Prayer is that the psalms in Evening Prayer are followed by a brief time for silent reflection. This practice is especially fitting at the end of the day. As the pace of the day slows down for the evening, the pace of worship is also slower, allowing time for personal reflection on the words of the psalm and for personal prayer. Following another ancient custom, each psalm and period of silent reflection is followed by a short *psalm prayer*, which highlights a key thought in the psalm and helps to put the Old Testament psalm in a New Testament, Christ-centered perspective.[105]

The next items in Evening Prayer are identical to the same section of the service in Morning Prayer. The psalm is followed by a Scripture reading. When a congregation uses Evening Prayer as an alternate to the regular Sunday services—for example, a Saturday night service that contains the same content as the next day's regular morning worship—then the Sunday's appointed readings may be read, using the same suggestions given earlier for Morning Prayer. A hymn is sung and, when a full-length service is observed, the sermon follows.

Morning Prayer offers the song "We Praise You, O God" ("Te Deum") or the Song of Zechariah as a response to the Word. Evening Prayer follows the reading and preaching of God's Word with the Song of Mary from Luke 1:46-55. Known by its first word in Latin, the "Magnificat" has been associated with *Vespers* since at least the sixth century.[106] *Christian Worship: Hymnal* includes two musical settings of this song: The first uses a refrain and chant tune, and the second is sung to a melody by the sainted Pastor Kurt Eggert. Mary's song, sung in the context of the news that she was to become the mother of Jesus, praised God for keeping his promises to his people and the great blessings he had given to Mary herself. In the same way, at the close of another day we praise God for keeping his promises to us and the personal blessings that he gave us during the day of grace about to end.

The conclusion of Evening Prayer is also similar to Morning Prayer. After an optional offering, a series of prayers is spoken and sung. The first is a longer form of the "Kyrie," or "Lord, Have Mercy." The text used in *Christian Worship: Hymnal* is based on an ancient Eastern church rite called the Liturgy of St. John Chrysostom.[107] One of two evening prayers is then spoken, followed by the Lord's Prayer, *Benedicamus*, and the Blessing.

Prayer at the Close of Day

Like its Daily Office counterparts, the late-evening service of Compline begins with prayerful responses. The minister begins with a short prayer for the close of day, "The Lord Almighty grant us a quiet night and peace at the last," followed by Psalm 92:1-2. The hymn, "Before the Ending of the Day" (*Christian Worship: Hymnal* 790), has a long-standing association with Compline and is suggested as the first hymn in the service, though other evening hymns are also appropriate.[108] The simple, prayerful text and chantlike melody ask for God's grace and peace as we fall asleep after another day. The hymn is followed by a confession of sins; we find peace with God by acknowledging our sins of the past day and hearing his unconditional pardon again.

Compline makes use of the psalms just as other the Daily Office services do. A sixth-century document shows that Psalms 4, 91, and 134 were associated with Compline.[109] Other psalms may also be sung. As in Evening Prayer, a time for silent meditation and prayer follows each psalm, concluding with a psalm prayer spoken by the minister.

A Scripture reading follows the psalms in all Daily Office services. The nature of Compline is such that a short Scripture reading is appropriate, although the occasion that the service is used for may call for something longer. Bible readings associated with Compline include Isaiah 61:1-3; Jeremiah 14:7-9; Matthew 11:28-30; John 14:27; Romans 8:38,39; Hebrews 13:20,21; and 1 Peter 5:6-9.[110] The reading is followed by a short set of responsive Bible verses that are appropriately called the Responsory. Psalm 31:5, a psalm that Jesus quoted in Luke 23:46 just before he gave up his life on the cross, is the main verse of the Responsory: "Into your hands I commend my spirit. You have redeemed me, O Lord, God of truth." Worshipers' thoughts are directed to the comforting truth that our souls and our lives are in the hands of a gracious God whether we fall asleep at the end of the day or we fall asleep in death.

After a hymn, Compline closes with a series of prayers, many of which are quotations from Scripture. The first set of responsive prayers is drawn from Psalm 17:1,8,15. One or more of several possible short prayers follow; these brief prayers come from a variety of sources from the ancient church to the 20th century.[111] The congregation then prays the Lord's Prayer and finally sings the Song of Simeon from Luke 2:29-32.

The Song of Simeon, or "Nunc Dimittis" (its first two words in Latin), is the canticle most commonly associated with the Prayer at the Close of Day. The Song of Simeon was already considered a prayer for the evening in the fourth-century document called the *Apostolic Constitutions*.[112] In Compline, the "Nunc Dimittis" is often framed by an *antiphon*—a liturgical term for a refrain that is sung before and after (and sometimes in the middle of) a psalm or another Scripture song. This particular antiphon-prayer came into Compline in the late Middle Ages and frames the Song of Simeon nicely: "Guide us waking, O Lord, and guard us sleeping, that awake we may watch with Christ and asleep we may rest in peace."[113] Once again, a common theme of Compline comes through this closing song: Simeon, who held the baby Jesus in his arms, was ready to die in peace now that he had literally seen and held the One who embodied his salvation. Once we have reviewed the mercy of God at the end of the day, we too are ready to rest in peace, both at the end of the day and whenever God brings us to the end of our lives.

The brief blessing that concludes the service is a blessing form from the medieval era.[114] While many Lutheran services add a short hymn after the final blessing, when Compline is truly used in a nighttime setting, it may be very effective to allow this simple blessing to be the final words on the ears of worshipers before they fall asleep.

Prayer at the Close of Day is especially striking when the service is conducted in a way that highlights time for quiet, unhurried meditation on God's Word. Lighting in the church may be dimmed. Ceremony may be kept to a minimum: Rather than using the altar and lectern, the minister may conduct the entire service seated at a chair facing the assembly. In many ways, Compline resembles the family gathering together in their living room for bedtime prayers led by their father but on a larger scale with a gathered congregation led by their pastor.

10

The Church Year

Just as our lives are guided by daily and weekly schedules, so they are also ordered after regular holidays and
events on our annual calendars. We welcome the New
Year on January 1, celebrate Valentine's Day with our significant other on February 14, and then welcome the start
of spring and its warmer weather in March. Americans
have unofficially bookended the start and end of summer
with Memorial Day on the last Monday in May and Labor
Day on the first Monday in September. In the middle
of summer, we participate in our community's Independence Day celebrations on July 4. The arrival of autumn
in September is followed by our children going through
the neighborhood to trick or treat on Halloween, October
31. Americans anticipate a national day of Thanksgiving

on the fourth Thursday in November, which ushers in the hustle and bustle of the Christmas shopping season for about four weeks. We finally end the year with a New Year's Eve celebration that leads into the next calendar year—and another annual cycle of holidays, celebrations, and other yearly routines. Scattered throughout that calendar and its national holidays are family birthdays, vacations, anniversaries, and other days and weeks that hold special significance in our personal lives.

Just as our personal lives are guided by an annual calendar, so the church's life is also guided by an annual calendar filled with seasons, holidays, and other special observances. But the church's annual calendar—simply called the Church Year—holds far more significance than days like Valentine's Day or Labor Day. The days and seasons of the Church Year are designed to provide an annual review of the life of Jesus Christ, from birth to ministry to death to resurrection and to his eventual return on the Last Day. Since Jesus' life contains the saving gospel in which we place our Christian faith, and since the gospel alone creates and strengthens our faith, it is only natural that Christians to use a tool like the Church Year to review the events of Jesus' life and be renewed in faith and love by those soul-saving events. In this chapter, we will take a closer look at the Church Year to better appreciate how it presents us the important gospel events from Jesus' life on a regular basis.

Lectionary

Before we look at the Church Year, it will be helpful to learn something about the system of Bible readings that take us through the seasons of the year and gives each season its unique emphases. That system is called the lectionary. Simply stated, a lectionary is a system of Bible readings designed to lead Christians through important sections of Scripture and the key events of Jesus' life on a repeating basis.

In chapter 7, we noted how the ancient Jewish synagogue service influenced the arrangement of Scripture readings in Christian worship. The Jews divided the Torah (the first five books of the Old Testament) into segments that were read in sequence over a year in some places and over three years in other places. That reading was paired with a reading that matched in theme from the Prophets—which, by the Jews' definition, included both prophetic and other historical books of the Old Testament. The sequential reading of the Torah and its accompanying reading from the Prophets were set aside whenever the Jews celebrated an important festival, and specific readings connected to the festival were read instead.[115] These concepts would find their way into the lectionaries that Christians developed for worship.

The regular reading of Scripture in Christian worship is not merely a remnant of synagogue worship. Paul instructed Timothy, "Until I come, devote yourself to the public reading of Scripture, to preaching and to teaching" (1 Timothy 4:13), and Paul told the Christians in Thessalonica, "I charge you before the Lord to have this letter read to all the brothers and sisters" (1 Thessalonians 5:27). Scripture itself tells us that it is meant to be read in public worship. Justin Martyr, writing around A.D. 150, gives further evidence of the regular reading of Scripture in the ancient church: "On the day called Sunday, all who live in cities or in the country gather together to one place, and the memoirs of the apostles or the writings of the prophets are read, as long as time permits; then, when the reader has ceased, the president verbally instructs, and exhorts to the imitation of these good things."[116] Though the quotation does not directly specify, it sounds as if books of Scripture were read in order over a period of time, just as the ancient Jews did with the Torah.

By the second century, there was an annual time set aside to celebrate Jesus' death and resurrection. By the third century, certain books of the Bible were read in connection with that celebration. By the fourth century, the legalization of Christianity gave far greater freedom in Christian worship and subsequently led to the formal development of the seasons of Advent, Christmas, Lent, and Easter. Specific Bible readings were assigned to those festive seasons and days. Soon written Bibles included marks in the margins to indicate the beginning and end of specific readings for specific occasions. Books with only the lectionary readings arranged by the Church Year began to appear in the sixth and seventh centuries.[117] Each lectionary reading came to be called a *pericope* (per-i'-ko-pee), coming from a Greek word that means to "cut out," since these selections were *cut out* of their original Bible book to be read publicly in Christian services.

By the year A.D. 800, Western Christianity had adopted a lectionary of two readings for each Sunday and festival with minor variations from place to place. This lectionary was used through the 20th century. Martin Luther suggested that congregations continue to use the readings that had come down to his day, though he was not completely content with some of the pericope choices. He envisioned a time when some useful revisions could be made but suggested that faithful preaching would need to make up for any deficiencies in the meantime.[118] The early Lutheran church made a few minor adaptations to the centuries-old lectionary: The Epiphany season ended with a celebration of Jesus' transfiguration, and the Church Year concluded with three Sundays that focused on the end of time and Christ's return.[119]

The lectionary of Western Christianity did not undergo any major revision for over a millennium. Although Luther had suggested a revision in the 16th century, the Roman Catholic Church called for a new lectionary during the Second Vatican Council (1962–1965). One of the liturgical committees from the council published their new lectionary in 1969. This lectionary extended over three years instead of one, and it included three weekly readings instead of two—typically from the Old Testament, the epistles of the New Testament, and a New Testament Gospel selection. Specific readings and books are read during the festive seasons of Advent, Christmas, Lent, and Easter, while more general, continuous readings through Bible books are common during the general seasons of the year. The three years of this lectionary are simply distinguished with the letters A, B, and C. Year A uses Gospel accounts primarily from Matthew, Year B from Mark, and Year C from Luke. John's Gospel is woven into all three years of the lectionary.

Many liturgical churches, including Lutherans, saw that the lectionary produced by the Second Vatican Council would be useful in their own denominations. Adaptations of the new Roman Catholic lectionary abound. The Inter-Lutheran Commission on Worship (ILCW) produced its own three-year lectionary in 1973. Several Protestant denominations jointly produced a further revision of the three-year lectionary, resulting in the Common Lectionary (1983) and then the Revised Common Lectionary (1994). WELS adapted the ILCW lectionary for inclusion in *Christian Worship: A Lutheran Hymnal*

(1993), along with a modest revision of the historic one-year lectionary.[120] WELS updated its own lectionary with a revision that appeared in *Christian Worship: Supplement* (2008). Now in *Christian Worship: Hymnal* (2021), a carefully revised and well-researched lectionary offers readings for each Sunday and festival that are united by a common emphasis, usually connected to the Gospel for the day.

Although the new three-year lectionary system has seen many adaptations among its users, its basic premises remain intact. The three-year lectionary provides a greater number of Scripture selections to worshipers, including Old Testament readings, and it carefully walks us through the life and ministry of Jesus each year utilizing the Gospels.

With the overview of the lectionary in mind, we now take a closer look at the seasons of the Church Year through which it guides us.

Advent

Several factors appear to have contributed to the development of the first season of the church year, Advent. A document from Spain in the year A.D. 380 reminded all Christians to attend church services daily from December 17 (one week before Christmas Eve) to January 6 (Epiphany Day). In the fifth century in Gaul (France), a customary fast was observed three days each week from November 11 (St. Martin's Day) until Christmas Day.[121] In Rome, the custom of Ember Days—days set aside four times each year for a public fast—predated Christianity. December was one of the months during which Ember Days occurred, at the time of their harvest. After these days were over, the Roman church observed a two-week time of preparation for Christmas. In order to curb the excessive feasting that some may have been tempted to engage in after the

December harvest and fast days, the church preached against sinful excess, encouraged a spirit of thanksgiving, and reminded Christians to be ready for the final judgment.[122] Finally, in A.D. 656 the church in Spain officially changed the date it celebrated the Annunciation—the angel Gabriel's announcement to Mary that she would be the mother of Jesus Christ (Luke 1:26-38). The date was moved from March 25 (which often occurs in the somber season of Lent) to December 18, one week before Christmas Day.[123]

While we cannot say with certainty how much each of these items played a role in Advent's development, we can see the themes of the Advent season previewed in these historical factors. Gregory the Great, writing in the late sixth century, speaks of a four Sunday Advent season in Rome.[124] By the tenth century, the merging of regional worship customs into one common practice resulted in a four-week Advent season in the entire Holy Roman Empire.[125] The lectionary documents from that general era included four major emphases from the Gospels which are still seen in worship today:

- Preparation for Christ's return at the end of the world,
- Jesus' Palm Sunday entrance into Jerusalem as a parallel to Christ coming to us now,
- The preaching and ministry of John the Baptist, and
- The events Mary experienced leading up to Jesus' birth in Luke 1.[126]

Our modern four-week Advent season, which begins four Sundays prior to Christmas Day, echoes these emphases. The word *advent* means "coming," and during the weeks before Christmas we prepare for the coming of Christ. Living in the New Testament era, we recognize that we are ultimately preparing for Jesus' final advent at the end of time, and so the readings of the first week of the season emphasize our preparedness for Christ's return. Congregations have the option of reading the Gospel account of Jesus' Palm Sunday procession on the First Sunday in Advent. This selection directs our thoughts to the truth that Jesus comes to us in several ways: As Jesus came to his people on Palm Sunday, so he has come to his people by his birth in the past, his means of grace now, and his return in the future. The Second and Third Sundays in Advent present us with the ministry and message of John the Baptist. John prepared people for the advent of Jesus' public ministry with his clear call to repentance. John's warnings are balanced by other Scripture selections, particularly on the Third Sunday in Advent, which point out our Christian joy in anticipation of our Lord's coming. Finally, the last Sunday of the season shifts our focus to the events just prior to Jesus' first advent at his birth.

In the American culture, *secular* Christmas is celebrated for several weeks before Christmas Day: Secular Christmas starts the day after Thanksgiving by some standards or even as early as the day after Halloween. This Christmas *before* Christmas often means that people are worn out with secular Christmas music and ambiance before Christmas even arrives. But the church season of Advent is not a pre-Christmas Christmas. Advent is a time of preparation more than celebration. The songs and customs of Advent anticipate and pray for Jesus' arrival. Advent teaches us patience as we wait for the Lord's good time—the time for Jesus' return and all the circumstances in our lives when we are tempted to become impatient or question God's wisdom.

The customs that have developed around Advent help to distinguish it as a time of preparation for Christ's coming into our world. Most churches have ornate colored cloths called *paraments* that adorn the altar and pulpit. The different colors represent different church seasons and their themes. The liturgical color used in Advent is either blue or purple. Purple was the historic color for Advent. As a color worn by ancient royalty, purple in Advent reminds us that our King is coming to us. Purple is also seen as a symbolic color for repentance, which is the emphasis we hear during Advent in John the Baptist's preaching. In more recent years, blue has become the predominant color for Advent. Blue is a color that symbolizes hope, which is another main theme of Advent: We hope for the Lord's coming into our world. Imagine Old Testament believers looking up to the heavens—the blue sky—and praying for the Messiah's arrival. Today we too look up to the blue heavens and pray that Christ returns as he promised and takes us home with him into heaven's glory.

A common symbol of the Advent season is the Advent wreath. This author has heard the theory that the Advent wreath developed in medieval northern Europe: People would remove wagon wheels from their carriages before winter, and instead of storing the bare wheels in their homes, the wheels would be decorated with evergreen branches and candles and hung from the rafters. While that theory is plausible, we simply don't know how the custom developed. What we can say is that this German custom began in people's homes and eventually found its way into churches.[127] The common custom today is for four candles to be placed around the wreath, one for each Sunday of Advent. A fifth candle, called the Christ candle, is placed in the center of many Advent wreaths and is first lit at Christmas. Lighting another candle every week symbolizes that Jesus "the true light that gives light to everyone was coming into the world" at his incarnation (John 1:9). The candles are usually the same color as the paraments in church: blue or purple—though some congregations use white candles. Sometimes the candle for the Third Sunday in Advent is rose (pink) to symbolize the emphasis of joy found in some of the readings for that Sunday. Since joy (represented by rose) is a strong contrast to repentance (represented by purple), it seems fitting to use a rose-colored candle if the paraments and other candles are purple. The center Christ candle is white to symbolize Jesus' purity; white is also the color for Christmas and the entire Christmas season.

Earlier we noted that the music of Advent, with its tone of anticipation, is different than the celebratory music of Christmas. One noteworthy example is the hymn "O Come, O Come, Emmanuel" (*Christian Worship: Hymnal* 327). This hymn comes from a set of seventh-century Advent texts called the *O Antiphons*. Antiphon is a liturgical term for "refrain." On the seven days before Christmas Eve, these antiphons were sung during Vespers (Evening Prayer) in connection with the Song of Mary. Each antiphon begins with the word O and then addresses Christ with an Old Testament title:

- **December 17:** O Wisdom, proceeding from the mouth of the Most High, pervading and permeating all creation, mightily order all things; come and teach us the way of prudence.
- **December 18:** O Adonai and ruler of the house of Israel, who appeared to Moses in the burning bush

and gave him the law on Sinai, come with an out-stretched arm and redeem us.

- **December 19:** O Root of Jesse, standing as an ensign before the peoples, before whom all kings are mute, to whom the nations will do homage, come quickly to deliver us.

- **December 20:** O Key of David and scepter of the house of Israel, you open and no one can close; you close and no one can open; come and rescue the prisoners who are in darkness and the shadow of death.

- **December 21:** O Dayspring, splendor of light everlasting, come and enlighten those who sit in darkness and the shadow of death.

- **December 22:** O King of the nations, the ruler they long for, the cornerstone for uniting all people, come and save us all, whom you formed out of clay.

- **December 23:** O Emmanuel, our King and our Lord, the anointed of the nations and their Savior, come and save us, O Lord our God.[128]

These refrains were paraphrased into the previously mentioned 12th century Latin hymn hymn. *Christian Worship: Hymnal* includes four of the original seven stanzas, using a modestly edited version of the English translation by John M. Neale and the 15th century melody that has become associated with the hymn text. Because of the original O *Antiphons'* use during the week before Christmas, "O Come, O Come, Emmanuel" is the traditional Hymn of the Day for the Fourth Sunday in Advent each year. The words of this hymn sing out one last note of Advent anticipation on the Sunday before we celebrate Jesus' birth.

Christmas

Jesus' incarnation and birth are the focus of the church's celebration of Christmas Day and the Christmas season. The account of Jesus' birth is described for us in the familiar Christmas story from Luke 2:1-20. Saint John expounds on the mystery and miracle of God becoming human in the opening verses of his Gospel, John 1:1-14.

Two theories suggest the origins behind the *timing* of the Christmas holiday. One theory comes from a presupposition that Christians inherited from Judaism, that the birthday and day of death for important religious figures is the same. Early Christians calculated the day of Jesus' death to be March 25. They also worked with a variation of the Jewish assumption just noted, believing that the day of Jesus' conception was the same as the day he died. This led to December 25 as the day to celebration Jesus' birth.[129]

A second theory suggests a Christian attempt to counteract ancient pagan religious festivals. Roman emperors of the third century introduced and promoted a holiday known as the Birthday of the Unconquered Sun to mark the late December winter solstice and the return of more sunlight each day. Christian theologians would have found little difficulty shifting the emphasis from the pagan holiday to a festival celebrating the birth of Jesus, the One who was unconquered by sin and whom we call the "Sun of Righteousness" (Malachi 4:2).[130] While we cannot know for certain to what extent each of these theories played a role in determining the timing of Christmas, an ancient document indicates that December 25 was celebrated as the birth of Christ in Rome as early as A.D. 336.[131]

Christmas is a day, but it is also a season. The development of the 12-day long Christmas season seems to come from the Western and Eastern centers of Christianity borrowing one another's holidays. Epiphany, celebrated on January 6, is a holiday that first developed in the Eastern church, possibly for reasons similar to the development of Christmas in the West.[132] Epiphany, which means to "reveal," observed a broader spectrum of ways that Jesus revealed himself as God, including God revealing Jesus to the Magi with a star (Matthew 2:1-12), Jesus' baptism at the start of his ministry (Matthew 3:13-17), and his first miracle at the wedding in Cana (John 2:1-11). As both geographical centers of Christianity accepted one another's holidays, the Epiphany celebration on January 6 led to a 12-day Christmas season from December 25 to January 5.[133] Keeping in mind that, in Jewish thinking, a day began at sunset on the previous night, the evening of December 24 marks the formal start of the celebration of Jesus' birth.

In many Lutheran congregations, one or more of their Christmas Eve services is led by the children of the congregation. Through songs and recitations of the Bible's Christmas story, the children fulfill the role of the angels on Christmas night and bring the good news of the Christ child's birth to the congregation. Some congregations also offer Christmas Eve services that are festive variations of established worship patterns like Vespers or Compline. Another well-established Christmas Eve worship tradition is a service of lessons and carols. This service has its origins in the Church of England in the late 19th century and is known today by the famous carol service held at and broadcasted from King's College in Cambridge, England.

This service traditionally begins with "Once in Royal David's City" and ends with "Hark! The Herald Angels Sing" and includes a series of nine Bible readings with beautiful choral music in response to each reading.[134]

Christmas Eve services tend to draw larger crowds and greater attention in our society, but it is beneficial for congregations to equally emphasize worship on Christmas Day. We could compare the purpose of the two days and their services this way: Christmas Eve celebrates the *facts* of Jesus' birth; Christmas Day celebrates the *miracle* and *mystery* of Jesus' incarnation. God became man so that mankind could become one again with God! "The Word became flesh and made his dwelling among us" (John 1:14). A festive Christmas Day service can be easily patterned after the traditional Christian Liturgy. A Christmas hymn such as "Angels We Have Heard on High" (*Christian Worship: Hymnal* 346) is a fine substitute for the traditional "Gloria in Excelsis" on Christmas morning. A generous use of Christ-proclaiming Christmas hymns throughout the service will be appreciated by worshipers. The second portion of the Athanasian Creed (*Christian Worship: Hymnal*, pages 284,285), which talks about the miracle of Jesus Christ being both God and man, provides a fitting confession of faith. Observing the Lord's Supper is also a fitting way to celebrate Christmas; on the day we celebrate the Word who became flesh, we personally receive his body and blood in the sacrament. The Lord's Supper would not be possible were it not for the miracle of Jesus' incarnation at Christmas!

The 12-day Christmas season includes 1 or 2 Sundays after Christmas Day. On these Sundays, we often hear some of the earliest events from Jesus' life: his dedication in the temple (Luke 2:22-40), his escape to Egypt after the Magi's visit (Matthew 2:13-15,19-23), and his visit to Jerusalem as a 12-year-old boy (Luke 2:41-52). Eight days after Christmas, on January 1, the Christian church calendar remembers how Jesus was circumcised and named on the eighth day of his life (Luke 2:21). This minor festival may be celebrated on the Sunday after Christmas when January 1 occurs on a Sunday. There are also other minor festivals with long-standing Christian tradition that occur on the three days after Christmas: These days remember Saint Stephen, the first martyr (December 26; see Acts 7); Saint John, the apostle (December 27); and the Holy Innocents, the little boys killed by King Herod as he attempted to murder the young Jesus (December 28; see Matthew 2:16-18). Except for the last minor festival of the three, these occasions do not have obvious connections to Christmas and are not observed frequently in our congregations, though our church calendars acknowledge these long-standing commemoration days from the ancient church.

The liturgical color used throughout the Christmas season is white. White is a symbol of purity and holiness, and so it is used especially for days and seasons that celebrate our holy and perfect Savior, Jesus Christ.

Epiphany

The festival of Epiphany, as noted earlier, began in the Eastern church. Epiphany is one of the oldest festivals in Christian history. Scholars believe that Epiphany was celebrated in Egypt and Asia Minor already in the second century.[135] Clement of Alexandria, writing at the end of the second century, speaks about a celebration of Jesus' baptism on January 6, which he also cites as the day of Jesus' birth. Eventually this festival spread to places in the Western church such as Gaul and Spain; by the second half of the fourth century, Epiphany was also being observed in Rome.[136]

The most common theories about Epiphany's origins are similar to those about Christmas. Some suggest that Epiphany developed as a Christian response to two Egyptian celebrations: the birth of Aion, the Egyptian god of time and eternity, and the festival of drawing water from the Nile, which was viewed as Egypt's source of life.[137] The other theory proposes that Eastern Christians calculated April 6 to be the date of Jesus death. Using the same assumptions described earlier, they would have calculated January 6 to be the day of Jesus' birth.[138]

Epiphany means "revelation" or "manifestation." God revealed himself to the world through his Son in many ways, and early observances of Epiphany seem to have included a broad range of events that revealed Jesus to be truly God. For example, in Egypt Epiphany's original emphasis was on the baptism of Jesus, even though their customs acknowledged the celebration of Jesus' birth and later expanded to include his first miracle (John 2:1-11) in their celebration. The first records of Epiphany in Gaul (France) describe an emphasis on Jesus' birth, but by the fifth century the focus had turned to three events: the visit of the Magi, the baptism of Jesus, and Jesus' first miracle. By the eighth century, a week was added to the celebration in France, and Jesus' baptism was commemorated at the end of the celebration.[139] In Milan, Italy, Jesus' transfiguration (Matthew 17:1-9) was celebrated in place of the miracle of changing the water into wine.[140] When Rome began to celebrate Epiphany in the latter half of the fourth century, the emphasis remained on Jesus' nativity: The birth account from Luke 2:1-20 with the visit of the shepherds was the focus on December 25, while the visit of the Magi in Matthew 2:1-12 became the emphasis on January 6.[141] Each of these biblical accounts reveals Jesus as the Son of God and our Savior in its own unique way.

This overview of Epiphany's history helps us understand how we celebrate Epiphany Day and Epiphany season today. Epiphany Day, January 6, marks the end of the Christmas season and transitions the Church Year from Jesus' nativity to Jesus' life. We hear the account of the wise men who visited Jesus when he was still a baby or toddler. If our Christmas celebration focuses on the *facts* of Jesus' birth and the *miracle* and *mystery* of his incarnation, then our Epiphany celebration focuses on the *application* of Jesus' birth. This miraculous Child, this Son of God, did not come for one race or an exclusive group of people; he came for all! The miraculous star that revealed the boy Jesus to the eastern Magi demonstrates that this truth equally applies to us today!

Because Epiphany is assigned to January 6, it frequently occurs on a day other than Sunday. As a result, it can easily be a forgotten festival. If there are two Sundays between Christmas Day and Epiphany Day, it may be wise to celebrate Epiphany on the Second Sunday after Christmas. Congregations might also consider if a midweek evening service is possible on January 6. Since Epiphany marks the end of the Christmas season, it is very appropriate that the church's Christmas decorations, including the Christmas tree and Advent wreath, remain in the sanctuary through the Epiphany celebration. This helps to underscore that the Christian Christmas celebration does not precede Christmas, but it begins with Christmas and lasts for nearly two weeks through Epiphany.

The First Sunday after Epiphany commemorates Jesus' baptism at the beginning of his ministry. God the Father's voice revealed Jesus as our Savior as he thundered from heaven, "This is my Son, whom I love; with him I am well pleased" (Matthew 3:17). Our remembrance of Jesus' baptism encourages us to remember our own baptisms. A few of the Bible readings assigned to this occasion in the lectionary encourage us to remember the blessings of Holy Baptism.

The Last Sunday after Epiphany remembers a similar event: Jesus' transfiguration. The baptism of Jesus and his transfiguration serve as bookends to the Epiphany season. As God the Father spoke his words of approval to Jesus at his baptism, so the Father speaks similar words of approval at Jesus' transfiguration. The Father said to Peter, James, and John: "This is my Son, whom I love; with him I am well pleased. Listen to him!" (Matthew 17:5). The grand display of Jesus' glory that his three disciples saw that day revealed Jesus' divine nature to them—a nature that he would humbly hide as they followed him on the journey to the cross after this event. That reality makes the transfiguration a fitting event to remember on the last Sunday in the Epiphany season just before the penitential season of Lent begins. Congregations may end the service with a short rite and hymn called "Farewell to Alleluia" that anticipates Lent on the horizon.

The season of Epiphany varies in length due to the moveable date for Easter Sunday. When Easter is earlier, Epiphany is shorter; when Easter is later, Epiphany is longer. During the middle Sundays of Epiphany, we hear about events from the beginning of Jesus' public ministry. The Second Sunday of Epiphany features a Gospel reading from John 1,2 each year; in one of the three years of the lectionary, worshipers hear the account of Jesus' changing water into wine. The remaining Sundays include accounts from the synoptic Gospels. In Year A, we hear excerpts from Matthew 4–6, including several selections from Jesus' Sermon on the Mount. In Year B, we read Gospel accounts from Mark 1,2 that especially highlight Jesus' miraculous deeds. Year C presents Gospel readings from Luke that often emphasize Jesus as a divine teacher of God's Word. Each series of accounts reveals different facets of the truth that Jesus is the eternal Son of God and our gracious Savior.

As with the Christmas season, the liturgical color for Epiphany Day is white. White is also used on the First and Last Sundays after Epiphany for Jesus' baptism and trans-figuration. All three of these days emphasize key events in Jesus' life, and so white is the natural color to use on those occasions to reflect the holy Son of God whose life and works we celebrate. The middle Sundays of the season fea-ture the liturgical color green. Green, symbolizing growth, is normally used during the general seasons of the year. While the middle weeks of Epiphany also reveal Jesus as our Savior, those weeks are not as direct in that emphasis as the first and last weeks of the season are. Yet the mid-dle weeks do reveal the growth of Jesus' ministry. We also grow in faith as we hear about Jesus' preaching, miracles, and teaching.

Lent

The name of the next church season, *Lent*, likely draws its name from an old English word for "spring," the time of year when the days *lengthen*.[142] In Lutheranism today, Lent is a 40-day season that extends from Ash Wednesday to the day before Easter, excluding Sundays.

Lent finds its origins in formalized periods of fasting observed among ancient Christians. In Egypt, a 40-day period of fasting developed after Epiphany, remembering Jesus' 40-day fast in the desert after his baptism (Mark 1:9-13).[143] In other locations, the custom of a week's fast prior to Easter became common as early as the third century. By the end of the fourth century, many documents describe a 40-day pre-Easter fast.[144] Specific lengths of time and customs varied from place to place, but the concept of a fast between Easter and Epiphany is well-documented and was widely practiced.

Two practices eventually developed in connection with this pre-Easter time of fasting. One was the reconciliation of penitents—Christians who had seriously lapsed from their faith, repented, and were going through a process to restore their fellowship. This process culminated in their participation in Holy Communion on Thursday of Holy Week. The other emphasis was on the instruction of catechumens—adult converts to the Christian faith who were preparing for their baptism at the vigil held on the night before Easter Sunday.[145] These two Lenten practices led to two major emphases of repentance and catechetical instruction in the faith.

In the seventh century, the beginning of Lent in Rome was officially established on the Wednesday prior to the sixth Sunday before Easter. This day eventually became known as Ash Wednesday from a custom that originated in Spain and France to impose ashes on the penitents who sought to restore their fellowship with the church. Although this custom did not formally originate with the start of Lent, it eventually became associated with the first day of Lent. Ashes, once reserved for the penitents, were eventually distributed to all worshipers. When this practice was decreed a universal custom in 1091, the name Ash Wednesday became associated with this day.[146] The establishment of Ash Wednesday as the beginning of Lent led to its 40-day season. There are actually 46 days from Ash Wednesday to Holy Saturday, but each Sunday is considered a little Easter and not included in the 40-day total, even though Sundays in Lent retain a solemn tone. The Sundays of this time are called Sundays in Lent, rather than Sundays of Lent, to note this distinction.

Ash Wednesday emphasizes a call to repentance at the beginning of our Lenten seasons. Luther was entirely correct in his Ninety-Five Theses that the entire life of a Christian is one of repentance, but there is also benefit in a special day and season to highlight our need for genuine repentance. Holy Week, the final week of Lent, will bring us spiritually face-to-face with all our Lord endured and suffered to win our salvation. As we stand on the horizon of those solemn events, it is entirely appropriate to have a day and season that highlight repentance. Ash Wednesday worship often begins with an extensive and thorough confession of sins and allows for the imposition of ashes as a devotional extension of the confession of sins. One common practice is for the minister to impose the ashes on worshipers' foreheads in the sign of a cross as he says, "Remember that you are dust, and to dust you shall return."

The penitential sense of Lent continues throughout the season by the omission of festive elements of the service. For example, it is a common custom to omit the main song of praise, the "Gloria in Excelsis," as well as any use of the word *Alleluia* in the service. These omissions create a more solemn sense to Lenten worship, though they are by no means a liturgical mandate. Luther himself was against the omission of Alleluia in Lent, although his comments connected that practice with other false practices that existed within the medieval Roman Catholic Church.[147] But when these omitted practices are done freely and with instruction, they can be useful ways to observe a solemn Lent and invigorate the joy of Easter when these customs return. The liturgical color purple, a symbol of repentance, is also used throughout the Lenten season. The color black, symbolic of sorrow and death, is an option for Ash Wednesday with its heightened penitential emphasis.

The catechetical aspect of Lent can be seen in the Sunday Scripture readings and themes. The emphases on the Sundays in Lent take us to central and fundamental teachings of Scripture. Mankind's fall into sin; Jesus' power over sin, death, and the devil; salvation by grace alone; the necessity of faith in Christ—these are among the fundamental Christian teachings heard during Sundays in Lent. Early Lutherans also held services during the week that included sermons based on the catechism.[148] Many modern American Lutherans are accustomed to midweek Lenten services that focus on the Passion History of Jesus. Although this is a different emphasis than the catechism, it presents the fundamental events of our salvation in an orderly way during Lent.

Holy Week

Holy Week is the final week of Lent. Although it is not a separate church season, it deserves additional emphasis because of its unique place in the Church Year. At the beginning of Holy Week, the church's celebration of Jesus' death, resurrection, ascension, and the coming of the Holy Spirit at Pentecost shifts into real time—we celebrate these events in the exact same time frame in which they originally occurred. Holy Week highlights the most important events of our salvation and serves as a bridge to the joyful Easter season that follows.

Lutherans have become accustomed to a review of Jesus' suffering and death through midweek services during Lent. Historically, that emphasis began not with Lent but with Holy Week. Palm Sunday, the first day of Holy Week, marked this transition from preparation to observance. The distinction between Lent and Holy Week was especially evident in Eastern Christianity: After observing Lent, there was a festive break with the celebration of Lazarus Saturday (John 11:1-44) and Palm Sunday, followed by a six-day fast on Monday through Saturday of Holy Week that preceded Easter Sunday.[149]

Palm Sunday has had two historic emphases. As its name indicates, Palm Sunday recalls Jesus' entrance into Jerusalem on a borrowed donkey, accompanied by the praises of the crowd that waved palm branches in his path (John 12:12-15). But the day had also been observed as Passion Sunday, the beginning of the week that commemorated Jesus' suffering and death. Over several centuries, the Palm Sunday emphasis overtook the Passion focus. Palm Sunday processions began in Jerusalem by the fourth century, became common in Western Christianity by the sixth century, and became full-scale city-wide processions in the eighth century. The hymn "All Glory, Laud, and Honor" (Christian Worship: Hymnal 412) became a part of these grand processions.[150]

Today's celebrations of Palm Sunday reflect many of these historic developments. Some congregations begin their Palm Sunday worship with a palm branch procession. The procession could include the entire congregation or a select group such as a choir or the children of the congregation. "All Glory, Laud, and Honor" is often used as a congregational hymn during these processions. The processional group carries palm branches, resembling the crowds on the first Palm Sunday, and deposits the branches before the altar or another designated place in the front of the church. If congregations want to note both emphases of the day, the service may include the reading of the Palm Sunday Gospel before the procession and the reading of the Passion History later in the service.

Holy Week leads into the celebration of the key events of our salvation that took place at the end of the week. Over several centuries, Christians developed a series of services for the last three days of Holy Week. These services are known as the *Triduum*, a Latin word meaning "three days." The *Triduum* especially refers to the interconnected services offered on Holy Thursday, Good Friday, and Holy Saturday.

Holy Thursday has also been called Maundy Thursday, a term derived from John 13:34. Jesus said to his disciples, "A new command I give you: Love one another." The Latin word for "command" is *mandatum*, from which *Maundy* is derived. Jesus' "new command" was a part of his lengthy address to his disciples on the original Holy Thursday (John 13:31–16:33).

There are several highlights of Holy Thursday represented in that day's worship. Jesus washed his disciples' feet as an example of humble service (John 13:1-17). His long discourse issued the new commandment to love one another as he has loved us. Jesus instituted Holy Communion in the context of the Passover meal (Matthew 26:26-29). After departing for Gethsemane, he prayed in anguish to his Father before being arrested by the Jewish religious leaders and abandoned by his disciples (Matthew 26:36-56).

Holy Thursday services bring these highlights together in a worship context. The minister's opening address and the confession of sins may include thoughts that reflect Jesus' foot washing and his new commandment. The greatest highlight, the institution of the sacrament, is brought to the forefront of our celebration of the Lord's Supper in this service. An ancient custom, the stripping of the altar, may conclude the service as a visual symbol of Jesus' abandonment in Gethsemane: As the altar furnishings are removed, we remember how Jesus—symbolized by the altar—was abandoned by his disciples at his arrest and betrayal. Psalm 88 is often sung as this ritual takes place. The service ends in silence and without a formal dismissal, anticipating the continuation of events and celebration at the next day's Good Friday services.

Good Friday is a unique day in the Church Year. On this special day, we celebrate the tremendous sacrificial love of our Savior, who took our place under God's law and was forsaken by his Father in heaven to win our forgiveness and obtain our salvation. Good Friday is the only day in the church calendar in which the main service is held, if possible, in the afternoon. This custom recalls the three hours of darkness that hung over the earth from 12:00 P.M. to 3:00 P.M. as our Lord endured hell on our behalf as our gracious substitute (Matthew 27:45). Afternoon services may include the solemn procession of a cross through the assembly, an ancient prayer called the Bidding Prayer that offers petitions for a wide range of people, and other elements that reflect the worship customs of Christians who have preceded us. Some congregations do not use the altar during worship on Good Friday to symbolize the continued abandonment of Jesus. The altar remains bare from the end of the Holy Thursday service, or it is draped in black paraments in contrast to the purple that was displayed throughout Lent.

Throughout Christian history, other devotional practices became connected with Good Friday. In the 17th
century, the custom developed of a three-hour long
service, held during the Good Friday darkness from
12:00 P.M. to 3:00 P.M. These carefully timed services are
built around the seven words Jesus spoke on the cross,
including sermons on each of the words, hymns, prayers,
and times for silent meditation. Another popular Good
Friday tradition is a service called *Tenebrae* (Latin for
"darkness") held in the evening, which features the gradual extinguishing of candles until the church is in total
darkness. This service may also focus on Jesus' seven
statements from the cross. The service sometimes ends
with a loud noise sounded in the darkness; this startling
sound may be understood to depict the earthquake at the
moment of Jesus' death (Matthew 27:51), the closing of
Jesus' tomb at his burial (Matthew 27:60), or even a fore-
shadowing of the rending of Jesus' tomb on Easter morning. Worship traditions like these often morph over time,
no longer mirroring their original sources from centuries
earlier but reflecting a meaningful way to celebrate our
salvation in our own time and place.[151]

The final day of the *Triduum*, Holy Saturday, marks the
transition from solemn Lent to joyful Easter. Although the
idea of an Easter Eve service may be new to many Lutherans, the Great Vigil of Easter is one of the oldest Christian
celebrations, dating back at least to the middle of the
second century.[152] Ancient Easter vigils featured the baptism and first communion of new converts to Christianity.
The baptism of new converts at Easter reflects Saint Paul's
words in Romans 6:3,4: "Don't you know that all of us
who were baptized into Christ Jesus were baptized into his
death? We were therefore buried with him through baptism

into death in order that, just as Christ was raised from the dead through the glory of the Father, we too may live a new life."

The Easter Vigil begins after sunset on Saturday, the start of Sunday by ancient Jewish standards. The vigil is divided into four segments: The first portion is the Service of Light, featuring the lighting and procession of the large paschal candle, a symbol of the risen Jesus. The second and longest portion of the vigil is the Service of Readings. Several Scripture selections from the Old Testament are read. These readings highlight God's great acts of deliverance in the past and anticipate his greatest act of deliverance in the resurrection of Jesus from the dead. The Service of Baptism follows. In this portion of the vigil, new converts to the faith may be baptized, or the worshipers may affirm their baptismal faith. After the service is three-fourths concluded, the mood dramatically changes to represent the moment of Jesus' resurrection. The relative quietness is ended with the announcement of Jesus' resurrection; church bells are rung, church lights are fully lit, and the congregation sings a song of praise to the risen Lord that begins the Service of Holy Communion. With a fully lit church, the white or gold paraments and festive Easter decorations suddenly make a joyful visual contrast to the previously bare sanctuary that worshipers viewed one day earlier.

Easter

In the great resurrection chapter of the Bible, the apostle Paul wrote, "If Christ has not been raised, your faith is futile; you are still in your sins. . . . But Christ has indeed been raised from the dead" (1 Corinthians 15:17,20). The resurrection of Jesus after his sacrificial death is essential for our Christian faith and hope. No wonder that Christians from earliest times chose Sunday as their day of worship. Every Sunday truly is a *little Easter!*

The celebration of Jesus' resurrection was not just a weekly event for the first Christians. Worship scholars generally agree that an annual celebration of Jesus' resurrection became common from the earliest times in Christian history. The annual remembrance of Jesus' death and resurrection coincided with the Jewish celebration of the Passover. In fact, the name *Pascha* was first given to this celebration. The noun *Pasch(a)* and adjective *paschal* are derived from the Hebrew word *pesach*, meaning "Passover."[153] The events of Israel's Passover, escape from Egypt, and deliverance at the Red Sea (Exodus 12–14) have strong parallels to the institution of the Lord's Supper, Jesus' death that freed us from sin's guilt, and his resurrection that delivered us from death.

This annual celebration quickly became a lengthy season of festive celebration. Already at the beginning of the third century, Tertullian (c. 155–c. 240) called the Easter season "the space of Pentecost" and "a most joyful space of exaltation." The reference to "space" and especially to "Pentecost," the 50th day of the season, indicates that Easter was an ongoing seven-week celebration and not just a single day. In fact, the name Pentecost initially referred to the 50 days of Easter before Pentecost Day became its own distinct holiday.[154]

One century later, the Easter season developed specific divisions within its seven weeks. The liturgical practice of an *octave*, a celebration that extended eight days from its first day to the same day of the next week, became associated with Easter. It appears that the Easter octave was set apart as a time for additional instruction of the newly baptized converts. The Ascension of Jesus 40 days after his resurrection (Acts 1:3) created another segment of the Easter season. Ascension was initially celebrated 50 days after Easter on the day of Pentecost, but as Pentecost Day began to focus more on the Holy Spirit, Ascension moved to the 40th day of Easter. Writings from the late fourth century and later indicate that Ascension had become its own holiday within Easter rather than a shared day with Pentecost. This adjustment occurred after Pentecost's emphasis had shifted from being viewed as the last day of the Easter season to becoming a day to commemorate the Spirit's outpouring on Jesus' disciples.[155]

Today, the Easter season remains the seven-week long celebration as it first began. Jesus' Ascension is celebrated on the Thursday that occurs 40 days after Easter Sunday. However, in many congregations, a Thursday night service in spring is impractical, and so the Ascension festival may replace the regular readings and focus for the Seventh Sunday of Easter. Pentecost Day, the Festival of the Coming of the Holy Spirit, brings the Easter season to its conclusion.

As the most significant festival in the Church Year, Easter worship is especially festive in nature. Some congregations hold two different services on Easter Sunday—an Easter Dawn (sunrise) service, followed by the main Easter Day festival service. After the Lenten absence of the song of praise "Gloria in Excelsis" and all uses of Alleluia, both return to weekly worship, often with special musical settings. A common custom that has developed among Lutherans is to sing the song "This Is the Feast" (*Christian Worship: Hymnal* 938) in place of the "Gloria" throughout the Easter season. Bright white paraments replace the dark purple and black of Lent and Holy Week. Gold is an optional color for the services of Easter Eve, Easter Dawn, and Easter Day. The paschal candle, a tall and ornate candle usually stationed next to the baptismal font and representing the risen Jesus, may be processed on Easter Sunday and is lit throughout the season. The paschal candle is either lit from Easter Day (or Holy Saturday) to Ascension or throughout the entire seven weeks of the season, according to local custom and preference. The paschal candle is also lit for baptisms and funerals, bringing to mind what St. Paul says about our baptismal connection to Jesus' death and resurrection in Romans 6:3-11.

We will be able to appreciate the Easter season more with an overview of each Sunday's focus. Easter Day clearly focuses on the resurrection of Jesus from the dead. The lectionary in *Christian Worship: Hymnal* suggests that John's account of the resurrection be read at Easter Dawn, while the appropriate synoptic Gospel (Matthew, Mark, Luke) is read at the main Easter Day service. The Second Sunday of Easter reviews the Doubting Thomas account that took place the week after Jesus' resurrection, along with its surrounding context in John 20:19-31. The Third Sunday of Easter presents us with another post-resurrection appearance of Jesus from the gospels.

The Easter season transitions on the fourth Sunday, called Good Shepherd Sunday. On that day, the Gospel accounts shift from resurrection *appearances* of Jesus to resurrection *themes*. Good Shepherd Sunday is especially cherished among Lutherans. We hear from Jesus' Good Shepherd discourse in John 10, and we sing Psalm 23 with its Good Shepherd thoughts. Both sections of Scripture include resurrection themes. Jesus said, "I am the good shepherd. . . . I lay down my life for the sheep. . . . The reason my Father loves me is that I lay down my life—*only to take it up again*. No one takes it from me, but I lay it down of my own accord. I have authority to lay it down and authority *to take it up again*" (John 10:14,15,17,18). Psalm 23:6 puts us in mind of our own resurrection as we sing, "I will dwell in the house of the LORD forever."

The fifth and sixth Sundays include Gospel selections from John 13–15. Although Jesus spoke these words on Holy Thursday, his discourse contains themes that are fitting for this segment of the Easter season. One of Jesus' predominant themes in this section is that he is preparing his disciples for his ascension and for the coming of the Holy Spirit at Pentecost. Jesus weaves other thoughts together with those themes, but the focus on his upcoming Ascension and the outpouring of the Holy Spirit are timely themes as Ascension and Pentecost approach.

The seventh and final Sunday of Easter, which comes after Ascension Day, presents us with an excerpt from Jesus' High Priestly Prayer in John 17, also spoken on Thursday of Holy Week. In that prayer, Jesus anticipates the time when he will be away from his disciples. He prays for the Father's blessing on them and on all from future generations who will believe in him. Once again, the themes expressed in this prayer lead it to be an excellent choice for this particular Sunday of the Church Year between Ascension and Pentecost.

Pentecost

Pentecost Day, the Festival of the Coming of the Holy Spirit, is the last major festival in the Church Year. As noted earlier, Pentecost was initially observed as the last day of the 50-day Easter season before it developed as a day to remember the outpouring of the Holy Spirit on Jesus' apostles (Acts 2:1-41).

The Christian Day of Pentecost coincided with an Old Testament harvest festival known as the "Festival of Weeks" (Exodus 34:22). On this occasion, Jewish believers were to offer the firstfruits of their wheat harvest to the Lord. This was one of three Old Testament festivals for which Jewish men were expected to travel to Jerusalem (Deuteronomy 16:16). This Jewish Pentecost-harvest festival took place 50 days after the Sunday that followed the Passover. God's divine timing and wisdom are clearly seen: As thousands of Jews and Jewish converts gathered in Jerusalem for this firstfruits harvest festival, the Holy Spirit brought about a firstfruits harvest of souls into the Holy Christian Church.[156] The Holy Spirit's miracle, enabling Jesus' disciples to speak in the languages of the many visitors in Jerusalem, brought the good news of the crucified and risen Jesus to all who were gathered in the city that day. Note the true significance of the Spirit's miracle: Speaking in tongues was not meant to impress the visitors of Jerusalem but to present them with the saving gospel message. The 3,000 who came to faith were baptized that same day. The real miracle of the day was all about the gospel—the means of grace—working in the hearts of people who needed to hear about their Savior, Jesus Christ!

The Spirit's arrival on the first Pentecost Day was accompanied by two additional miracles: the sound of a rushing wind and the appearance of tongues of fire on the disciples' heads. The Greek and Hebrew words for "spirit" and "wind" are the same, and so this miraculous announcement of the Holy Spirit's arrival carried unique associations to the witnesses of Pentecost. The tongues of fire were a visual testimony to the different languages, or *tongues*, that the disciples were enabled to speak that day. The liturgical color used on Pentecost Day is red, recalling the tongues of fire that appeared on the disciples' head. Red also reminds us of the many martyrs throughout history whose blood was shed for their confession of faith in Christ. For these reasons, red is not only used for Pentecost but for most major church festivals and celebrations.

Pentecost is both a day and a season—just like Christmas, Epiphany, and Easter. The season after Pentecost is the longest part of the Christian calendar, comprising about half of the year. The length of the season varies based on the date of Easter. Notice how the date of Easter affects the length of both the Epiphany and Pentecost seasons. An earlier date for Easter results in a shorter Epiphany season and longer season after Pentecost; a later date for Easter lengthens the Epiphany season and shortens the time after Pentecost.

The first half of the church year, sometimes called the Half-Year of our Lord, presented us with the life of Christ—his birth, life, ministry, passion, death, resurrection, and ascension. The second half of the year, sometimes called the Half-Year of the Church, presents us with God's Word concerning the life of the church and the life of the Christian in light of the life, death, and resurrection of Jesus Christ. During the second half of the Church Year, our growth in Christian faith and sanctified living is highlighted in a variety of ways and themes, but this emphasis never overshadows the source and strength of our faith and lives, the gospel of Jesus Christ. The liturgical color green, used for the season after Pentecost, visually emphasizes the season's focus on growth in faith and godly living.

In the previous section on Easter, we noted how significant Christian festivals were sometimes observed for an eight-day period called an octave. Another festival day occurs one week after Pentecost Day, which brings its octave to a festive conclusion. Trinity Sunday is celebrated annually on the First Sunday after Pentecost. Unlike nearly all other Christian festivals that celebrate an *event*, Trinity Sunday highlights a *doctrine*: the mystery of our majestic God, who is three distinct persons—Father, Son, and Holy Spirit—and yet one God. Trinity Sunday is a relatively late addition to the Church Year. Regional celebrations existed in medieval Christianity, but there was some resistance to the idea of a universally held observance simply because every Sunday's worship acknowledges and celebrates the triune God.[157] Trinity Sunday was finally declared a universal celebration in 1334.[158] The liturgical color for this occasion is white, symbolizing the holiness and perfection of our triune God. Many congregations speak the Athanasian Creed on Trinity Sunday, especially for the first half that confesses the Bible's truth about the triune God.

The Second Sunday after Pentecost begins the green season with its more general emphasis on Christian faith and life. Although there is not a specific focus for the season after Pentecost, worship planners can detect several multi-week segments with a common theme within the season. The Gospel accounts resume in each synoptic Gospel from approximately the place they left off in the Epiphany season. We read Matthew's gospel in Year A of the lectionary, Mark in Year B, and Luke in Year C. One exception is in Year B: Shortly after the weekly readings present Mark's account of the feeding of the 5,000 (Mark 6:35-44) and Jesus walking on the water (Mark 6:45-56), the lectionary switches to John 6 for a few weeks. This chapter records Jesus' Bread of Life discourse, which followed the miracles chronologically, but it is not recorded in the other Gospels.

As the Church Year nears its conclusion, the Pentecost season devotes its last few Sundays to a focus on end-of-time matters such as judgment day and eternal life in heaven. At the beginning of this chapter, we noted that early Lutherans added this focus to the end of the Church Year. Before the Reformation, if the season after Pentecost was long due to an early date for Easter, the readings from the last few Sundays after Epiphany that had been omitted were inserted near the end of the Church Year.[159] Rather than reassigning those Epiphany season readings, Lutherans gave an end time focus to the conclusion of the Church Year.

There are also a few special occasions that may be observed at this time of the Church Year. On the last Sunday in October, congregations may commemorate the Lutheran Reformation of the church. Within 15 years of Luther first posting the Ninety-Five Theses on October 31, 1517, there were celebrations of the Reformation among Lutherans. The actual date for the observance varied: Among the dates for the Reformation celebration were the eve of Luther's birth (November 10, 1483), the anniversary of Luther's death (February 18, 1546), or the Sunday after the anniversary of the presentation of the Augsburg Confession (June 25, 1530). Reformation observances fell into disuse during the Thirty Years' War (1618–1648) but were later restored in 1667 by Elector John George II of Saxony. The elector selected October 31, the anniversary of Luther posting the Ninety-Five Theses, as the commemoration day. Among Lutherans, the common practice that resulted was to celebrate the Reformation on October 31 or the previous or succeeding Sunday.[160] Red, the color for church celebrations, is used on Reformation Sunday.

Another well-established Christian holiday occurs the day after Reformation Day. All Saints' Day is November 1 and may be celebrated on the first Sunday in November. All Saints' Day has its roots in the ancient Christian church as a day to remember the martyrs who gave their lives for their confession of faith. This commemoration was held on different dates throughout several centuries, but in 835, November 1 was officially designated as a festival day to commemorate all saints.[161] All Saints' Day encourages us to look back in time and give thanks to God for the Christian saints and martyrs who have preceded us. The liturgical color white is used to remember that Jesus has made his saints pure and holy forever. The color white also recalls John's vision of the saints in heaven: "Before me was a great multitude that no one could count, from every nation, tribe, people, and language, standing before the throne and before the Lamb. *They were wearing white robes* and were holding palm branches in their hands" (Revelation 7:9).

The final Sunday of the Church Year (occurring between November 20 and 26) may emphasize the general end-of-time focus that is common throughout the last Sundays of the Pentecost season. There is also an option to observe the final Sunday of the year as Christ the King Sunday. This is a relatively new addition to the Christian calendar. In 1925, Pope Pius XI decreed this festival for the last Sunday in October as a Roman Catholic response to increasing communism and fascism in the world. The Roman Catholic Church moved the festival of Christ the King to the last Sunday of the Church Year with the worship reforms that came out of the Second Vatican Council.[162] Many Protestant calendars adopted this festival as a festive conclusion to the Church Year. A Lutheran celebration of this day would not focus on political concerns but on spiritual concerns. Our emphasis would be on Jesus Christ, who reigns in our hearts as the King of kings and Lord of lords and will reign gloriously in heaven for all eternity. As a festival day remembering Christ, the liturgical color for the day is white.

Minor Festivals

The Church Year helps us walk through the life of Jesus and the primary teachings of Scripture on an annual basis. One useful addendum to the Church Year that deserves our attention is the calendar of Minor Festivals that congregations may celebrate from time to time. A list is included on page VIII in the front section of *Christian Worship: Hymnal.*

Many events in Jesus' life and ministry are covered in the Church Year. However, there are several events that relate to Jesus' birth which are observed through the calendar of Minor Festivals rather than the Church Year. The dates chosen for these celebrations all relate to December 25, the date on which we celebrate Christ's birth. For example, on March 25, nine months before we celebrate Christmas, we observe the Annunciation of Our Lord, when the angel Gabriel announced to Mary that she would conceive and give birth to the Son of God (Luke 1:26-38). Shortly thereafter we remember the Visitation on May 31, when Mary visited Elizabeth, the expectant mother of John the Baptist (Luke 1:39-56). Since John was born about six months before Jesus (Luke 1:36), the birth of John the Baptist is celebrated on June 24, six months before Christmas. January 1, eight days after Christmas, is set aside in the Minor Festival calendar to celebrate the Circumcision and Name of Jesus (Luke 2:21). On February 2, 40 days after Christmas, we celebrate the Presentation of Our Lord, a day which commemorates when Jesus was presented in the temple as Mary's firstborn son in accordance with Jewish ceremonial laws (Luke 2:22-40). Because these occasions relate to the birth of Jesus, the holy Son of God, the color for these days in white.

Several other minor festivals recall significant apostles, evangelists, and saints in Scripture. These festivals reflect the encouragement given in Hebrews 13:7: "Remember your leaders, who spoke the word of God to you. Consider the outcome of their way of life and imitate their faith." We do not always know why specific dates were chosen to remember individual people. Sometimes the date chosen is believed to be the anniversary of the day when an apostle's earthly remains were moved to their final resting place; sometimes the date is the anniversary of the dedication of a significant church building with that saint's name. When church history informs us that a saint died as a martyr, the color red is used on their commemoration date to remind us that their blood was shed for their confession. On other saints' days, the color white reminds us that these men and women, whose souls now rest in heaven's peace and perfection, have been made holy and pure by God.

There are additional days in the Minor Festival calendar that fall outside the two categories of nativity events and saints' days. Two dates recall Lutheran church history: the Presentation of the Augsburg Confession (June 25) and Reformation Day (October 31). September 29 has been designated to remember Saint Michael (Jude 9; Revelation 12:7) and All Angels as early as the fifth century.[163] The great apostles, Peter and Paul, share a common commemoration date (June 29) because they were believed to be martyred on the same day in different years.[164] Because of their shared commemoration date, they are also given their own individual dates in January that recall a significant moment in their lives.

When a minor festival date occurs on a Sunday, a congregation may consider replacing the usual Sunday focus with the minor festival.

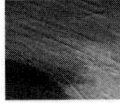

11

Symbolism[165]

The Independence Day parade is about to march down Main Street in your hometown. A member of the armed forces from the city carries the American flag at the front of the parade. As the flag approaches, everyone stands, removes their hats, and holds their hands over their hearts. Several enlisted servicemen and veterans follow behind the flag, dressed in military attire. The crowd claps and cheers for them, some of whom are getting well along in years. Only after the veterans and active servicemen pass does the crowd sit to watch the rest of the parade.

The church bells peal to mark the start of the wedding. The guests have taken their seats inside the church. The music begins as each bridesmaid walks gracefully down the center aisle, met by her respective groomsmen halfway to the front of the church. The bride enters, dressed in white and escorted by her father down the aisle. The assembly stands to honor her on her special day. The assembly sits as the spoken wedding rite formally begins. The couple makes their marriage vows: They hold hands, speak their promises to God and each other, and exchange wedding rings. Finally, the officiant proclaims them to be husband and wife.

Parades and weddings are just two examples of events in which symbolism plays a major role. An American Independence Day parade without the American flag and with no opportunity to honor our servicemen and veterans would seem odd, even disrespectful. Many couples would be disappointed if the festive formalities of the bride's special gown, the procession, and the exchange of rings were not a part of their wedding ceremony. Symbolic objects, such as the American flag, and symbolic actions, such as the ceremonies of a wedding, are powerful ways to communicate the significance of what we are observing or celebrating. Symbolism is even a part of less formal events. We blow out symbolic candles on our birthday cake, representing the number of years we have enjoyed God's gift of life. We watch the championship-winning sports team hoist the trophy that symbolizes their victory and accomplishments. Clearly symbolism with objects and actions is a normal part of our experience.

Symbolism is also a significant part of Christian worship. In this chapter, the first of several chapters dealing with practical worship matters, we will explore symbolism in the context of Christian worship. When we understand how symbolism works and consider examples of Christian symbolism in public worship, our worship experience will be enriched.

Background of the word

Our English words *symbol* and *symbolism* come from the Greek word *symballo*. The roots and meanings of a source word in one language do not necessarily determine its meaning in English, but in this case, the background of the word provides a useful illustration about symbolism. The Greek prefix *sym* means "together." The Greek verb *ballo* means "throw." The compound verb, *symballo*, has several possible definitions, including "to confer, to consider, to draw conclusions about, to compare."[166]

An illustration that brings out the concept of symbolism is that of a broken coin. An ancient military commander might break a coin into two pieces and give half of the coin to one of his generals. If the general sent a messenger back to the commander, the messenger would bring the general's half of the coin with him. The commander would "throw together" or compare the two halves of the coin, and when they matched, he could draw the conclusion that this was a legitimate messenger sent by his general. The most important aspect was not that the coin halves fit together but that the matching pieces of the coin revealed a more important truth—in this case that the messenger could be trusted. The commander could not look into the heart of the messenger to detect his honesty, but the coin served as a testimony to his legitimacy.

As we consider the intersection of symbolism and Christian worship, this illustration helps us to understand that the most important part about symbolism is not the symbolic object or action itself but what that object or action *communicates*. Symbolism points us to greater divine truths. Symbolism allows us to visually depict and communicate realities that we cannot literally see.

Symbolism as communication

It is useful to understand that symbolism is a *form* of communication and to recognize *how* symbolism communicates. To help us understand how symbolism communicates, we need to recognize that God has designed our human minds with two distinct, unique hemispheres. In popular language, people sometimes talk about the left brain and the right brain. Of course, we do not have two brains; we have two *hemispheres* of the brain, each with its own unique purpose. The left and right hemispheres of our brain work together to help us function in our daily lives. The following quotation from the psychologist Bessel van der Kock provides a helpful description of the two hemispheres:

> We now know that the two halves of the brain do speak different languages. The right is intuitive, emotional, visual, spatial, and actual, and the left is linguistic, sequential, and analytical. While the left half of the brain does all the talking, the right half of the brain carries the music of experience. It communicates through facial expressions and body language and by making the sounds of love and sorrow. . . . The right brain is the first to develop in the womb, and it carries the nonverbal communication between mothers and infants. We know the left hemisphere has come online when children start to understand language and learn how to speak. This enables them to name things, compare them, understand their interrelations, and begin to communicate their own unique, subjective experiences to others.[167]

To summarize, the left hemisphere is *cognitive*, functioning with logic and reason, and communicating with words. The right hemisphere is *affective*, centering on our emotions and often expressing itself through the arts.

As pastors preach and teach, they strive to speak to both hemispheres of the brain. To borrow a popular expression, pastors aim to speak to both the head (left hemisphere) and the heart (right hemisphere). A pastor unpacks the meaning of a Bible verse or explains the original definition of a Greek or Hebrew word in the sermon to clarify what the Bible says. He also uses illustrations, figures of speech, and applications that make a powerful impact on his listeners. Good preaching and teaching engages both hemispheres of our brain.

The same is true in public worship. Lutheran worship at its best speaks to our cognitive and affective sides—to head and heart. The words of worship proclaim biblical truths and teachings about sin, forgiveness, the triune God, the work of Christ, and the power of the means of grace. The symbolism of worship in music, ceremony, and art impresses those same truths to us in a way that touches our emotions. As words and symbols are used side-by-side in public worship, we avoid the extremes of an overly intellectual church service on one hand and an exclusively emotional spiritual experience on the other. The *words* of worship speak primarily to our cognitive side. *Symbolism* speaks especially to our affective side.

Another useful distinction that will help us understand symbolic communication is the difference between the concepts of a *sign*, a *signal*, and a *symbol*.

- A *sign* simply provides information and does not require a response. For example, as you drive along the freeway, you may see blue signs with the drawing of a gasoline pump or eating utensils. Those signs tell you that a gas station or restaurant are available at an upcoming exit. You can use that information if you need to fill up your tank or if you're hungry. But if you just ate lunch and filled up your car with gas, you can safely ignore the sign and the information it provides.

- A *signal* requires you to give a single response. As you drive along city streets, you encounter a stop sign. Though it is called a sign, it is really a signal. You must stop at the intersection (unless you want to pay a fine!). Once you have stopped and checked for other traffic, you may continue forward. The signal you encountered, the stop sign, requires nothing else from you.

- A *symbol* invites us to think and ponder about something in a meaningful way. When we see the American flag at the head of an Independence Day parade, what thoughts come to mind? Few people would see the stars and stripes and limit their thoughts to the nation's 50 states and 13 original colonies. The flag leads us to ponder our nation's history and the freedoms we enjoy. For a veteran, it reminds him of his military service and the sacrifices he and others were willing to make to protect his country's freedoms. For the wife of a deployed serviceman, it reminds her of her husband as she and her children pray for his safety each day and his safe return. A new immigrant may think of the freedoms and opportunities that are now available after emigrating to the United States.

These distinctions are helpful so that we do not let the symbolism in church turn into mere signs or signals. When we see the cross, we ought not treat it as a sign that can be ignored if we so choose. When we stand for the Gospel, we ought not treat it only as a signal, standing because the pastor directed us to stand without recognizing what this practice symbolizes. Symbols are intended to engage us, especially our right brain, in the meaning and celebration of Christian worship.

As a positive example of the way symbolism communicates, consider the paschal candle, the large ornamented candle that is traditionally stationed near the baptismal font. The paschal candle is lit during the Easter season as a symbol of the risen Jesus among his followers. Scripture uses light as a symbol of life (John 1:4), and so the candle is an ideal symbol of the risen and living Jesus among his people. Some paschal candles have other symbols on them, such as the Greek letters alpha and omega (Revelation 1:8) and five nails that represent Jesus' five wounds: the crown of thorns on his head, the nails in each hand, the nail driven through his feet, and the spear wound in his side after he died. To note the truth that our baptism connects us to Jesus' death and resurrection (Romans 6:3-11), this symbol of the risen Jesus is lit not only for the Easter season but also for baptisms and funerals, expressing our baptismal hope and confidence that Jesus' resurrection has conquered death for us.

While the previous paragraph may provide new and useful information to some readers, we would miss the value of the paschal candle if our understanding of it stopped with this information. What does that candle communicate? To the parents of a newly baptized infant, the paschal candle may remind them of the miracle of faith and new life that the Holy Spirit has worked in their child. To the widow who mourns the loss of her husband, the paschal candle points her to the sure hope of a blessed reunion in heaven even in the midst of her sadness. To the young man struggling with addiction and guilt, the paschal candle is a symbol of Jesus' power over sin and ability to dispel its darkness from his heart.

Which one of these interpretations of the symbol is correct? The answer is "Yes!"—in other words, there is not a single meaning that the paschal candle should invoke. When a proper understanding of the truths of Scripture have been proclaimed regularly from the pulpit, then the symbolic connections that individual believers make in worship will reflect a proper understanding of God's Word and will help them to apply Scripture's truths in a personal and meaningful way. Faithful preaching and teaching *must* be present for symbolism to communicate properly. When that is the case, symbolism becomes much more meaningful to worshipers.

Biblical examples

The Holy Spirit used symbolism throughout the Old Testament to proclaim God's message of sin and grace. Rather than a *direct* description of the coming Savior's sacrificial death on the cross, the very first gospel promise in the Bible uses *symbolic* language. God described Satan's ultimate destruction and the suffering Jesus would endure with this prophecy: "I will put enmity between you and the woman, and between your offspring and hers; he will *crush your head*, and you will *strike his heel*" (Genesis 3:15). God directed his prophet Ezekiel to symbolize the siege of Jerusalem and the exile of the Jews with unusual object lessons that Ezekiel literally acted out before the people (Ezekiel 4,5,12). The worship customs and temple rituals that God prescribed for the Israelites were also filled with ceremonies that expressed various truths about the coming Savior in symbolic ways.

Briefly consider just one example of a symbolic ceremony from the Old Testament: the sacrifices and rituals God prescribed for the annual Day of Atonement (Leviti-

cus 16). After the high priest carried out the regular morning sacrifice, he ceremonially washed himself, dressed in
special linen garments, and offered the divinely appointed
sacrifices. He first offered a bull as a sin offering for himself
and his family. Two goats were then presented to the high
priest; one was chosen by lot to be a sin offering to atone
for the sins of the people, while the other was designated
to be the scapegoat. The blood of the sacrificed bull and
goat were ceremonially sprinkled inside the Most Holy
Place, the innermost area of the temple in which only the
High Priest could enter and only once a year. Then the
high priest put his hands on the head of the scapegoat,
confessed the sins of the nation over the goat as if to trans-
fer the people's guilt to the scapegoat, and then the goat
was led away and released into the wilderness to die.

Think about how many spiritual truths God expressed
through this annual Old Testament ceremony. Mankind's
sinful condition prevented anyone from approaching a
holy God on his own merits. The blood of a sacrifice was
the only way by which someone else could approach God.
The sins of mankind needed to be transferred to another
and taken away by a substitute. Each of these biblical
truths was powerfully communicated through the symbolism in the ceremonies on the Day of Atonement.

With New Testament hindsight, we can more clearly
see the striking symbolic previews of Jesus' saving work in
these ceremonies. The book of Hebrews, specifically chapters 9 and 10, offers an extended commentary about the
Day of Atonement. This explanation helps modern readers
to more fully understand the striking symbolic messages
from the Day of Atonement.

A unique example of symbolic communication in the
New Testament occurs in 1 Corinthians 11:2-16. In this

section, the apostle Paul discusses the Corinthian practice of women wearing a veil or covering on their head in public worship. Because it was a commonly understood cultural custom among the Corinthians, Paul urged the women of the congregation to observe this custom because it was perceived as an acknowledgement of a women's calling within the roles that God designed for the genders.

At the end of the discussion, Paul concludes, "If anyone is inclined to be contentious, we have no such practice, nor do the churches of God" (1 Corinthians 11:16 ESV). Paul encouraged the Corinthians to follow their local custom but acknowledged that churches in other cities and regions didn't have such a practice. The symbolism behind veils and head coverings for women would not have made sense in other places because it was not their custom. Paul was not about to establish a universal ceremonial law for women. Instead he urged the Corinthians to follow a local cultural practice that symbolized their respect for a larger biblical principle.[168]

This example is especially useful because it shows us that symbolic communication is not always a universal language. The custom in Corinth would not have made sense in other cities. In the same way, symbolic customs in the United States may not necessarily translate well in Africa or India or vice versa. The customs in Wisconsin might not be perceived the same way in Maine, Texas, or Hawaii. While we respect, appreciate, and even use customs from other times and places in Christian history, we are not quite as concerned with specific symbolic practices as we are with the perception and meaning that those practices will have among a particular group of people.

Symbolism in worship today

Symbolism is also a mode of communication in Lutheran worship today. Earlier in this book, we noted examples of symbolism such as the Advent wreath, the paschal candle, and the worship customs of Holy Week. We now look at several other examples of symbolic communication in worship. These examples are not meant to be a comprehensive list of worship symbolism, nor are they prescriptions for what ought to be observed in every congregation. Some examples will be less common than others, but all of these examples will help us see concrete examples of symbolic communication.

Vestments

An example of symbolism in Lutheran worship that requires a more complete level of explanation is the custom of vestments, that is, the special garments worn by participating ministers. In early Christian history, ministers simply wore the same type of clothing that was commonly worn by the larger population. Clergy were to use a separate set of clean, dignified-looking clothing for worship, but they were still the same garments worn by the rest of society. As clothing styles changed, Christians retained the garments from the past and designated them as vestments for ministers to wear in worship.[169]

The most basic Christian vestment is the *alb*. The term comes from the Latin word for "white." Although it morphed through variations in its forms over time, the alb was essentially a simple white tunic. A document from the late sixth century confirms that the alb had become a clergy vestment by that time, distinct from the regular clothing of the day. Today the alb has become the most common vestment used in liturgical worship. It is worn by both ministers and laypeople assisting with the service.[170] From a devotional perspective, one might view the alb as a symbol of the perfect, white robe of Jesus' righteousness that covers up our sin (Revelation 7:9).

A vestment associated with the pastor is the *stole*. The stole may have begun as something of a handkerchief, a rectangle-shaped linen worn around the neck, over the shoulder, or over one's forearm. Servants would use it to clean vessels; in worship, it may have been used to clean the vessels used for Communion. By the fourth century, this large cloth was folded lengthways to be a long, thin band, which became a symbol of a deacon's office rather than a servant's cloth. By the seventh century, different ways of wearing the stole symbolized different offices in the church—deacon, priest, bishop.[171] Other scholars suggest that the stole originated in one or two colored stripes that first-century Roman senators and officials wore on their albs as a sign of their office.[172] In modern practice, the stole matches the liturgical color of the season and is worn by ordained pastors over the shoulders with two panels extending to the knees or lower. Knowing its possible origins as a servant's cloth or a symbol of official office, we may think of it as a symbol of the pastor's divinely called role as a servant of Christ.

A third common vestment is the *chasuble*. This poncho-shaped garment, with roots as far back as the sixth century B.C., was a sleeveless outer cloak. Saint Paul likely had that type of garment in mind when he asked Timothy to bring him his cloak in 2 Timothy 4:13. In the fourth century, Sylvester, bishop of Rome, recommended its use for clergy both as an everyday garment and while conducting church ceremonies, even during the celebration of Holy Communion. By the early fifth century, the chasuble was recognized as a vestment.[173] In modern use, the chasuble also reflects the liturgical color of the day or season. Use of the chasuble today is not as common for Lutherans as the alb and stole are. In congregations where chasubles are customary, the pastor who presides at the Lord's Supper wears the chasuble over his alb and stole.

Other vestments have come into use over Christian history, but the alb and stole have become standard vestments among many Lutherans today. A generation ago, it was common in the WELS for pastors to wear a black academic robe as they presided at worship. These robes were once the professional garb in the medieval academic world. In American courtrooms today, the judge who presides over a trial also wears the black academic robe from medieval academia. In both cases, the clothing of a past era becomes a visual statement of an important office or role that an individual is fulfilling.

A merging of these two customs can be seen in another set of vestments used in some congregations: a looser white robe over a close-fitting black robe. The black robe is called a *cassock*, and it comes from the same family of origin as the black academic robe. The white robe worn over it is called a *surplice*; the surplice is a stylized version of an alb, designed to fit over another clerical robe.

In addition to serving as a symbol of a minister's office, worshipers may also view these vestments as a symbol of our connection to Christian believers from past eras who share our confession of faith in Christ.

Liturgical Colors

Colors have symbolic significance in many aspects of our lives. Schools and sports teams show their pride by wearing their school and team colors. People may wear colored ribbons on their clothing to symbolize their concern for a special cause that is represented by a color: Pink for breast cancer, yellow for military support, and silver for mental illnesses are just a few of many possible examples. Even the colors of our clothes can make a statement. We may wear black at a funeral to express sorrow, or red and green at a Christmas party because American society identifies those colors with Christmas. A combination of red, white, and blue, matching the American flag, are common on days of national celebration in the United States.

In our discussion of the Church Year, we noted that there are liturgical colors associated with the days, seasons, and festivals of the year. For the first eight centuries of Christian history, there was not a formal system of liturgical colors. By the turn of the 13th century, the Western Church developed a custom of colors at the direction of Pope Innocent III. We can see similar customs to our modern practice in the practice at that time: White was used for high festivals, including Christmas and Easter. Red was for Pentecost and days to remember the apostles and martyrs. Black was used for the seasons of Advent and Lent, for funerals, and for other sorrowful occasions. Green was assigned to regular weekdays when there was not a major festival being observed. The color violet was used for just a few rare occasions at that time.[174]

The liturgical colors have not remained static throughout history, but a fairly common practice has developed among Lutherans today. The following chart describes the symbolic understanding behind the colors that were discussed earlier in connection with the Church Year:

White   Color of the Godhead and eternity; color of the robe of the glorified Christ and of the angels and saints in heaven; color of perfection, joy, and purity.

Black   The absence of color; symbolic of death.

Red   Color of fire, fervor, blood, martyrdom; the victorious truth of Christian teaching based on the blood of Christ.

Green   The color of life and nourishment; the basic color of nature.

Purple The color of royal mourning and repentance.

Blue   The color of the sky and hope.

Gold   The color of royalty, riches, and victory.[175]

Chancel furnishings

The *chancel* refers to the front area of the church from which the pastor preaches and presides. Lutheran congregations typically have several significant and symbolic pieces of furniture in the chancel.

The *altar* is a symbol of Jesus. Many worship scholars view the altar as the *main* symbol of Jesus in the chancel. Just as many Old Testament sacrifices were carried out on the altar in the temple, so Jesus was the ultimate sacrifice for our sins, to which all Old Testament sacrifices pointed. The body and blood that he once sacrificed for us on the cross now come to us miraculously in the Lord's Supper, which takes place at the altar.

The *pulpit* is the podium from which God's Word is preached. Many older congregations also have a separate *lectern* from which the Scripture readings are spoken. A recent trend is to have a single location for reading and preaching the Word of God, sometimes called an *ambo*. Each of these are symbols of the importance of God's Word.

The *baptismal font* is the place where new believers are brought into the family of God through Holy Baptism.

A recent trend among Lutherans is to have fonts of sub-stantial size that can hold a large amount of water. Some congregations always keep water in the font, not just when there is a baptism. The sight of a substantial amount of water in the font and the *weightiness* of the font visually symbolize the weighty importance of Baptism.

Notice how our proper focus on the means of grace—the gospel in Word and sacrament—can be symbolized by the chancel furnishings.

Processions

Many cities in the United States begin their Indepen-dence Day celebration by watching a parade through the streets. Professional sports games begin with a parade of the starting lineup running onto the field or arena. Birthday parties may include someone carrying the birthday cake with its lit candles into the room where family and friends are singing "Happy Birthday." Each of these is, in its own way, a symbolic procession to celebrate a special event or occasion.

Some congregations have the custom of processional hymns to begin the service. The service participants walk down the center aisle as the opening hymn is sung, while the first person in the procession carries a processional cross. This practice helps us to remember that were it not for Jesus' sacrifice for our sins, we could not approach God in worship and prayer. The cross is often placed next to the pulpit or ambo to symbolize the central message of Chris-tian preaching as written by Paul, "We preach Christ cruci-fied" (1 Corinthians 1:23).

If the service ends with a recessional hymn, the sight of the participants exiting the sanctuary behind the cross may remind us of Jesus' call to take up our cross and follow him

(Mark 8:34) and our responsibility to "Lift High the Cross" (*Christian Worship: Hymnal* 900) and proclaim the good news of salvation in our daily lives.

Minister's direction

In chapter 5, we discussed the distinction between *sacramental* and *sacrificial* parts of the service. In short, the parts of the service in which God speaks to us are called *sacramental*; segments of the service in which we respond to God are called *sacrificial*.

The presiding minister's posture in front of the altar symbolizes this distinction. This distinction is especially evident when a church has a wall altar, located alongside the chancel's front wall. In that situation, everything in the service that is conducted at the altar must be done in front of the altar. When the minister faces the altar, his posture visually depicts that he is speaking to God; when he faces the congregation, his posture symbolizes his role as God's spokesman to the congregation. Even in churches with a freestanding altar, with space between the wall and altar, the pastor may conduct a portion of the service in front of the altar, such as the confession and absolution, before taking his place behind the altar for the rest of the service.

Many aspects of worship involve a conversation between God and his people. Even something as simple as the direction that the pastor faces can symbolize the conversation that is taking place in public worship.

Sign of the cross

The pastor makes the sign of the cross with his hand several times throughout the service. This brief gesture is often noted in the hymnal with a cross (†) inserted into the minister's spoken words.

After the opening hymn, the pastor makes the sign of the cross at the invocation. These are the same words first spoken at our baptism (Matthew 28:19). The sign of the cross connected with these baptismal words symbolizes the truth that our baptism connects us to Jesus' death (Romans 6:3,4). Following Luther's suggestion in the Small Catechism, some worshipers make the sign of the cross over their head and heart at that moment to symbolize their personal baptismal connection to Jesus' death.

The cross is signed again during the absolution, reminding us that Jesus' death is the sacrifice that has forgiven our sins (1 John 2:2).

The pastor may make the sign of the cross as he speaks the Words of Institution, consecrating the bread and wine for the Lord's Supper. There the cross communicates the real presence: The very body and blood Jesus' sacrificed for us will be miraculously given to us in the sacrament.

The pastor makes the sign of the cross one final time at the closing blessing, visually communicating that the blessings of God's providence, grace, and peace can only be enjoyed because Jesus died on the cross on our behalf.

Final thoughts on symbolism

The preceding examples of symbolism are hardly exhaustive. Much more could be said about the examples given, and many more examples could be listed. The purpose of these examples has not been to wire worshipers' minds so that they recollect the background of certain symbols whenever they encounter them. That would miss the point! That would turn devotional symbols into pragmatic signs and signals. Rather these examples are meant to show how various symbols in worship can encourage one's own devotional thoughts and applications.

In the discussion about symbolism in worship, we will do well to remember Jesus' warning, lest we turn useful devotional customs into legalistic man-made rules (Matthew 15:7-9). We also do well to view symbolism and ceremonies with the same view that our Lutheran forefathers confessed: "Ceremonies should be observed both so that people may learn the Scriptures and so that, admonished by the Word, they might experience faith and fear and finally even pray. For these are the purposes of the ceremonies."[176]

May the symbolic actions and objects of worship continually teach us to treasure the soul-saving gospel truths of Christ, crucified and risen for us and our salvation!

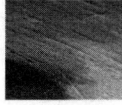

12

Music in Worship

Music surrounds us. Our favorite television sitcoms begin each episode with a theme song, use music to transition from one scene to another, and replay the theme song as the screen displays the closing credits. Some radio stations play music all day; other stations, devoted to news and talk radio, use "bumper music" to transition in and out of commercials. Grocery stores, department stores, and restaurants play music as we shop and dine. We play music in the car as we drive from place to place. Sports stadiums play music as players are introduced at the start of a game, after plays in which the home team scores, and during intermissions. Countless other examples could be listed, but let it suffice to say that music is a major part of our lives.

Music is also a significant part of Lutheran worship. Except for unique circumstances, it seems highly unlikely that a church service would occur without some use of music.

There are countless practical issues that ministers and musicians encounter in the intersection of worship and music. In this chapter, we will consider some of the most important musical issues that congregations consider. Our overview will be divided into four categories: the *texts* (particularly hymn texts) we sing as an assembly, the *music* by which we sing those texts, the *instruments* that accompany our singing, and the role of *choirs* to assist our participation.

Text issues

The most important aspect about music in worship is not the music itself, but the *words* that we sing. The first chapter of this book spoke about the importance of proclaiming the gospel in public worship. Two Bible verses cited in that chapter deserve our attention again, especially as we consider the intersection of text and music.

The apostle Paul wrote in Colossians 3:16, "Let the message of Christ dwell among you richly as you teach and admonish one another with all wisdom through psalms, hymns, and songs from the Spirit." Paul encouraged the Colossians to instruct each other by means of the songs they sung together in corporate worship. The psalms from the Old Testament and the New Testament compositions they sung had the ability to teach the truths of God's Word to one another. The audience for these song texts extends beyond God. Paul stated in a parallel Bible verse, Ephesians 5:18,19: "Be filled with the Spirit, speaking to one another with psalms, hymns, and songs from the Spirit." Just as the Holy Spirit works in our hearts through the written and preached Word and the sacraments, so the Spirit also fills our hearts with the gospel message that we sing *to one another*. This is why the *texts* we sing matter so much: When we sing Christ-proclaiming texts to one another, the gospel is present to strengthen our faith.

Martin Luther recognized the great importance of musical texts that proclaimed the Word of God. In a preface to a symphony by Georg Rhau (1488–1548), a significant Lutheran musician at the time of the Reformation, Luther wrote,

> It was not without reason that the fathers and prophets wanted nothing else to be associated as closely with the Word of God as music. Therefore, we have so many hymns and Psalms where message and music join to move the listener's soul, while in other living beings and [sounding] bodies music remains a language without words. After all, the gift of language combined with the gift of song was only given to man to let him know that he should praise God with both word and music, namely, by proclaiming [the Word of God] through music and by providing sweet melodies with words.[177]

Luther thought so highly of the "Te Deum," the main song of praise from the Matins service, that he counted it alongside the Nicene and Athanasian Creeds as creeds of Christendom.[178] In a letter to George Spalatin (1484–1545) written in 1523, Luther expressed the great need at the time for hymns to be in the German language so that it would put the Word of God on the lips of the people.

> [Our] plan is to follow the example of the prophets and the ancient fathers of the church, and to compose psalms for the people [in the] vernacular, that is, spiritual songs, so that the Word of God may be among the people also in the form of music. Therefore we are searching everywhere for

poets. Since you are endowed with a wealth [of knowledge]
and elegance [in handling] the German language, and
since you have polished [your German] through much use,
I ask you to work with us on this project.[179]

If the songs we sing are able to bring the gospel to God's
people, does this mean the gospel must be present in all
of our songs? Does each song we sing need to poetically
expound on the birth, life, death and resurrection of Jesus?
Does every song need to present the whole council of God?

We can articulate a wise answer to those questions
by looking at the Spirit-inspired hymnal of the Old
Testament—the Psalms. The book of Psalms is very comprehensive in its content. Because it proclaims Christ
clearly and reflects all of Scripture's content, it is no
wonder that Luther called the Psalms "a little Bible."[180]
Within the Psalms, we encounter songs that confess sin
and ask for God's pardon, depict the future saving work of
Christ, express faith and trust in God, confess confidence
in the last moments of life, bring prayers and petitions
before God, and give thanks to God for his blessings.

The book of Psalms is comprehensive in its content,
but individual psalms are more specific. Not every psalm
is a prophecy of Christ, a confession of sins, a prayer for
God's help, or a statement of thanksgiving. But collectively, the book of Psalms presents all these thoughts and
more, and it concludes with a very simple statement of
praise in Psalm 150.

If we were to suggest that every hymn had to present
the whole council of God, then we would have a problem
with God's inspired Old Testament hymnal. If we were
to suggest that every hymn must be rich in doctrinal content, then we would have to delete Psalm 150 from the
Bible. On the other hand, if we were to suggest that the

songs and hymns we sing need not richly reflect the truths taught in God's Word, we would fail to take to heart the example that the Holy Spirit placed in the Old Testament's hymnal. We would also fail to take to heart Saint Paul's inspired encouragement to teach the faith to one another through the songs that we sing in worship.

The steady diet of hymns and songs we use in worship could be compared to a meal. There is no harm in an appealing appetizer or delicious dessert, but our main course and side dishes need to nourish our bodies with the vitamins and nutrients needed for good health. A simple hymn of praise that is not necessarily rich in teaching content may be fine to include in a service, but if the majority of our hymns did not teach the faith in some way, we would be missing an opportunity to nourish our souls with the truths of Scripture and the gospel of our Savior. We strive for hymns that teach the faith and proclaim the good news of Jesus, not as a mandate but as a beautiful way to bring the faith-strengthening gospel to those gathered in worship.

We should also note that a hymn's simplicity or complexity doesn't necessarily reflect the level of its gospel content. The children's hymn, "Jesus Loves Me, This I Know," is a very simple text, but this stanza from the song is clear in its gospel content:

> Jesus loves me—he who died
> Heaven's gate to open wide;
> He has washed away my sin,
> Let this little child come in.[181]

Just as music texts can be used for noble purposes, music texts can also be used for sinful purposes. In fact, the very first poem in the Bible was a text about sin. Lamech boasted about murder in Genesis 4:23,24:

"Adah and Zillah, listen to me;
  wives of Lamech, hear my words.
I have killed a man for wounding me,
  a young man for injuring me.
If Cain is avenged seven times,
  then Lamech seventy-seven times."

This negative example, and the Bible's frequent reminders to watch out for false prophets and false teaching, remind us that we need to be wise and discerning about the songs we use in public worship. While it is highly unlikely that a song promoting sin, like Lamech's song, would be sung within the context of Christian worship, it is often more difficult to detect the sometimes subtle strains of false doctrine found in some popular Christian songs today. Whenever we consider song texts for public worship, we do well to ask some thoughtful diagnostic questions about those texts. Our concern is the faithful proclamation of God's Word for the benefit of our congregations. Our concern is also the clear proclamation of God's truths to guests who may not yet know God's truth. Some useful questions include these:

1. Does this text confess the triune God?

2. Does this text address the issue of sin and our sinful condition?

3. Does this text proclaim the forgiveness of sins in Christ Jesus?

4. Does this text confess God's work through the means of grace?

5. Does this text properly proclaim and distinguish between law and gospel?

6. Does this text contain phrases that might be understood as false teaching?

7. Does this text view God primarily as our Savior and Redeemer?

8. Does this text recognize that my Christian life is empowered by the gospel?

9. Does this text demonstrate the truth that praise is proclamation?

10. Does this text communicate in a way that the whole congregation can sing its message as a body, or is its message limited to an individual perspective?[182]

Although there are song texts that may cause us concerns, we can be thankful for the many poets and musicians who have prepared other songs, past and present, that are fit for Lutheran worship. The Lutheran church has been blessed with many fine hymn writers of its own and has been able to incorporate some of the best hymns of other post-Reformation poets.

In addition to Luther himself, Paul Gerhardt (1607–1676) deserves special mention. Many consider Gerhardt to be the most gifted hymn writer in Lutheran history. The English Congregational minister Isaac Watts (1647–1748) wrote many psalm paraphrases and hymns. Another well-known English hymnwriter was Methodist minister Charles Wesley (1707–1788), who may have written some 6,500 hymns, many with a sincere emotional appeal and evangelistic character. In more recent years, American Lutheran pastors and poets of the 20th century have added to the Lutheran church's repertoire of excellent hymns. Among the names worth noting are Jaroslav Vajda (1919–2008) and brothers Martin (1907–1976) and Werner Franzmann (1905–1996). Many hymns from these writers are included in *Christian Worship: Hymnal*.

Music issues

A pastor was leading a Bible class in his congregation about the subject of worship. At the start of one class, he asked the participants to spend 60 seconds writing down as many different musical styles that are played on the radio as they could recall. When the class shared their answers, the collective list from all the participants numbered nearly two dozen styles. The pastor then pointed out the irony that, in discussions about church music, people often talk about only *two* styles: traditional or contemporary.

It is no surprise that through 2,000 years of church history, the church has found a wide range of musical styles for its hymns and canticles. *Christian Worship: Hymnal* contains hymns representing a diverse range of genres, including Gregorian chant, German Lutheran chorales, hymns from England and Scandinavia, African-American spirituals, gospel hymns, spiritual folk songs, and modern Christian songs. A broad spectrum of hymnody with roots in different locations and eras brings to light the truth that the holy Christian church and the faith its members confess span time and space.

So what stylistic characteristics make a hymn suitable for use by an assembly in public worship? To answer this question, it is helpful to note three broad cultural categories in which music, and art in general, may be categorized: high/classical, folk, and pop/mass. The descriptions that follow define very broad categories of music and art, rather than the narrower, time-specific styles that use the same names.[183]

- Music from a *high/classical culture* attempts to depict transcendent matters (things that are beyond our experience and full comprehension), often communicating through the symbolism of music when words seem insufficient. It is music that can be accepted across generations and tends to focus on the common human experience rather than the individual, but it is not necessarily accessible to the average person. This type of music is ideal for a choir or orchestra to perform in a sacred concert rather than being sung by a congregation in worship, but these works live on in performances for many generations after they were first written.

- Music from *folk* culture also tends to focus on the transcendent, be multi-generational, and focus on communal experiences, but it is more accessible to the average person than high/classical music. The purpose of folk music within a culture is to pass on the culture's values and traditions from one generation to the next. Because of its intent and nature, it is more accessible. By this definition, the vast majority of Christian hymns, even across many times and places, would fall into this category. Hymns are written for assembly participation. The best hymns stand the test of time and continue to be used long after they were first written.

- Finally, music that identifies with *pop/mass culture* focuses more on the imminent, the here and now, rather than the transcendent. This music is also very accessible, but it tends to be popular only with a single generation and speaks from an individual rather than communal perspective. Pop music, as a broad category, is designed to be entertaining to the listener, who tends to be a consumer of the music more than a participant with the music.

Popular music finds a home today on the radio and in other electronic media.

The description of these broad categories already suggests the basic style of music that is most appropriate for public worship. The label *folk music* may be a bit confusing, because readers may think of a specific style, like American folk music, instead of the broader category of folk music at large. When we think of hymns from the church's past and present that enable the assembly's participation, show respect for the church's experience over time, and bring the transcendent gospel message to generations of worshipers, we are describing music that fits into the broad category of *folk music*.

Some readers may enjoy music that is a product of the high/classical culture. Many great musical works from the past that express the Christian faith fall into this category. As an example, the cantatas by Johann Sebastian Bach (1685–1750), *The Messiah* by George Frideric Handel (1685–1759), and Felix Mendelssohn's (1809–1847) *Hymn of Praise* (Symphony No. 2) are great works of musical art that require much rehearsal and preparation from the performers. These works deserve to be performed by choirs and orchestras, but in the context of worship, they would be beyond the abilities and even appreciation of many in the assembly. These musical works are better suited for a sacred concert performed by a well-rehearsed choir and orchestra.

Other readers may also enjoy music produced in the context of the pop/mass culture. The specific genre of Christian contemporary music often reflects this category. Not everything that was said previously about music from the pop/mass culture necessarily applies to every Christian contemporary song today, and a clear line between folk music and popular music is sometimes hard to define. When modern Christian songs are written with accessible melodies for an assembly, combined with a faithful and clear Christian text, they may find their way into Christian worship today. The hymns of composer Keith Getty, author of "In Christ Alone" (*Christian Worship: Hymnal* 510) and "Speak, O Lord" (633), are examples of contemporary songs that work well with an assembly because of their folk-like qualities and substantial Christian message.

Other contemporary songs might not work as well in a worshiping assembly, especially if the song was designed more for performance or media consumption. The range of the notes and the syncopated rhythms of some Christian contemporary songs make them better suited for the radio than for assembly singing.

A basic understanding of these broad categories of music and culture will prove useful as pastors, musicians, and church leaders make decisions about music within worship. There are also some additional thoughts about musical styles that are worth our consideration.

Music often carries associations that listeners recognize. For example, the melodies of "Joy to the World" (*Christian Worship: Hymnal* 353) and "Amazing Grace" (576) have the same meter (pattern of syllables and lines of text). In theory, we can sing the words of "Amazing Grace" to the melody of "Joy to the World" and vice versa. It fits—and yet it doesn't. The melodies have become associated with their respective texts, and the mood of both melodies accurately reflects the mood of the texts with which they are associated. Readers who remember the 1960s television show *Gilligan's Island* will note that the melody for the show's theme song also fits the words of "Joy to the World" and "Amazing Grace," but the theme song's style does not match well with the message of either hymn!

A generation ago, veterans of World War II and others who vividly remember the war may have felt uncomfortable with the hymn "Glorious Things of You Are Spoken" (*Christian Worship: Hymnal* 857). The tune of that hymn is the same melody used for the German national anthem, composed by Joseph Haydn (1732–1809) long before the 20th century. While any association with Adolf Hitler and World War II has largely faded away from the tune, we can easily understand how the mental associations connected to that melody would have evoked strong negative reactions especially among those who served in the United States' armed forces during World War II.

These and other possible examples help us understand that music and melodies often carry their own association. The melody is often a musical symbol of the text with which it is associated. We may not be able to provide a scientific, left brain explanation of the way we perceive musical styles, but we are wise to recognize that different musical styles and melodies will communicate different messages. Worship planners serve their congregations well when they strive to discern what kinds of music will support the gospel message, and what kinds will get in the way of gospel proclamation.

Does this call for discernment mean that we should not try new hymns and melodies in worship? Of course not! Just as we appreciate great hymns from the church's past, so the church may expand its repertoire with the best hymns and songs from today. Everything that is old and familiar to us now was once new. "God's Word Is Our Great Heritage" (*Christian Worship: Hymnal* 640) and "For All the Saints" (880) were new to WELS members when *The Lutheran*

Hymnal was published in 1941.[184] The Christmas hymn "Where Shepherds Lately Knelt" (345) and the Lenten hymn "My Song Is Love Unknown" (397, also 399 with an alternate tune) came into the WELS musical repertoire when *Christian Worship: A Lutheran Hymnal* was published in 1993. WELS was introduced to a powerful, alternate melody for "Jerusalem the Golden" (889) and the lilting hymn of trust titled "Day by Day" (803) with the 2008 publication of *Christian Worship: Supplement*. Time will tell which hymns from *Christian Worship: Hymnal* will become the new favorites in our congregations. As the church moves forward in time, we retain the best of the old and add the best of the new that will preserve our confession of faith in song for the next generation.

Organ and other instruments

Worshipers benefit from musical instruments that accompany and support their singing. The instrument most commonly associated with Lutheran worship is the organ. The impressive versatility of the organ is likely why the Austrian composer Wolfgang Amadeus Mozart (1756–1791) called the organ "the king of instruments." The organ's keyboards (called manuals), combined with the pedalboard (played by the feet), enable an organist to play a wide range of sounds that vary in color, pitch, and volume. The result is an instrument that allows one person to function as a full orchestra.

The primary reason why the organ is so useful in worship is that it produces a *sustained* sound. When someone plays notes on a piano or strums chords on a guitar, the sound immediately begins to fade. But when the notes of an organ are played, the sound continues at the same volume until the keys are released. This sustaining sound helps worshipers to feel more supported, and therefore more confident, as they sing.

Besides supporting congregational singing, its wide range of sounds enable the organist to play *attendant music*—music before and after the service, during the offering, and during the distribution of Holy Communion. Attendant music is especially useful when it highlights the melodies of hymns in the service and musically symbolizes the focus of a particular service or the overall season of the Church Year.

The pipe organ appears to be the first instrument used in Christian worship, perhaps as early as the start of the second millennium.[185] Pipe organs continue to be the most ideal instruments for worship, even in an age of digital instruments and speakers. Pipe organs are almost always designed for the specific space in which they will be played. The natural sound produced by wind traveling through the pipes can fill a church sanctuary more evenly and completely than digitally produced or amplified sound.

The challenge for many congregations is that a new pipe organ can be an expensive investment. But this investment pays dividends over time: A pipe organ's initial cost at installation will likely be offset over several decades and generations because, unlike digital instruments, well-maintained pipe organs can last for centuries. Over the longer life of a congregation, the purchase of a pipe organ will prove to be wise stewardship.

If financial resources prevent a church from obtaining a new pipe organ, other options are still available to them. A significant marketplace for used pipe organs has developed in recent years. Churches that have closed or no longer use the pipe organ in their sanctuary may have an instrument suitable for another church's facility. When a used organ proves to be a good match for another building, this option may allow a church to obtain a fine pipe organ for pennies on the dollar. Digital organs can also be a fine choice. Advances made with digital church organs in recent years have been impressive. Digital instruments can now produce sounds that are very imitative of an actual pipe organ. A proper speaker system and installation process will ensure that a digital instrument serves a congregation well for many years.

The organ is an excellent instrument to accompany choirs and congregations alike, but by no means should it be the only instrument in public worship. Psalm 150 encourages believers to praise God with trumpets, harps, strings, pipes, and cymbals. Lutheran worship at its best strives to use the best of God's gifts by incorporating many instruments. The piano rightly deserves to take its place alongside the organ. Music in a pianistic style provides a beautiful contrast to the organ. Some song styles work well with guitars, which may also join the piano to create a fuller sound. Many church music publishers produce music for brass, woodwinds, strings, and percussion instruments. Handbell choirs may play their own anthem or add their sounds with the organ and other instruments for special pieces of music. When many instruments and singers perform a hymn or anthem together, we enjoy a unique fulfillment of Psalm 150:6: "Let everything that has breath praise the LORD."

The role of the choir

Instruments are not the only musical resources to assist God's people in worship. Just as valuable is the role that the choir performs.

In the past, many Lutheran church choirs performed *anthems* almost exclusively. Anthems are individual musical pieces sung by the choir. They may be performed *a cappella* (without accompaniment) or supported by the organ, piano, or other instruments. Ideally, choral anthems should reflect the Scripture readings and focus for a specific service or at least the theme of the church season in which the service takes place.

More recently, the WELS Commission on Worship has encouraged church choirs to take a more active role in the music of the Liturgy. This shift from an *anthem choir* to a *liturgical choir* may be a new concept in some congregations, but it reflects a more traditional role for the choir. A liturgical choir fulfills its role by participating especially in the musical aspects of the Proper. Chapter 5 defined the Proper as the parts of the service that change from week to week. Practically speaking, what does this look like?

Liturgical choirs may participate in the Psalm of the Day. The choir's involvement in the psalm adds musical variety and helps chanted psalm texts to move at a steady pace. Verses from psalm settings in *Christian Worship: Hymnal* may be sung responsively between the choir (or soloist) and congregation. *Christian Worship: Psalter*, another publication to support the services of the hymnal, provides musical settings for all 150 psalms, and often multiple settings for a single psalm. Choirs and congregations will find the Psalter to be a very useful resource for psalm variety. Many other published resources provide similar musical settings of psalms for choirs and congregations. More complex chant settings are available for choirs that have the ability and desire to sing more challenging music. Some composers have set the psalms to easily accessible melodic styles. Many anthems have been published with texts from the psalms; these anthems could easily be sung as the Psalm of the Day in a service. There are a wide range of musical possibilities for the choir's performance of the Psalm of the Day.

Liturgical choirs may sing the Gospel Acclamation, also called the Verse of the Day. As worshipers anticipate the Gospel, the choir sings a short Bible verse, typically framed with multiple alleluias. This musical fanfare announces the coming of our Savior-King who speaks to us in the Gospel. Many church music publishers have provided settings of the Gospel Acclamation for service use. Available musical settings for these acclamations range from simple unison arrangements with an easy keyboard accompaniment to majestic four part harmony with organ and brass. The resources that support *Christian Worship: Hymnal* provide many accessible musical settings to enable choirs and soloists to perform the Gospel Acclamation.

If a choir wants to sing an anthem in the service, one of the most fitting locations for the anthem is after the Gospel. Following all three Scripture readings, the anthem serves as a musical commentary on the readings and especially the Gospel.

Another item in which liturgical choirs can participate is the Hymn of the Day. As the main hymn of the service, the Hymn of the Day deserves special treatment when possible. As discussed in chapter 7, the Hymn of the Day can be accompanied by a *concertato*, a festive musical arrangement of a hymn that may involve the choir and other instruments.

The choir may also serve as a *teacher* of the congregation. Before the congregation sings a new hymn, the choir may sing one or two opening stanzas. The choir could also sing the hymn as an anthem in a service before the congregation sings the hymn for the first time. By alternating how each stanza is performed, a new hymn could easily be treated like a choir anthem: Some stanzas could be sung in harmony, others in unison, and still others with just the men, women, or a soloist. The organist can change the registration (group of sounds) used to accompany each stanza. Some stanzas can be accompanied while others are sung *a cappella*. In this way, the choir helps a congregation become comfortable with a new hymn even before they all sing it. Adult and children's choirs can both fulfill the role of music teacher in worship.

While some church choirs have a large number of singers and an ability to perform more difficult music, many church choirs have a small number of singers and may not be able to perform anthems on a regular basis. Choirs with limited resources may discover that it is relatively easy to function as a liturgical choir. The choir's involvement in the Psalm of the Day, Gospel Acclamation, and Hymn of the Day can be done in harmony or unison with complex or simple musical settings. Children's choirs can function as liturgical choirs just as easily as adult choirs. Soloists can even fulfill the role of a liturgical choir, and choirs with greater ability and resources may also discover that they can easily sing their parts of the Liturgy alongside the anthems that they prepare.

Some singers may feel that the role of a liturgical choir is not as fulfilling or challenging as the role of an anthem choir. But in this writer's experience, the people who especially appreciate a liturgical choir are the listeners—the worshiping assembly. By adding interest and variety to psalms and hymns, the choir can inspire and invigorate the congregation's singing. Just as many instruments in worship reflect the thoughts of Psalm 150, so the role of the liturgical choir can be a fitting application of Ephesians 5:18,19: "Be filled with the Spirit, *speaking to one another with psalms, hymns, and songs* from the Spirit."

13

Myths About Lutheran Worship

Do you believe everything you hear in the news? Do you trust everything you read on the internet? Do you accept every statement from a person who claims to have learned about something through the grapevine?

Your answer to each of these questions is likely "No! Not at all!" News stories can be slanted with a political bias. Social media posts only tell so much of the story and are often limited to the part of the story that supports the poster's perspective. Each person who hears a verbal story remembers a segment of the details, interprets what they mean, and then passes on his own summary to the next person, leaving portions of the original account untold. There is good reason to be hesitant to believe everything we hear and read. A dose of healthy skepticism can be beneficial.

Do you believe every quote attributed to Martin Luther? Do you trust every person's assessment about Lutheran worship? Do you accept every claim made about the practices of the Lutheran church?

It comes as no surprise that there are many myths about Lutheran worship. Some of those myths have already been addressed in the pages of this book. Myths about worship often contain an element of truth, but they also fail to tell the whole story. Sometimes an honest misunderstanding turns fiction into fact. Perception becomes reality, even if it's not true, and a myth about worship becomes widely accepted conventional wisdom.

In this chapter, we continue our look at practical worship matters by examining and correcting several common myths about Lutheran worship.

Myth #1: *Martin Luther used bar tunes and other secular music for his hymns.*

A frequently repeated myth about Luther is that he used secular tavern tunes for some of the hymns he composed for worship. A similar myth is that Luther once rhetorically asked, "Why should the devil have all the good music?" Although these are commonly held assumptions about Luther, both are false.

These two claims both seem reasonable at first glance. Luther advanced the principle that the congregation should be active participants in worship. His German service and hymns enabled worshipers to participate more meaningfully. If that's the case, why wouldn't he have encouraged familiar secular melodies that people enjoyed?

However, the claim that Luther used bar tunes is a misunderstanding of his practice. Luther used *bar form*, a style of German poetry and music common in the Middle

Ages. Bar form consisted of three lines or phrases; the first two were identical in meter and melody, and the third was different (represented by the letters A A B). Another version of bar form added a fourth line that was a variation of the first two lines (A A B A¹). Bar form was a musical and poetic structure; it had nothing to do with taverns![186] Many of Luther's hymns, including his famous "A Mighty Fortress Is Our God" (*Christian Worship: Hymnal* 863,864), followed this version of bar form:

A   A mighty fortress is our God, a trusty shield and weapon;
A   he helps us free from ev'ry need that has us now o'ertaken.
B   The old evil foe now means deadly woe; deep guile and great might are his dread arms in fight;
A¹ on earth is not his equal.

"Dear Christians, One and All, Rejoice" (557) also follows this pattern:

A   Dear Christians, one and all, rejoice, with exultation springing,
A   and, with united heart and voice and holy rapture singing,
B   proclaim the wonders God has done, how his right arm the vict'ry won.
A¹ How dearly it has cost him!

A related myth is the rhetorical question falsely attributed to Luther, "Why should the devil have all the good tunes?" If the quotation were true, it would have implied that Luther advocated for secular-styled music to be used in worship. The historical record suggests otherwise.

First, this quotation was not uttered by Luther but by English evangelist Rowland Hill (1744–1833).[187] Second, Luther's own hymns demonstrate that this was not his practice. Among all the hymns penned by Luther, only once did he use an existing secular folk tune, for the hymn "From Heaven Above to Earth I Come" (331). The reason he used a secular tune was likely because the song was originally written for a children's Christmas pageant, not public worship.[188] The words of the first stanza resembled the words of the original folk song. The first hymnal in which Luther's text appears was published in 1535 and includes the secular folk melody, but another hymnal published four years later included Luther's own tune.[189] Luther's melody is the one that appears today in *Christian Worship: Hymnal*. Luther was reported to have become uncomfortable as he heard the melody for his Christmas hymn used in secular contexts. This situation led to the new melody he penned for his hymn.[190]

Finally, Luther's own words indicate that he believed the church should have distinct music from secular culture. In the preface to the first Lutheran hymnal, published in 1524, Luther wrote,

> I . . . have with the help of others compiled several hymns, so that the holy gospel which now by the grace of God has risen anew may be noised and spread abroad. . . . And these songs were arranged in four parts to give the young—who should at any rate be trained in music and other fine arts—something to wean them away from love ballads and carnal songs and to teach them something of value in their place, thus combining the good with the pleasing, as is proper for youth.[191]

It is entirely correct that Luther wanted worship to be accessible to the laity, but it is a myth that he used secular bar tunes to accomplish that goal.

Myth #2: *Lutherans do not celebrate the Lord's Supper on a weekly basis.*

The Lutheran church broke away from the Roman Catholic Church in the 16th century because of the concerns that Luther and the Reformers had about false teachings and unscriptural practices in the Roman Catholic Church. Luther was not shy or subtle in his writings condemning what was wrong in the Catholic Church. But as Luther guided the Reformation, he did not simply reject a doctrine or practice because it was associated with the Roman Catholic Church. Rather he accepted or rejected doctrine and practice on the basis of Scripture.

Considering Reformation history, Lutherans today might assume that whenever our common practice is different than the practice of the Roman Catholic Church, it reflects a deliberate choice to observe a different practice. That is *often* the case but not *always* the case. The frequency that we celebrate Holy Communion is a good example of this type of issue, and it serves as the topic for our second Lutheran worship myth.

Within the WELS, it is currently most common for congregations to celebrate Holy Communion twice each month on designated Sundays (for example, the first and third Sundays of each month), in addition to a few selected holidays. Some of our churches have a less frequent observance of the sacrament, perhaps monthly. Another smaller portion of congregations celebrate the Lord's Supper more frequently, even weekly. Since the majority practice is less than weekly, people might incorrectly assume that our frequency of celebrating the sacrament is intentionally different than the Roman Catholic Church's frequency. Another variation of this myth is that a less frequent reception of the Lord's Supper will make the sacrament more meaningful.

Even after the Reformation had begun, the Lutheran church held the Lord's Supper in very high regard. In the Augsburg Confession of 1530, our Lutheran forefathers confessed the following regarding Holy Communion and the service in which it was celebrated called the Mass:

> Our churches are falsely accused of abolishing the Mass. The Mass is held among us and celebrated with the highest reverence. . . . Because the Mass is for the purpose of giving the Sacrament, we have Communion every holy day, and if anyone desires the Sacrament, we also offer it on other days, when it is given to all who ask for it.[192]

The corresponding section in the Apology of the Augsburg Confession also states, "We do not abolish the Mass, but religiously keep and defend it. Masses are celebrated among us every Lord's Day and on the other festivals. The Sacrament is offered to those who wish to use it."[193] (The "Lord's Day" is another name for Sunday.) These quotations from the Lutheran Confessions show us that the early Lutheran church continued the common practice throughout previous Christian history to offer the sacrament every Sunday and festival.

The practice of offering the sacrament less frequently did not begin as a reaction to Catholicism but out of a movement that began among Lutherans in the late 1600s called Pietism. Pietism was a response to legitimate concerns in the Lutheran church that developed during and after the Thirty Years War (1618–1648). Three decades of religious warring between Lutherans and Catholics had devastated Germany. The strong doctrine-focused preaching of the Reformation didn't seem relevant in light of the war and its aftermath. Pastors who were fortunate to have survived the war tried, with greatly reduced manpower, to rebuild Lutheran congregations. They found church discipline to be difficult at best under these circumstances. Legal mandates requiring church and Communion attendance only made a bad situation worse, as impenitent people worshiped and received the sacrament merely out of obligation.[194]

Pietists correctly identified these problems and genuinely wanted to fix them. However, their proposed solutions created new problems. Pietism incorrectly identified the clergy, doctrine, liturgy, and the sacraments as the causes of dead orthodoxy. In exchange, Pietism placed new emphases on personal prayer, sanctification, and one's own emotional response to the gospel. Although these things are proper and good as genuine fruits of faith, Pietism's emphases essentially *replaced* the objective truths of Scripture and the means of grace with the believer's own subjective experiences and feelings. This development led to several negative consequences among Lutherans, including a devaluation of the Lord's Supper.[195]

The founders of the WELS were Pietists. Not surprisingly, the early history of WELS was rooted in this movement. But not long after its founding, thanks to the positive influence of the Wisconsin Synod's second president, John Bading, and C. F. W. Walther, the founder and first president of the Lutheran Church—Missouri Synod, the Wisconsin Synod began to adopt a more confessional Lutheran position and abandon its pietistic thinking. Unfortunately, pietistic tendencies in worship remained for many decades to follow. Among those tendencies were infrequent celebrations of the Lord's Supper and a lack of appreciation for the Lutheran Liturgy.[196]

As we look over approximately 170 years of WELS history, we see a steady increase in the frequency that the Lord's Supper is offered, which is a product of a deeper appreciation for the sacrament fostered over time. Early in WELS history, it was common for churches to offer Holy Communion only four or six times a year; now it is offered twice monthly in most churches and even weekly in some. There is no biblical mandate regarding frequency, but the tremendous blessings of the sacrament encourage us to celebrate and receive it often.

Congregations are wise to study this issue for themselves. The great blessings of the Lord's Supper may lead a congregation to celebrate the sacrament on a weekly basis. At the same time, worship is often the first point of contact for many visitors in North American churches. Recognizing this reality, a congregation may offer several services throughout the year to which they invite their community. The service follows the first half of the Liturgy and presents a clear gospel message, but the sacrament is not offered since the many hoped-for guests would not be able to participate. With this perspective, a congregation may choose to offer the sacrament twice a month and then schedule special services advertised in the community on non-Communion Sundays. In this situation, it is not lack of appreciation for the sacrament that leads to the practice but a deliberate plan to reach out to the local community through specific services during the year.

Christian charity is in order when we note different practices within the churches of our synod on this matter. We need not assume that a church that celebrates the sacrament weekly is exhibiting Roman Catholic tendencies, nor that a church that does not celebrate the sacrament weekly is exhibiting pietistic tendencies. Situations vary from church to church and location to location. We cannot discuss every possible situation that would lead to one decision or another. What matters most is that we place a high value on the Lord's Supper and adopt a practice that reflects our understanding of the sacrament. The Lord's Supper does not become more special by a less frequent observance, nor should it become routine because of a more frequent observance. The sacrament's blessings are not dependent on our subjective feelings toward it but on the objective blessings received through it. For those blessings—forgiveness of sins, life, and salvation—we give thanks to God!

Myth #3: *Lutherans do not display crucifixes.*

The myth that Lutherans do not display a crucifix, a cross with the crucified body of Jesus on it, is also a common myth about Protestant churches in general. Anecdotally, one is more likely to encounter artistic crucifixes in Roman Catholic and Orthodox churches than in Lutheran and other Protestant churches. This is not a universal rule, since many American Lutheran churches of the past and present display a crucifix on the altar or somewhere else in the front of the church, but anecdotal experiences may contribute to this myth.

The cross and crucifix may at first seem like odds symbols for Christianity—or for anything! The cross was an instrument of death! Wearing a cross as jewelry or displaying a crucifix would be as unusual in the first century as wearing a pendant of an electric chair today or displaying a portrait of a criminal after he has been executed! Roman ruins, possibly from the second or third century, contain a graffiti-like picture of a mock-crucifix ridiculing the Christian faith. The drawing among the ruins depicts a crucified man with the head of a donkey and a person kneeling before the cross with these words: "Alexamenos worships his God."[197]

Despite their unusual nature as symbols, it is no surprise that the cross and crucifix became Christian symbols. The cross was used already from earliest times in Christian history. The earliest known example of a crucifix as Christian art dates to the second half of the sixth century.[198] The choice for these symbols is clear as we read these words from St. Paul:

> The message of the cross is foolishness to those who are perishing, but to us who are being saved it is the power of God.

> Jews demand signs and Greeks look for wisdom, but we preach Christ crucified: a stumbling block to Jews and foolishness to Gentiles, but to those whom God has called, both Jews and Greeks, Christ the power of God and the wisdom of God.

> I resolved to know nothing while I was with you except Jesus Christ and him crucified. (1 Corinthians 1:18,22-24; 2:2)

In the early years of the Lutheran Reformation, some of Luther's colleagues took a radical approach to the Reformation, even toward matters like crucifixes and other church art. Led primarily by Andreas Carlstadt (1486–1541), the radical reformers wanted to rid the church of anything that remotely resembled Roman Catholicism, even resorting to coercion and violence to bring about these changes.[199]

Luther was in hiding after the Diet of Worms (1521) to protect his own life when radical Reformation violence broke out in Wittenberg, the German city where Luther was a professor for most of his career. Luther came out from hiding in early 1522 to respond to the radicals' tactics.[200] Church historians Philip and David Schaff wrote:

> [Luther] saw the necessity of some changes, but regretted
> the violence with which they had been made before pub-
> lic opinion was prepared, and he feared a reaction which
> radicalism is always likely to produce. . . . But about cler-
> ical vestments, crucifixes, and external ceremonies, he
> was indifferent; nor did he object to the use of pictures,
> provided they were not made objects of worship. In such
> matters he asserted the right of Christian freedom, against
> coercion for or against them.[201]

The Lutheran church today has benefited from the pastoral approach that Luther took during the Reformation. Following the principle that we may use the best of God's gifts to his glory, especially the gift of art, Lutherans have not hesitated to produce artistic expressions of Good Friday in paintings and crucifixes. Many older, historic parishes display a crucifix in the front of the church that has been a part of their buildings since their founding. The chapel of Wisconsin Lutheran Seminary (Mequon, WI) features a processional crucifix in the chancel, while the chapel of Martin Luther College (New Ulm, MN) has a large painted cross above the altar which displays a *corpus*, a picture of the crucified Jesus, during fitting seasons of the church year.

Sometimes the myth about crucifixes has been stated this way: We don't display a crucifix because Jesus is no longer on the cross; he is risen. No confessional Lutheran would suggest that Jesus is not risen! But the fact that Christ is risen does not keep us from depicting his redeeming work on the cross through art. At Christmas time, we have no trouble realizing that Jesus is no longer in the manger even though the baby Jesus is in the manger in many nativity displays. The same is true of any display of Christ on the cross.

The crucifix can be a stunning visual testimony to the gospel. Lutheran congregations today are free to display such art at their discretion.

Myth #4: *Lutherans do not make the sign of the cross.*

If an observer compares a Roman Catholic Mass and a WELS Lutheran liturgical service, he would notice a similar outline or progression. He would also notice several differences in the specific details of the service. One of the most frequently noted observances this author has heard from others is that Roman Catholic worshipers make the sign of the cross over themselves at various times throughout the service, while that practice is quite rare in WELS congregations.

Is the sign of the cross just a Roman Catholic custom? Is it a religious superstition? Or has this been a part of Lutherans' experiences in the past? Do Lutherans today follow this practice or not? Is this something that only the pastor does in worship, or do all worshipers make the sign of the cross?

In the Small Catechism, Martin Luther suggests a pattern for a person's daily devotions in the morning and evening. At the beginning of these devotional times, Luther envisions that a Christian makes the sign of the cross over himself while speaking the words we normally call the invocation. Luther writes, "In the morning, when you rise, you shall bless yourself with the holy cross and say, 'In the name of God the Father, Son, and Holy Spirit. Amen.'" Luther makes the same suggestion for a person's evening devotion.[202]

In other contexts, Luther explains how the sign of the cross can be used as a devotional encouragement to oneself. For example, in comments on Psalm 118:5, Luther wrote,

If the devil puts it into your head that you lack the holiness, piety, and worthiness of David and for this reason cannot be sure that God will hear you, make the sign of the cross, and say to yourself: "Let those be pious and worthy who will! I know for a certainty that I am a creature of the same God who made David. And David, regardless of his holiness, has no better or greater God than I have."[203]

In a sermon based on a portion of the first chapter of John's Gospel, Luther said,

Whenever [troubling] thoughts come to pious hearts, fill them with grief, and cause them to be sorry and to lament deeply—as many psalms testify concerning their numerous shortcomings—then we have no other recourse than to cling to Christ and to take comfort in the evangelist's words: "But to all who received Him." Then we rely firmly on his statement, and in the name of Christ we call upon God the Father to make the sign of the cross over us and say: "They are sinners, neither as pious nor as pure as they should be. But because they believe in My only-begotten Son, who is full of grace and truth, I shall not be angry with them. None of their sins harm them if they continue in faith."[204]

The cross is a rich symbol of the sacrifice Jesus made for us to be our Savior. By making the sign of the cross, worshipers give themselves a tangible reminder of the source of their true comfort and identity as children of God. Notice in the second quotation above how Luther says that God makes the sign of the cross on us: Worshipers make the gesture over themselves, but the real comfort comes from the grace of God seen in the cross of Christ!

The sign of the cross is customarily used in baptismal services. Luther included the sign of the cross in the two baptism services he published during his career, and the sign of the cross continues to be used in Lutheran baptism rites today. Prior to administering the Sacrament of Holy Baptism, the minister makes a single cross over the baptized person from head to heart and shoulder to shoulder, saying, "Receive the sign of the cross on the head and heart to mark you as one redeemed by Christ the crucified." As explained in chapter 11, the sign of cross in connection with Baptism recalls how our baptism connects us to Jesus' death, as Paul explains in Romans 6:3,4. When we hear the words of the invocation, which were attached to the waters of our own baptism, and make the sign of the cross, we are recalling our baptismal connection to Jesus' death with this personal gesture.

There are several moments in the service when the pastor makes the sign of the cross over the congregation. These moments are typically when the actions of worship reflect the believers' reception of God's forgiveness and blessing through the means of grace. The sign of the cross is customarily made at the invocation, the absolution, the dismissal from Holy Communion, and the closing blessing. These moments in worship are usually marked with a cross (✝) within the minister's words at the time when he makes the sign. Worshipers who find the practice beneficial may personally make the sign of the cross on themselves.

Although Luther encouraged the practice, and while some Lutheran congregations have become accustomed to making the sign of the cross, it is not presently a widespread practice in the congregations of the WELS. The issue, of course, is not whether we make the sign or not but that we treasure the blessings of our baptismal connection to Christ. Those who find the practice to be a devotionally helpful reminder of their baptism should make the sign freely. Those who do not prefer the custom should also be free to omit it. Even though Luther encouraged the practice and prescribed it in his baptism services, he also recognized that the sign of the cross was an outward custom that could be included or omitted. Commenting on his own baptismal rite, Luther said, "External things are the least important, such as . . . signing with the cross . . . and whatever else has been added by man to embellish baptism. For most assuredly baptism can be performed without all these."[205]

Myth #5: *Lutherans do not applaud.*

The audience applauds at the entrance of the conductor onto the stage and after each musical work in the concert is completed. A gathered assembly of family and friends applauds after the class valedictorian and salutatorian finish their speeches. The massive crowd of fans claps for the retired athlete at his induction ceremony into the Hall of Fame.

The children's choir sings an anthem in worship. Does the assembly clap or not? The pastor deliberately declares a final "Amen," marking the conclusion of his sermon. Is it appropriate to applaud at this point? New members are received into the congregation with a brief welcoming rite. Should the congregation applaud when this membership ceremony is finished?

The situations in the previous two paragraphs are parallel to one another, yet the different contexts of secular events and sacred settings cause us to pause and ask ourselves some questions about applause in the context of worship.

Let it be said upfront that it is a fallacy to say that Lutherans never clap. Practices regarding applause in worship vary from church to church and region to region.

Questions about applause in worship cannot be answered with a simple yes or no. There is diversity of opinion about applause generally among Lutherans and specifically within WELS, but it would be false to say that Lutherans *never* applaud.

Any matter that is not decided by the Word of God deserves careful study and brotherly discussion. Will applause in a secular situation, such as at the end of a graduation speech, be perceived in the same way in a parallel sacred situation, such as a sermon? Could applause suggest that worship, especially music in worship, is merely a public performance and not an act that gives all glory to God? Could the lack of applause after the formal reception of new members into a congregation be perceived as socially cold and an unwelcoming statement—the very opposite of what we intend at that moment? Questions like these help us to understand that there are many facets to consider in the discussion.

Here is a related myth that approaches the issue from the opposite perspective: In 2 Samuel 6, King David publicly danced for joy when the ark of the covenant was carried into Jerusalem. According to this example, since David danced before the Lord (and even defended his actions to his wife, who found his behavior offensive), we should encourage dance in public worship.

Whenever we look at sections of the Bible that relate an event, we need to remember that *descriptive* accounts of Bible history are not necessarily *prescriptive* commands that Christians must imitate today. David's dancing, his clothing, or anything else in this account is not meant to be a command that New Testament Christians must duplicate.

There are verses in the psalms that speak about dancing and clapping. Psalm 47:1 says, "Clap your hands, all you nations; shout to God with cries of joy." Psalm 150:4 says, "Praise him with timbrel and dancing." If the outward actions of dancing and clapping were inherently sinful, the psalms would not include these encouragements. At the same time, we recognize that a true fulfillment of these encouragements to praise God is not found in prescribed mandates. We do not fail to praise God as Psalm 150:3 describes if there are no blaring trumpets, or if the harp and lyre are replaced with piano and organ. Rather we capture the true spirit of these psalms of praise when our whole being is engaged in joyful thanksgiving to the God of our salvation.

We may find a more satisfying solution to this apparent tension if we discuss the matters of clapping and dancing from a comparative cultural perspective. Experts in cultural studies make a distinction between *high-context cultures* and *low-context cultures*. Simply stated, a high-context culture is one in which symbolic actions and nonverbal communication are strong communication tools. We could say that in high-context cultures, actions really do speak louder than words. Conversely, in low-context cultures, verbal communication is more significant than symbolic communication. In these settings, words matter more than actions.[206]

In some Asian cultures, a person shows sincere respect for another by bowing toward the other person; the lower the bow, the greater the level of respect. In many African cultures, ritual dance is a significant part of celebrations in religious and secular life. Recent videos on social media have enabled WELS members to see the authentic ritual dance and music of our Lutheran brothers and sisters in Africa. These are examples of high-context cultures.

In contrast, the low-context culture of the United States does not place significance on the depth of one's bow toward another, and dancing tends to be a social activity rather than a ritual experience. America's low-context setting does not mean that we do not value any nonverbal communication; we still have our own forms of symbolic communication. We remove our hats and hold our hands over our hearts for the national anthem. Military personnel salute the president, their commander-in-chief, as a sign of respect. We stand at a funeral when the casket is carried out of the church to show our respect for the deceased and our solidarity with the deceased person's family and friends. But in comparison, American culture relies more on verbal communication and does not have as many widely accepted forms of symbolic communication.[207]

Different styles of communication among different cultures show us that two outwardly different actions may communicate the same message. The polite and awe-filled silence after performance of a choral work in one setting can be the cultural equivalent to appreciative applause in another setting. Likewise, the same basic action in two different cultures could communicate very different messages. Ritual dance in many cultures is a respectful and joyful form of celebration, but social dancing in the United States cannot be called a cultural equivalent and may even be perceived as disrespectful in more formal settings.

These insights help us address the myth that began this discussion. Our response to this myth is not as simple as saying "Lutherans don't clap" or "Yes, we do!" Rather we ask ourselves what message is sent by the choices we make. Will silence be perceived as respect or apathy? Will applause be perceived as thankfulness for the gospel message or approval of a public performance? What biases do I bring to the discussion, and am I willing to acknowledge them? What concerns do my fellow Christians have that I have not yet considered? What options have we not considered that may help address this healthy tension in a God-pleasing manner? We make no universal rules about applause in worship, but we ask these searching questions so that whatever we do in public worship ultimately gives honor, glory, and praise to God.

Myth #6: *The Liturgy means "page 15."*

Many Lutherans are familiar with the well-established musical setting of the Liturgy that begins on page 15 in both *The Lutheran Hymnal* (1941) and *Christian Worship: A Lutheran Hymnal* (1993). *The Lutheran Hymnal* calls its page 15 service "The Order of Holy Communion," while *Christian Worship: A Lutheran Hymnal* uses the title "Common Service." The musical settings of the main canticles from this rite now appear in The Service, Setting One in *Christian Worship: Hymnal*, pages 154-171. Because this musical setting has survived for so long (also appearing in the *Lutheran Service Book* (2006) of the Lutheran Church—Missouri Synod), some might assume that this version is the gold standard of Lutheran liturgical services. While the "page 15" service that is retained in current hymnals has served the church well for many decades, the story behind the service helps us understand that this is simply one possible musical setting of the Liturgy, and it was never meant to be elevated above others as the ideal standard.

As European Lutherans came to the United States, they continued to worship using settings of the Liturgy in the languages with which they were familiar. But the longer Lutherans were in the United States, adopting English as their primary language in everyday life, the greater the need became for orders of service in English. Many saw the benefit in a standardized English text of the Lutheran Liturgy based on the 16th century German orders of service from the Lutheran Reformation. The most significant and successful attempt for a common Lutheran order of service resulted in the Common Service, published in 1888 by three East Coast-based Lutheran church bodies.[208]

WELS worshipers will likely think of the Common Service as a musical arrangement of the Liturgy, but the original Common Service of 1888 was a set of worship *texts*. In addition to texts for the Liturgy, the Common Service included texts for *Matins, Vespers,* a historic responsive prayer called the Litany, and the Propers used in the services.[209]

Musical settings of the 1888 Common Service were soon prepared and published. *The Chorale Service Book,* published in 1901, provided chant-based music for the texts of this service.[210] This setting was included in the 1906 edition of *Evangelical Lutheran Hymn-Book* published by the English Synod of Missouri. (The English Synod became the English District of the Lutheran Church—Missouri Synod in 1911.)[211]

A 1912 edition of the *Evangelical Lutheran Hymn-Book* used a different musical arrangement based primarily on 16th century German sources, except for the Scottish chant used for the "Gloria in Excelsis."[212] This musical setting was also included in the Wisconsin Synod's 1917 *Book of Hymns,* even though evidence suggests that this specific service was not widely used by the synod's congregations at the time.[213] This same setting of the Common Service also appeared in *The Lutheran Hymnal* from 1941 and, with minor adaptations, in *Christian Worship: A Lutheran Hymnal* from 1993. Both books included this setting on page 15, which explains why many WELS members simply refer to this musical setting and service as "page 15." WELS hymnals have included this arrangement in our circles for over 100 years, making it a very familiar musical setting among several generations of WELS worshipers.

Although this specific Common Service musical setting has become comfortable within WELS and is sometimes viewed as the ideal setting of the Lutheran Liturgy, it reached this status by mistake! The subcommittee that prepared the services in *The Lutheran Hymnal* did not want music to be printed with the texts of the service. Instead they wanted three different musical settings of the songs to be printed elsewhere in the hymnal, so that congregations could follow a text-only version of the service and sing any of the three musical settings written for it. Their suggestion was not followed in the final printed version of *The Lutheran Hymnal*, and the musical setting with which we are familiar became the only setting for the service.[214]

The unfortunate result of this situation is that for several decades only one musical setting of the Lutheran liturgical rite was readily available to the Lutheran church bodies that produced this hymnal. The late Walter Buszin (1899–1973), professor of worship at Concordia Seminary in St. Louis (1947–1966),[215] noted that worshipers found that the single setting of the Liturgy for all seasons and occasions of the year had become monotonous and lifeless within a short time. He noted that what worshipers most appreciated was not variety in service *texts* but in *musical settings*.[216] Unfortunately, *The Lutheran Hymnal* did not provide the kind of musical variety that worshipers would have appreciated and its Subcommittee on Liturgics recommended.

The irony of *The Lutheran Hymnal's* single musical setting of the Liturgy is that such lack of musical variety represented the exact opposite of the situation in early

Lutheranism. Pastor Bryan Gerlach, director of the WELS Commission on Worship since 1995, writes,

> During the 17th century over 150 settings of the liturgy were published for use by German Lutheran choirs. In addition to new settings by Lutherans, other settings from the past and from other countries remained acceptable through the strength of tradition and because the texts were the common property of both Lutherans and Catholics. From published collections and inventories of music held by various churches, we gain an impression of vigorous and dynamic variety.[217]

Fortunately, current resources published by the WELS Commission on Worship encourage healthy musical variety for the Liturgy. The long-standing music from the "page 15" service takes its place alongside two other musical settings of the Liturgy in *Christian Worship: Hymnal*. Several more musical settings of the Liturgy are also available through the digital resources that accompany the hymnal. These settings permit the texts of the service to be sung in a variety of possible styles and with a variety of accompanying instruments.

The musical setting attached to the Common Service has served WELS congregations for many years. Yet this setting is simply one of many possible musical versions of the Liturgy. The music of this or any other setting does not define the Liturgy for us. Rather the Liturgy is the overall progression and common texts of worship discussed in chapters 5 through 8, which can be set to a variety of fitting musical styles. Lutherans are wise to identify several musical versions of the Liturgy that will encourage variety and vitality in their congregations.

Myth #7: *A Lutheran service is incomplete without a rite of confession and absolution.*

Law and gospel are the two most important teachings in Scripture. Chapter 2 discussed the importance of law and gospel in connection with worship. We could not truly appreciate our Savior's tremendous substitutionary sacrifice without the law's stern sentence of hell for all who fail to obey God perfectly. We would never enjoy peace with God were it not for Jesus' gracious saving work, from his conception and birth to his death and resurrection. The forgiveness of our sins that Jesus won for us would be meaningless if the law had not led us to repentance and the gospel was not present in the means of grace to apply Jesus' gifts to our hearts.

One of the clearest presentations of law and gospel within the Liturgy is the rite for confession and absolution that occurs near the beginning of the service. Our prayers of confession acknowledge our sinful condition and the many ways sin manifests itself in our lives, all deserving God's eternal condemnation. The beautiful words of absolution that follow leave no doubts behind for repentant souls: God's called servant brings us a message from the Lord himself that Jesus Christ has forgiven our sins! This regular part of the service is a tremendous comfort to hurting souls and a vivid example of law and gospel at work in worship.

Two forms for confession and absolution are included in each setting of The Service in *Christian Worship: Hymnal*, but not all the services include confession and absolution. The services of Morning Prayer and Evening Prayer, rites from the Daily Office, do not include a formal confession and absolution. The new Service of Word and Prayer (pages 266-269) also does not include confession and absolution. A pastor may prepare an order of worship for a special occasion; the service follows the basic flow of the

Liturgy but does not contain a specific rite for confession and absolution.

Many pastors have heard the concern that a church service feels incomplete without a formal rite for confession and absolution. While the custom is a valuable and worthy practice, can we say that a service is deficient without a formal prayer of confession and an absolution statement from the pastor? Are my sins not forgiven—or were they somehow forgiven less—if this is not included in the service?

It may have surprised some readers to learn in chapter 6 that confession and absolution are relatively new additions to the Liturgy. Luther did not include a rite for confession and absolution in either his 1523 Latin service or his 1526 German service. Some of the other most significant orders of service produced among Lutherans during the Reformation also did not include a confessional prayer and absolution statement.[218]

Worshipers do not need to wonder if they have received the full measure of God's grace if they attend a service that does not include a corporate confession and absolution. It is not merely a specific ritual that proclaims law and gospel, but the entire service! The customary song texts of the Liturgy collectively speak about our need for God's mercy and praise him for his grace for us in Christ. Scripture readings present us with a picture of law and gospel in the context of each service's specific emphasis. A proper Lutheran sermon is essentially a text-specific call to repent of our sins and a proclamation of Christ's forgiveness. One could argue that confession and absolution already takes place in the Communion portion of the Liturgy: The words we sing in the "Agnus Dei" plead for Christ's mercy and acknowledge that he takes away the sin of the world; then we tangibly receive his forgiveness in his body and blood, given to us in the sacrament.

Related to this myth about confession and absolution is a similar thought that proper preparation for the Lord's Supper suggests that a Communion service should include this rite. Once again, while this is a fine and worthy practice, we want to be careful that we do not turn it into liturgical law. An outward ritual of confession may be beneficial, but it is certainly not a required precursor to the sacrament. A humble and repentant heart, of course, *is* necessary to properly receive the sacrament. But a humble and repentant heart that looks to Christ for forgiveness is synonymous with faith! Luther points out in his Small Catechism that the one true preparation for the Lord's Supper is faith in Jesus' words and promise regarding the Supper:

> Who, then, is properly prepared to receive this sacrament?
>
> Fasting and other outward preparations may serve a good purpose, but he is properly prepared who believes these words: "Given" and "poured out for you for the forgiveness of sins."
>
> But whoever does not believe these words or doubts them is not prepared, because the words "for you" require nothing but hearts that believe.[219]

Even though we do not require that confession and absolution are present in every service, we realize the great blessing this practice is within the context of public worship. We also realize that some services have not included confession and absolution—including some of the most important services produced within our Lutheran heritage. Festive occasion services in our circles sometimes feature a responsive dialogue of Scripture passages in place of the customary Confession, Absolution, and "Kyrie." These responsive dialogues are meant to highlight the special focus of the day, sometimes even with thoughts of confession and absolution woven into their overall progression.

If you attend a service in which a rite for confession and absolution was not included, did you miss something? Did you leave church without forgiveness? Were you any less forgiven than a service that did include a formal ritual of confession and absolution? Of course not! God's grace is richly presented in so many ways in the Liturgy. A service without a formal confessional prayer and absolution statement still delivers God's grace in Scripture, sermon, song, and sacrament. We make no rules about a corporate confession and absolution, but we treasure the practice and encourage its use as one of many ways that God's grace is showered on us.

Myth #8: *Liturgical worship is a hindrance to evangelism.*

Our Lord Jesus has given his church two important tasks: reaching out to lost souls with the gospel and proclaiming that same gospel to strengthen the faith of God's people. The important tasks of outreach and nurture drive the mission of our congregations.

Unfortunately, sometimes these two proper emphases are pitted against each other. Pastors and congregations are thought to focus on one area at the expense of the other. Excelling in worship sometimes leads to an unfair accusation that a church doesn't care for the lost. Excelling in evangelism may also lead to the accusation that worship and faithfulness to Christian teaching aren't important in that congregation. These are unfair assumptions that spring out of a false dichotomy. Worship and outreach are equally important tasks of the church that work in harmony with one another.

One way this false dichotomy manifests itself is in the assumption that liturgical worship is a hindrance to evangelism. Some may be concerned that the ritual and ceremony of liturgical worship doesn't communicate well with the unchurched and may turn them off to Christianity before we even get a chance to share our faith with them. Some Lutherans, with a genuine concern for the lost, may see the many non-liturgical megachurches with full parking lots and auditoriums on Sunday and assume that the Lutheran Liturgy is deflecting people away from their churches to those other congregations.

On one hand, it is true that worship is meant especially for the believer. Worship is the regular gathering of God's people around the means of grace for their forgiveness and the strengthening of their faith. On the other hand, so much of worship's content—particularly liturgical worship—provides unchurched visitors with the very things their souls need! The truths of law and gospel are proclaimed in confession and absolution; the songs we sing echo the truths of Scripture; God's divinely inspired Word proclaims his grace and guidance; faithful preaching presents believer and unbeliever alike with the law's call to repent and the gospel's promise of forgiveness for Jesus' sake.

The Liturgy provides both Christian and non-Christians what they need to hear. Yes, it may be ideal to teach an unbeliever the basic truths of the faith in a Bible class before they experience public worship, but the simple reality of our day is that worship is the most common way for an unchurched person to learn more about a Christian congregation. Yes, we may prefer that a Bible class prepares someone for the sacrament before he or she attends a Communion service, but we realize that most guests will attend a service with the sacrament before they can commune. For that reason, we find clear and polite ways to explain our biblical practice of closed Communion and then invite them to study with us so that they too can participate in the Lord's Supper with us in the future.

The concern that the Liturgy is a hindrance to evangelism may reveal a way of thinking that assumes worship should do things it was never meant to accomplish. While the Liturgy supports outreach, it cannot replace the authentic evangelism work of the congregation. While the sermon proclaims the gospel, it cannot replace study time in God's Word that explores, learns, shares, and applies a wide range of biblical truths to those who have gathered for study. While God's Word always comforts the soul, a service cannot replace the work of pastoral counseling that personally applies God's grace and guidance to someone facing a difficult situation.

An interesting anecdote demonstrates the importance of letting worship accomplish its unique purpose. In 1995, Sally Morgenthaler wrote a book called *Worship Evangelism*. Her book promoted contemporary worship settings as congregations' best possible means for evangelism. She presented many "Worship Evangelism" seminars around the country. But in 2005, just a decade after the book was published, she stopped her presentations. One year later, her "Worship Evangelism" website was no longer publicly available. In a periodical article from 2007, she acknowledged that she was reconsidering her own perspectives on worship and evangelism. She realized that the approach she had once promoted was discouraging congregations from doing active evangelism work. Following her model, churches had turned evangelism into a Sunday morning activity and then failed to evangelize their communities the rest of the week. She wrote, "We have become convinced that the primary meeting place with our unchurched friends is now outside the church building."[220]

The myth that liturgical worship is not helpful for evangelism may also be driven by an assumption that people are drawn to congregations with a particular style of worship. The assumption that contemporary worship—a concept we'll discuss further in the final myth—is especially attractive to the unchurched seems reasonable, especially when one considers the large churches where services with Christian contemporary music are the norm. Yet research suggests this assumption is not correct. In a book called *Surprising Insights from the Unchurched*, Thom Rainer describes the unexpected data drawn from extensive interviews with 353 formerly unchurched people who had joined a congregation within two years of the survey. When these people were asked, "What factors led you to choose this church?" the top two answers given were the pastor and his preaching (90%) and the church's doctrine (88%). Worship and music style was the second-to-least given answer (11%).[221]

Lutherans base their practice on the truths and principles taught in Scripture, not on research statistics or poll results. But these results are very telling! There is no reason to think of liturgical worship as a hindrance to evangelism when new church members openly acknowledge that worship style was one of the least significant reasons they affiliated with a congregation.

Another source of insightful information comes from the WELS Leadership Forum, an event held in late 2008 sponsored by the WELS Board for Parish Services (now simply called Congregational Services). The forum studied the common characteristics of the 30 fastest growing con-gregations within the WELS. "Excellence in worship and relevance in preaching" was among the common traits of these growing congregations, but a specific worship style was not. A majority of congregations represented in the forum exhibited a strong commitment to liturgical worship done well.[222]

Recognizing that liturgical worship can support out-reach, Lutheran churches are wise to put their best foot forward in worship. Guests may not understand every-thing that happens the first time they visit your congrega-tion—and that's okay! A new visitor cannot be expected to grasp everything in worship any more than those who have never watched a specific sport can grasp the rules and intricacies of the game on their first viewing. But just as the crowd's enthusiasm sends a message about the sport and the team they support, so a congregation's enthusias-tic participation, friendliness, and sincerity send a strong and compelling message to first-time visitors and returning guests. A pastor's faithful message from the pulpit and the musicians' best efforts within the service also send a com-pelling message that worship is important!

Lutherans need not apologize for liturgical worship. Rather we offer our best efforts in worship to the glory of God and pray that he blesses those efforts for the benefit of members and guests alike.

Myth #9: *Liturgical worship is unattractive to younger generations.*

The discussion of the previous myth reminded us that use of God's Word within the Liturgy, especially law and gospel, ensures that our worship contains what is needed for nurturing believers and engendering faith in the unbeliever. The same can be said about different age groups. The law and gospel content of God's Word and the proper use of the sacraments ensure that our worship contains what is needed for people of all ages—from youth to adults, from grandparents to grandchildren.

An often expressed assumption about liturgical worship is that it is unattractive to younger generations, especially millennials. (The Pew Research Center defines millennials as those who were born between 1981 and 1996.)[223] While the atmosphere of liturgical worship may have varying degrees of formality and informality, nevertheless the culture of worship is quite different from the popular culture teens and young people live in each day. The music of worship is quite different from the music to which teens and millennials typically listen. Does this mean that the Liturgy will not be able to resonate with younger generations?

Thom Rainer, previously cited in this chapter, has also researched the perspectives of millennials. He and one of his sons are coauthors of a book titled *The Millennials: Connecting to America's Largest Generation*. Because of his research, he is often asked if millennials, as a group, have a preference toward a particular worship style. Many are surprised to hear his response: No! Millennials generally do not look at worship along the two-perspective dichotomy of traditional and contemporary. Rainer describes millennials' worship perspectives with these three points:

1. They desire the music to have rich content. They desire to sing those songs that reflect deep biblical and theological truths. It is no accident that the hymnody of Keith and Kristyn Getty has taken the millennials by storm. Their music reflects those deep, rich theological truths.

2. The millennials desire authenticity in a worship service. They can sense when congregants and worship leaders are going through the motions, and they will reject such perfunctory attitudes altogether.

3. This large generation does want a quality worship service, but that quality is a reflection of the authenticity noted above and adequate preparation of the worship leaders both spiritually and in time of preparation. In that sense, quality worship services are possible for churches of all sizes.[224]

Once again, it needs to be stated that our practice as Lutherans is determined by our theology, not research surveys. But once again, it benefits us to observe that liturgical worship is not a deterrent to young people, as many may assume. Rather *liturgical worship and preaching done well* will resonate with millennials—and many other generations too!

Every Sunday night at 9:30 P.M., a church in Seattle, Washington, offers a late evening Compline service. The service is almost entirely chanted by an unaccompanied men's choir, which sings from a back corner in the large cathedral. The dark church, illuminated by candles, and the otherwise silent sanctuary, filled with the sounds of chant, create an atmosphere that is quite unlike daily life in Seattle or any major United States city. Yet this quiet, late evening service is attended by hundreds each week— the majority of which are college students and young adults! This author attended one of the services sung by the Compline Choir.[225] While the music was peaceful and calming, the large crowd of young people was concrete and striking evidence that often held assumptions about younger generations' preferences are frequently myths.

The assumption that younger generations do not find certain forms of worship and styles of music attractive contributes to a practice in some churches to offer services in several different styles aimed at different demographic groups. While we can appreciate the concern for reaching the lost and retaining our youth that drives the concept, we may also rightly ask if this is the best practice for the church's worship life. Saint John's inspired picture of heaven depicts "a great multitude that no one could count, from every nation, tribe, people and language" (Revelation 7:9). Among those different groups mentioned by John are people from every generation throughout history! All of them, united despite their former earthly demographic differences, are gathered in heaven and engaged in thankful worship of their Savior.

Worship on earth will always be a dim reality and insufficient representation of worship in heaven, but doesn't Saint John's description of the heavenly gathering of God's people encourage us to reflect the same in our services as much as we can? How blessed we are if we find ourselves in a setting where multiple ethnicities and age groups worship together as the body of Christ, learning to know and love one another's music and poetry as expressions of their common faith! Michael Horton writes:

> We need to embrace diversity and cultivate both tolerance and discrimination. Far from being antithetical notions, these skills are twin virtues sired by wisdom. There will be people on both sides of the debate who will want to make this easy: Just accept the new or just reject it; style has to fit the culture of marketing or style has to fit the culture of a bygone era. . . . We have to reject the market segmentation that sets father against son and mother against daughter not for the sake of the gospel but for the sake of target marketing. And at the same time, we have to understand

our cultural habits. Some of these habits we may use to help us improve on the past, while others we will recognize as worldly accommodation of which we must repent. We will have disagreements about specific applications—and that is as helpful to future generations as it is frustrating for us. We cannot rush headlong into the future or hold nervously to the past. Those two options are no longer available to those who would be faithful today to God's drama of redemption.[226]

Rather than catering to assumptions that may not be correct, consider how we can encourage our younger members to be active and intentional participants in Lutheran worship. Include a unit on worship in Catechism instruction and youth Bible classes. Involve young people in worship at an early age, whether as acolytes, ushers, altar committee assistants, or musicians. Music is an especially ideal way for involving our younger members. Many are taking music lessons and participating in band or choir in high school and college. They are practicing their musical skills on a regular basis, and in many cases may be among the best musicians in a congregation! When we intentionally involve our younger members in public worship, we send them an important message: Not only is Lutheran worship for you, but we need in you Lutheran worship!

Myth #10: *Lutherans are against contemporary worship, or, Lutherans are in favor of contemporary worship.*

Have you ever been engaged with someone in a conversation in which you and the other person kept talking past one another? You tried to make your point in several different ways, but the other person never seemed to understand what you were saying. You listened carefully to what he was telling you, but you couldn't grasp his point. Sometimes that happens when two people are using the same word, but each person has a different definition in mind. When your vocabulary and definitions aren't the same, it is easy to talk past one another.

Christians can easily talk past one another in a discussion about contemporary worship and traditional worship. The reason for the confusion is simple: What does contemporary worship mean? What does traditional worship mean? A randomly chosen group of Lutherans would likely produce more definitions of these terms than the number of people in the group! Do these phrases describe an order of service? Do they refer to musical style? Do they define the era in which the service or its music was written? Or do they mean something else?

As the previous chapter noted, we create a false dichotomy and greatly limit our understanding of worship if we describe its content within the categories of two vaguely defined musical styles. An anecdote from another WELS pastor demonstrates this difficulty. A pastor who served a mission congregation outside the Midwest noticed that his church's services were described as two ways: Members of the community in which he was reaching out considered the congregation's worship to be traditional because the pastor wore vestments and the pattern of worship followed the Liturgy. WELS visitors from the Midwest described his congregation's service as contemporary because the musical settings of the liturgy were written in more recent years and were drawn from musical resources beyond the hymnal.[227]

A blanket statement that Lutherans are for or against contemporary worship is not possible when the expression embodies different definitions to different people. To assist us in this discussion, we will look at two common ways the terms *traditional* and *contemporary* are used: as descriptions of musical styles and as descriptions of the pattern or outline of the service.

When the phrase contemporary worship refers specifically to the *music* of the service, then the thoughts in the previous chapter would apply to our discussion. What words and message does the music support? Do the songs clearly proclaim the gospel or other important truths of Scripture? Does the musical style enable the congregation to participate and unite as a worshiping assembly? Does the music's style match well with the message it proclaims? Do the song texts edify the congregation, or are they more suited as someone's personal expression?

If the songs we sing reflect solid scriptural content, enable the congregation's involvement, and exhibit a fitting relationship between text and music, then the era in which the music was written need not be a significant concern. Some texts for public worship have been set to countless musical settings over many generations, past and present. The songs of the Liturgy—the "Kyrie," the "Gloria," the "Sanctus," and the "Agnus Dei"—continue to be published with new musical settings in our time. In many cases, these new musical arrangements of the Liturgy can be accompanied by the traditional sounds of organ, brass, and timpani or the contemporary sounds of pianos, guitars, woodwinds, and percussion, depending on a congregation's musical resources and abilities. Several services from *Christian Worship: Hymnal* and its digital resources were deliberately designed to support this type of musical flexibility, allowing the same melodies to be supported by the classic sounds of the organ or the fresh sounds of a modern ensemble. Various composers have treated traditional hymns in the same way, writing music that accompanies familiar hymns with new instrumentation.

We welcome new songs, sounds, and settings in Lutheran worship, but we also recognize that caution is in order any time we explore something that has not had the chance to stand the test of time. Music from past eras that has survived to our day has gone through the natural vetting process of history: Valuable contributions are retained for future generations, while songs of lesser quality are discarded. The vetting process that music from the past has experienced is a process we are living through as new music is tried and tested in public worship today. We are wise not to dismiss new songs out of hand, but we are also wise to be judicious about the modern musical selections we choose today.

Lutherans welcome the best of old and new music in worship. We send a message when edifying music from the past and present finds a home in Lutheran worship today: The holy Christian church spans time, and the range of our musical choices across different eras reflects that truth. Likewise, we send a message when edifying music from various places and cultures are used in Lutheran worship: The holy Christian church also spans across the globe, and we subtly confess that truth when we use music drawn from different places around the world.

Another common use of the phrase contemporary worship refers to a *form* or *pattern* for public worship. Previous chapters have explained the pattern of the Liturgy and the services of the Daily Office. In casual conversations, the Liturgy and Daily Office are often called traditional worship. In contrast, contemporary worship may be used to refer to nonliturgical services that follow a notably different pattern. When the terms are used in this way, it can be somewhat confusing, because liturgical, *traditional* services can still be done with modern musical compositions, and nonliturgical, *contemporary* services can still include traditional songs and hymns. Liturgical worship does not automatically assume historic music, and contemporary worship does not necessarily require contemporary music. Nevertheless, this terminology, which seems to describe to *time* and *style*, is often used to refer to worship *forms*.

For the sake of clarity, we will use the term *praise service* to refer to the definition of contemporary worship that focuses on its format or outline. The praise service is commonly used among Protestants and Evangelicals today. Although its outline is not as clearly defined as the services from the Liturgy and Daily Office are, there is a basic outline that can be observed throughout most Evangelical praise services.

- A praise service begins with several songs in sequence. Prayers and comments may be included among the songs.
- A variety of items may follow the opening group of songs, including special prayers, the offering, the distribution of bread and wine for the Lord's Supper, or other presentations that are unique for a specific Sunday.
- The opening songs and any items that follow lead up to the sermon. In these services, sermons are typically longer than those preached in Lutheran congregations, and their format is often closer to an informational Bible class than a proclamatory sermon. A focus on the Christian's life tends to predominate over the life and saving work of Christ.
- The sermon may be followed by a final prayer. The prayer is often an invitation to encourage worship-

ers to invite Jesus into their hearts, reflecting the decision theology professed by many Evangelicals.

• A final praise song frequently concludes the service.

The preceding description is not rigidly followed in every nonliturgical service among American Christians, but it is a basic, common outline for praise services.

As we compare the praise service format with the format of liturgical services, we note an important distinction. Liturgical services are built around the means of grace and gospel proclamation. The service includes absolution, three related Scripture readings, sung responses and songs from Scripture, gospel-centered preaching, a confession of faith in the triune God that echoes biblical truths, and the reception of Holy Communion. The congregation does respond to God's gospel gifts with prayer and praise throughout the service, but the majority of the service focuses on God's grace to us. The main purpose of worship is assumed to be proclaiming the gospel through God's Word and sacraments—*God to us.*

In contrast, praise services are built around a different assumption. In the praise service format, the purpose of worship is assumed to be *my praise to God* rather than *God's service to me.* Praise, prayer, and preaching that speaks to our sanctified Christian lives is the main emphasis of this worship format. The main purpose of worship is assumed to be our adoration of God—*us to God.*

The late Robert Webber (1933–2007) was a leading voice for worship renewal among Evangelical Christians. He once voiced his concern about the direction of worship among his Evangelical brothers and sisters in faith:

> I have attended many evangelical worship services in which the underlying drama of Christ's work has not been central and clear. I have longed to hear the words, "Christ has overcome all the powers of evil. Be at peace." But this message, the very central proclamation of the faith, is frequently missing. Often the service tells me what *I* have to do rather than celebrating what *Christ* has done. I'm told to live right, to witness, to get myself together, to forgive my enemies, and to give more money. But that's only part of the story. I also need to hear and experience the triumphant note that God has put away evil through his work in Christ. This is the word that gives me the peace of the Lord and stimulates me to offer my life in the service of Christ.[228]

Does this observation mean that it is inherently wrong to follow a form of worship that begins with several songs, offers an extended sermon, and concludes with a prayer and final song? No. We would become legalistic if we established a rule where Scripture has not. But when we understand the theological reasoning that led to the development of this type of service—focusing on our praise of God more than his service to us—we are wise to question the benefit of this form of worship among Lutherans who recognize a different purpose for worship.

A second quotation from an Evangelical voice will be helpful to emphasize this concern. Donald Hustad (1918–2013) was another leader in Evangelical worship. In the preface of a book about praise services, Hustad noted the theological assumptions behind this form of worship. His preface *discouraged* Christians with different theological beliefs from using praise service concepts in their public worship! Hustad wrote,

> Praise and worship music itself originated with the Charismatic Renewal Movement; all of the approaches identified in these chapters . . . are carefully devised according to

charismatic theology and Scripture interpretation and are expected to lead to characteristic pentecostal experiences. . . . Charismatic believers have a right to develop their own worship to match their own theology and exegesis, and they have done this well. *Noncharismatics should not thoughtlessly copy or imitate their worship formulae,* unless they expect to enter the same "Holy of Holies" in the same way. Instead, they *should develop their worship rationale based on their scriptural understanding, and then sing up to their own theology!*[229]

In chapter 4, we were introduced to the Latin phrase *lex orandi, lex credendi:* "The form of praying is the form of believing." That phrase conveys the truth that the way we pray—and by extension, the way we worship—reflects what we believe. Because worship is a direct reflection of our beliefs, we strive for worship forms that are built around those beliefs. Although the New Testament establishes no rules or laws about public worship, Lutherans are wise to use and adapt forms for public worship that are rooted in the means of grace. Let forgiveness be proclaimed richly! Let God's Word be read and preached generously! Let the blessings of Baptism be revisited regularly! Let the faith-strengthening sacrament of our Savior's body and blood feed our souls frequently! Let our forms of worship utilize these means of grace faithfully!

The discussion about these two frequently used meanings for contemporary worship show us why this matter isn't answered with a simple yes or no. We must first define what we mean so that two different people or groups are not talking past each another. We have discussed two common definitions, but someone might have something else in mind with the expression contemporary worship, and in Christian courtesy we should listen to what is meant before making any false assumptions. If the matter is about musical styles, we recognize that there are many fine musical contributions to the church in past and present generations, and we exercise a bit more caution with music that has not yet stood the test of time while not dismissing it simply because it is new. If the matter is about forms of worship, we recognize that forms are built on a set of beliefs, so we strive for forms that put God's gospel gifts of the means of grace at center stage in our public worship life.

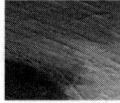

14

A Glossary of Worship Terms

If you enjoy watching or playing hockey, you know that there is terminology someone needs to know in order to understand the game. You need to know what is meant by icing, offside, faceoff, and power play. You need to know the difference between the wings, the defensemen, the center, and the goaltender. You need to know hockey's vocabulary.

If you follow local, state, or national politics, you also understand that knowledge of political terms is helpful as you follow the news. Knowing the meaning of terms like bipartisan, filibuster, primary, and slate will enable you to understand what political commentators are saying on radio and television.

The study of worship also presents us with a wide range of new vocabulary terms. You have encountered many of these terms throughout this book. What follows is a simple glossary of common worship terms that will be helpful as you read, learn, and discuss what you have learned about Christian worship.[230]

Absolution: An announcement of Christ's forgiveness to another person or an assembly of Christians.

Academic Robe: A black robe that was more commonly worn by some past generations of Lutheran ministers as a vestment; this style of a robe was the professional academic garb of medieval universities and is still worn today in graduation ceremonies and by judges presiding at a trial.

Adiaphora: A Greek word meaning "indifferent things," referring to anything that has not been commanded or forbidden by God in Scripture. Singular is *adiaphoron*.

Advent: The church season before Christmas, beginning four Sundays before Christmas Day and extending until Christmas Eve.

Agnus Dei: Latin for "Lamb of God," a penitential song based on John 1:29 sung just before the distribution of Holy Communion in the Liturgy.

Alb: The long, white robe traditionally worn by those presiding or assisting in the service.

Altar: The table in the front of the assembly that symbolizes Christ and his sacrifice, on which the bread and wine for the Lord's Supper are placed.

Altar Cloth: A linen cloth that covers the altar.

Ambo: The podium from which God's Word is read and preached. This term is especially used when a church has a single podium rather than a separate lectern and pulpit.

Anthem: A song sung by the choir.

Antiphon: A refrain sung with a psalm or canticle. Sometimes the term *antiphon* may be used to refer to a refrain that is only sung at the beginning and end of a psalm or canticle; in contrast, the term *refrain* may be used to indicate a refrain that is also sung within the psalm or canticle.

Antiphonal: The manner of singing a psalm or canticle responsively between two people or groups.

Ascension: The festival celebrating Jesus' triumphant return to heaven on the 40th day after his resurrection from the dead. (Easter Sunday is counted as the first of the 40 days.)

Benedicamus: Latin for "Let us praise the Lord." This statement, and the congregational response of "Thanks be to God," traditionally concluded the services of the Daily Office.

Benediction: Blessing.

Benedictus: The Latin title for the Song of Zechariah (Luke 1:68-79), the main song of praise in *Lauds* from the Daily Office.

Canticle: A prose song, often taken from biblical texts.

Cassock: A robe worn by clergy, often but not always black, and usually worn beneath a surplice.

Celebrant: The title for the minister who officiates at a service, especially at a service in which Holy Communion is celebrated.

Chalice: The cup of wine used for Holy Communion.

Chancel: The area in a church where the ministers are stationed during worship, in front of the assembly.

Chasuble: A poncho-shaped vestment worn over the alb and stole by the presiding minister at a service with Holy Communion.

Christmas: The day and season during which Jesus' birth is celebrated. Christmas Day is December 25. The Christmas season lasts 12 days, from December 25 to January 5.

Ciborium: The container in which Communion hosts (bread) are stored on the altar.

Collect: The historic name for the Prayer of the Day.

Compline: The late evening service from the Daily Office that was historically observed before going to sleep for the night.

Concertato: A festive arrangement of a hymn usually including participation by choir, congregation, organ, and other instruments.

Creed: A statement of faith. In the Liturgy, the congregation speaks a statement of faith in connection with the reading and preaching of God's Word, normally the Apostles' Creed or the Nicene Creed.

Crucifix: A cross on which the body of Christ is affixed or pictured.

Daily Office: The series of seven or eight daily prayer services that originated in medieval monasticism.

Doxology: A short statement of praise, usually addressed to the triune God, often the last stanza of a hymn.

Easter: The day and season during which Jesus' resurrection is celebrated. Easter Day occurs on the first Sunday after the first full moon in spring. The season lasts for seven full weeks.

Easter Vigil: A ceremony-rich service on Easter Eve that celebrates Jesus' resurrection from the dead.

End Time: The name given to the last four weeks of the Church Year in *Christian Worship: A Lutheran Hymnal*, during which worship focused especially on preparation for the end of the world and Christ's return on judgment day. Even though this is the regular emphasis at the end of the Church Year, a formal seasonal title for these weeks was unique to *Christian Worship: A Lutheran Hymnal* (1993). Most other hymnals, including *Christian Worship: Hymnal* (2021), incorporate this emphasis into the end of the Pentecost season.

Epiphany: The day that Christians remember the visit of the Magi to the boy Jesus (Matthew 2:1-12), and the season of the Church Year in which Christians remember the different ways Jesus reveals himself to us as our Savior and God.

Epistle: A letter in the New Testament, specifically the books from Romans to Jude in traditional New Testament sequence. In the Liturgy, this term is sometimes used to refer to the Second Reading in the service, which is usually an excerpt from one of the letters of the New Testament.

Eucharist: Another name for the Lord's Supper, drawn from the New Testament's word for "thanksgiving."

Eucharistic Prayer: A prayer of thanksgiving for the Lord's Supper spoken during a Communion service.

Flagon: The pitcher in which the wine for Communion is stored on the altar.

Font: A large stand with a water basin at which baptisms are conducted.

Geneva Robe: Another name for the academic robe.

Gloria in Excelsis: The Latin title for the main song of praise near the beginning of the Liturgy, "Glory to God in the highest."

Good Friday: The Friday before Easter Sunday, on which Christians commemorate Jesus' death.

Gospel: The good news about Jesus Christ, our Savior. In the Liturgy, the word refers to the third reading in the service, drawn from one of the four Gospels in the New Testament: Matthew, Mark, Luke, or John.

Gospel Acclamation: A Bible verse framed with Alleluias (except during the season of Lent) used as an acclamation before the reading of the Gospel in the Liturgy.

Gradual: The historic name for the Gospel Acclamation.

Holy Week: The seven days before Easter Sunday.

Invocation: The words spoken at the beginning of the Liturgy that first were spoken to us in Holy Baptism: "In the name of the Father and of the Son and of the Holy Spirit."

Kyrie: A Greek word meaning "Lord," referring to the phrase "Lord, have mercy," often prayed near the beginning of the Liturgy.

Lauds: A prayer service at sunrise from the Daily Office.

Lectionary: The system of readings from Scripture used for Sundays and festivals during the Church Year.

Lectern: The podium from which God's Word is read.

Lent: The 40-day season, excluding Sundays, from Ash Wednesday to Holy Saturday, during which Christians emphasize God's call to repentance for our sins and God's grace in the sacrificial death of Jesus Christ for sinners.

Litany: A lengthy responsive prayer, often with a repeating refrain spoken or sung by the congregation.

Liturgy: An order of worship developed and adapted throughout Christianity which centers on the use of God's Word and sacraments.

Magnificat: The Latin title for the Song of Mary (Luke 1:46-55), the main song of praise in Vespers from the Daily Office.

Matins: A prayer service held early in the morning before sunrise from the Daily Office.

Maundy Thursday: Thursday of Holy Week, on which Jesus instituted the Lord's Supper. Also called Holy Thursday.

Narthex: The gathering space, lobby, or entrance adjacent to the nave of a church building.

Nave: The portion of a worship space where the main congregation is gathered.

None: A prayer service from the Daily Office, held at 3:00 P.M.

Nunc Dimittis: First Latin words of the Song of Simeon (Luke 2:29-32), a song historically connected with Compline from the Daily Office and sometimes used after the distribution of Holy Communion in the Liturgy.

Officiant: The title for the minister who presides at a service, especially a wedding or funeral.

Ordinary: The portion of the Liturgy that remains the same from service to service, especially the five texts known by their Greek or Latin titles: "Kyrie," "Gloria in Excelsis," "Credo," "Sanctus," and "Agnus Dei."

Paraments: The colored cloths on the furnishings in the chancel that symbolize the seasons and festivals of the Church Year.

Paten: The plate used to hold the Communion hosts (bread) distributed during Holy Communion.

Pax Domini: Latin for "The peace of the Lord." This is an abbreviation for the statement, "The peace of the Lord be with you always," traditionally spoken by the minister before the congregation sings the *Agnus Dei* in the Liturgy, prior to the reception of Holy Communion.

Pentecost: The seventh Sunday after Easter Day, which concludes the Easter season and celebrates the coming of the Holy Spirit on the early Christian church (Acts 2); also the general season of the Church Year that begins on Pentecost Day and extends through the remainder of the Church Year.

Pericope: A selection from a Scripture book, especially one to be read on a specific Sunday or occasion.

Preface: The opening responses of the Sacrament (Holy Communion) portion of the Liturgy.

Presider: An abbreviated term for "presiding minister."

Presiding Minister: The title for the minister who presides in public worship, especially at liturgical services.

Prime: A prayer service from the Daily Office held just before the start of a day's work.

Proper: The Scripture readings and other texts that change in an order of service based on the occasion being celebrated.

Pulpit: The podium from which the sermon is preached.

Purificator: A cloth used to wipe the rim of the chalice after people drink from it.

Rubrics: The directions for conducting a service. In many hymnals, the rubrics are printed in red.

Sanctuary: The worship space. In some worship traditions, the sanctuary refers only to the chancel.

Sanctus: Latin for "holy," referring to the song of praise during the Holy Communion portion of the service based on Isaiah 6:3 and Matthew 21:9.

Sext: A prayer service from the Daily Office, held at noon.

Stole: The long, colored scarf worn by a pastor over his shoulders as a symbol that he has been ordained into the public ministry.

Surplice: A white robe, looser than an alb, meant to be worn over a cassock.

Te Deum Laudamus: The Latin title of the main song of praise from *Matins*, "We Praise You, O God."

Terce: A prayer service from the Daily Office, held at 9:00 A.M.

Triduum: A Latin word meaning "three days," usually referring to the services of Holy Thursday (Maundy Thursday), Good Friday, and Holy Saturday (Easter Eve).

Verse of the Day: Another name for the Gospel Acclamation.

Vespers: The prayer service from the Daily Office held at sunset.

Vestments: The special clothing worn by ministers while presiding and assisting in a service.

Words of Institution: The words of Jesus establishing Holy Communion, compiled from Matthew 26:26-28; Mark 10:22-24; Luke 22:19,20; and 1 Corinthians 11:23-25.

Conclusion

From one perspective, this book has barely scratched the surface on the topic of Christian worship. From another perspective, we have considered so many different factors about worship that it is hard to summarize our study into a few concluding thoughts. But as our study concludes, it is beneficial for us to review and remember the most important truths about public worship. These truths will guide us as we make practical decisions for the worship life of our local congregations. To guide our closing thoughts, we refer to three quotations from the Apology of the Augsburg Confession to help us review the fundamental truths of public worship.

Christian worship is more than a set of traditions, rituals, and readings. Worship accomplishes so much more than enabling us to remember Jesus or praise him. Worship presents us with the blessings of his grace. God's Word does not merely relate the historical events of Jesus' death and resurrection; it also delivers God's forgiveness and

Jesus' righteousness into our hearts. The Lord's Supper is not simply an action during which we remember Jesus; it is also our reception of the very body and blood he gave and shed, and the Spirit's application of Christ's forgiveness to us at the same time. In other words, worship is not just a trip down memory lane! Worship brings Christ's gifts, won for us in the past, to us today. Speaking about the Lord's Supper, the Apology of the Augsburg Confession states,

> Remembering Christ is not the useless celebration of a show. It is not something set up for the sake of example, as the memory of Hercules or Ulysses is celebrated in trage-dies. Rather, it is remembering Christ's benefits and receiv-ing them through faith, to be enlivened by them.[231]

Christ is present with his gathered people as they con-nect to him through the means of grace! His Holy Spirit works in the Word and sacraments to enliven and enrich our faith in Jesus. As counterintuitive as this may sound, in public worship we primarily *receive* God's gracious gifts:

> God wants Himself to be known, He wants Himself to be worshiped, so that we *receive benefits from Him* and receive them because of His mercy, not because of our merits.[232]

Consider the gifts you *receive* in Christ's Word and sac-raments. The burden of sin is lifted from your heart. In its place, you receive Christ's righteousness and forgiveness. The uncertainty of your status before God is replaced with faith in the Son of God who loved you from eter-nity, redeemed you by his sacrifice, and assures you of your place at his side for all eternity. As the Holy Spirit sustains your faith in Christ through his gospel gifts, you are truly enabled to worship God!

A third quotation from the Apology shows us how faith—in this example, the faith of the sinful woman who came to Jesus in sincere repentance (Luke 7:36-50)—is the greatest form of worship:

> The woman came with the opinion that forgiveness of sins should be sought in Christ. *This worship is the highest worship of Christ.* She could think nothing greater about Christ. To seek forgiveness of sins from Him was truly to acknowledge the Messiah. To think of Christ this way, to worship Him this way, to embrace Him this way, is truly to believe.[233]

So public worship is first *receiving* of God's gifts of forgiving grace. But when we consider the great gifts of God that he delivers in his Word and sacraments, we are naturally inspired to worship him—both with our collective prayers and praise in public worship and lives that glorify him in word and deed for his rich grace. In other words, public worship inspires and enables our daily lives of worship. The good news that we proclaim inspires our praise to God.

May the gracious gifts of God in Christ inspire us to treasure corporate worship for the great blessings it provides our souls! May the gracious gifts of God in Christ inspire us to glorify him with daily lives of worship! May the gracious gifts of God in Christ inspire us to give our best efforts to his glory as we plan and carry out corporate worship for the benefit of Christ's people!

Endnotes

[1]Portions of this chapter are based on lecture outlines prepared by James Tiefel for worship classes at Wisconsin Lutheran Seminary and for the WELS School of Worship Enrichment, a regional weekend worship seminar offered by the WELS Commission on Worship. Tiefel served as professor at Wisconsin Lutheran Seminary from 1985 to 2020.

[2]The nontraditional names for worship used in this paragraph were based on actual names for worship used in advertising by a few Christian churches around the United States.

[3]Carl L. Lawrenz and John C. Jeske, *A Commentary on Genesis 1-11* (Milwaukee: Northwestern Publishing House, 2004), pp. 204-206.

[4]Martin Luther, *Luther's Works,* edited by Jaroslav Jan Pelikan and Helmut T. Lehmann, American Edition, Vol. 35 (St. Louis: Concordia Publishing House; Philadelphia: Fortress Press, 1955–1986), p. 254.

[5]Stephen Geiger, "Exegetical Brief: Colossians 3:16—Teaching and Admonishing with Music," *Wisconsin Lutheran Quarterly,* Vol. 109, No. 1 (Winter 2012), pp. 53-57.

[6]Several of the biblical worship principles in chapters 2-4 of this book are similar to the principles described in chapter 3, "The

Principles of Lutheran Worship," and chapter 4, "Lutheran Worship Principles and *Christian Worship*," of *Christian Worship: Manual*, edited by Gary Baumler and Kermit Moldenhauer (Milwaukee: Northwestern Publishing House, 1993), pp. 21-66.

[7]Francis Pieper, *Christian Dogmatics*, Vol. 3 (St. Louis: Concordia Publishing House, 1953), p. 106.

[8]*Luther's Catechism: The Small Catechism of Dr. Martin Luther*, (Milwaukee: Northwestern Publishing House, 2017), p. 9.

[9]The Large Catechism, Part 4, Baptism: 44, *Concordia: The Lutheran Confessions*, edited by Paul T. McCain, 2nd ed. (St. Louis: Concordia Publishing House, 2006), p. 427.

[10]*Luther's Works*, Vol. 36, p. 59.

[11]Apology of the Augsburg Confession, Article XIII (VII): 4, *Concordia: The Lutheran Confessions*, p. 184.

[12]*Christian Worship: Hymnal* (Milwaukee: Northwestern Publishing House, 2021), pp. 168,186,202.

[13]The Large Catechism, Part 5, The Sacrament of the Altar: 12-14, *Concordia: The Lutheran Confessions*, pp. 432,433.

[14]The Large Catechism, Part 5, The Sacrament of the Altar: 23,24,27, *Concordia: The Lutheran Confessions*, pp. 434,435.

[15]*Luther's Works*, Vol. 53, p. 11.

[16]Augsburg Confession, Article XXIV: 1,2,9: *Concordia: The Lutheran Confessions*, pp. 47,48.

[17]*Luther's Works*, Vol. 53, pp. 47,48.

[18]Bengt Hagglund, *History of Theology*, (St. Louis: Concordia Publishing House, 1968), pp. 239,240.

[19]*Luther's Works*, Vol. 13, p. 168.

[20]*Luther's Works*, Vol. 53, pp. 323,324.

[21]*Luther's Works*, Vol. 53, pp. 315,316.

[22]This is the translation used in *Christian Worship: Hymnal* for "The Service," Setting Two (pp. 176,177) and Setting Three (pp. 191-193).

[23]*Luther's Works*, Vol. 53, p. 30.

[24]Luther D. Reed, *The Lutheran Liturgy*, revised edition (Philadelphia: Fortress Press, 1960), p. 261.

[25]Frank C. Senn, *Christian Liturgy: Catholic and Evangelical* (Minneapolis: Fortress Press, 1997), p. 184.

[26]Reed, *The Lutheran Liturgy*, pp. 262,263.

[27]Reed, *The Lutheran Liturgy*, p. 252.

[28]The Small Catechism, Morning Prayer, *Concordia: The Lutheran Confessions*, p. 344.

[29]Reed, *The Lutheran Liturgy*, p. 253.

[30]Thomas O'Loughlin, *The Didache: A Window on the Earliest Christians* (London; Grand Rapids: Society for Promoting Christian Knowledge; Baker Academic, 2010), p. 170.

[31]Reed, *The Lutheran Liturgy*, p. 256.

[32]Senn, *Christian Liturgy*, p. 352.

[33]*Christian Worship: Hymnal*, p. 154,172,188.

[34]*Luther's Works*, Vol. 31, p. 25.

[35]Senn, *Christian Liturgy*, p. 121.

[36]Reed, *The Lutheran Liturgy*, pp. 268,269.

[37]Alexander Roberts, James Donaldson, and A. Cleveland Coxe, editors, *The Ante-Nicene Fathers, Volume VII: Fathers of the Third and Fourth Centuries: Lactantius, Venantius, Asterius, Victorinus, Dionysius, Apostolic Teaching and Constitutions, Homily, and Liturgies* (Buffalo, N.Y.: Christian Literature Company, 1886), p. 478.

[38]Reed, *The Lutheran Liturgy*, p. 274.

[39]John O'Brien, *A History of the Mass and Its Ceremonies in the Eastern and Western Church* (New York: The Catholic Publication Society Co., 1881), pp. 205,206.

[40]Reed, *The Lutheran Liturgy*, p. 273.

[41]*Luther's Works*, Vol. 53, pp. 23,72.

[42]Senn, *Christian Liturgy*, pp. 69,70.

[43]Senn, *Christian Liturgy*, pp. 139,140.

[44]Reed, *The Lutheran Liturgy*, pp. 279,282,283.

[45]Reed, *The Lutheran Liturgy*, p. 281.

[46]Reed, *The Lutheran Liturgy*, pp. 490,492.

[47]Reed, *The Lutheran Liturgy*, p. 288. Like many statements in a brief overview of the Liturgy such as this book, this summary of the development of the liturgical readings' pattern is an oversimplification. For example, in *The Sunday Lectionary: Ritual Word, Paschal Shape* (Collegeville, Minn.: The Liturgical Press, 1998), Normand Bonneau points out the varying customs in the

ancient church, in which different regions had the tradition of three, four, five, or even six readings (p. 12).

[48]*Luther's Works*, Vol. 35, p. 254.

[49]Reed, *The Lutheran Liturgy*, p. 264.

[50]Reed, *The Lutheran Liturgy*, p. 295.

[51]Reed, *The Lutheran Liturgy*, p. 295.

[52]O'Brien, *A History of the Mass*, p. 221.

[53]Senn, *Christian Liturgy*, p. 187.

[54]Reed, *The Lutheran Liturgy*, pp. 299,300.

[55]F. Bente, *Historical Introductions to the Symbolical Books of the Evangelical Lutheran Church* (St. Louis: Concordia Publishing House, 1965), p. 13.

[56]Bente, *Historical Introductions to the Symbolical Books*, pp. 10-13.

[57]Reed, *The Lutheran Liturgy*, p. 303.

[58]Senn, *Christian Liturgy*, p. 185.

[59]Reed, *The Lutheran Liturgy*, p. 311.

[60]The Large Catechism, Part 5, The Sacrament of the Altar: 70, *Concordia: The Lutheran Confessions*, p. 439.

[61]Philip H. Pfatteicher. *Commentary on the Lutheran Book of Worship: Lutheran Liturgy in Its Ecumenical Context* (Minneapolis: Augsburg Fortress, 1990), pp. 158,159.

[62]Reed, *The Lutheran Liturgy*, pp. 325-328.

[63]Pfatteicher, *Commentary on the Lutheran Book of Worship*, p. 161.

[64]*Luther's Works*, Vol. 53, p. 21. Emphasis added.

[65]C. F. W. Walther, *Pastoraltheologie* (1897), pp. 170f, quoted in Arnold Koelpin, "The Sacramental Presence in the Theology of the Synodical Conference," *Our Great Heritage*, Vol. 3 (Milwaukee: Northwestern Publishing House, 1991), p. 284.

[66]Text authored by Johnold J. Strey, edited by the Rites Committee of the WELS Hymnal Project, and included in The Service, Setting Three in *Christian Worship: Hymnal*, p. 201. The Prayers of Thanksgiving from the other two settings of The Service (pp. 168,185) are abbreviated and adapted from ancient Eucharistic prayers.

[67]*Christian Worship: Hymnal*, pp. 168,186,202.

[68]*Luther's Catechism: The Small Catechism of Martin Luther*, p. 14.

[69]Quoted in Arnold Koelpin, "The Sacramental Presence in the Theology of the Synodical Conference," pp. 283,284.

[70]Justin Martyr, "The First Apology of Justin," in *The Ante-Nicene Fathers,* Vol. I, *Apostolic Fathers with Justin Martyr and Irenaeus* (Buffalo, N.Y.: Christian Literature Company, 1885), p. 185.

[71]*Luther's Works,* Vol. 53, pp. 28,29.

[72]Reed, *The Lutheran Liturgy,* p. 368.

[73]Pfatteicher, *Commentary on the Lutheran Book of Worship,* p. 189.

[74]*Luther's Works,* Vol. 38, p. 123.

[75]Reed, *The Lutheran Liturgy,* p. 374.

[76]*Christian Worship: Hymnal,* pp. 170,187,203.

[77]Armin W. Schuetze and Irwin J. Habeck, *The Shepherd under Christ: A Textbook for Pastoral Theology* (Milwaukee: Northwestern Publishing House, 1974), p. 94.

[78]Reed, *The Lutheran Liturgy,* p. 377.

[79]Reed, *The Lutheran Liturgy,* p. 381.

[80]*Christian Worship: Hymnal,* p. 170.

[81]Reed, *The Lutheran Liturgy,* p. 388.

[82]J. H. Maude, *The History of the Book of Common Prayer,* edited by Leighton Pullan, Oxford Church Text Books, Second Edition (London: Rivingtons, 1900), p. 54.

[83]O'Loughlin, *The Didache: A Window on the Earliest Christians,* p. 166.

[84]Lucien Deiss, *Springtime of the Liturgy,* translated by Matthew J. O'Connell (Collegeville, Minn.: Liturgical Press, 1979), pp. 150-153.

[85]Pfatteicher, *Commentary on the Lutheran Book of Worship,* pp. 343,344.

[86]Reed, *The Lutheran Liturgy,* p. 389.

[87]Pfatteicher, *Commentary on the Lutheran Book of Worship,* pp. 343-345.

[88]Pfatteicher, *Commentary on the Lutheran Book of Worship,* p. 344.

[89]Reed, *The Lutheran Liturgy,* p. 389.

[90]Reed, *The Lutheran Liturgy,* p. 390.

[91]*Luther's Works,* Vol. 53, pp. 37,38.

[92]*Luther's Works,* Vol. 53, pp. 68,69.

[93]Pfattiecher, *Commentary on the Lutheran Book of Worship*, pp. 347-348.

[94]This Scripture quotation and several others that follow in this chapter are taken from the translation used in *Christian Worship: Hymnal*.

[95]Reed, *The Lutheran Liturgy*, p. 409.

[96]Pfatteicher, *Commentary on the Lutheran Book of Worship*, p. 375.

[97]Pfatteicher, *Commentary on the Lutheran Book of Worship*, p. 417.

[98]*Luther's Works*, Vol. 34, pp. 201,202.

[99]J. Dowden, "Te Deum Laudamus," edited by George Harford, Morley Stevenson, and J. W. Tyrer, *The Prayer Book Dictionary* (New York: Longman, 1912), p. 777.

[100]Reed, *The Lutheran Liturgy*, pp. 416-418.

[101]Pfatteicher, *Commentary on the Lutheran Book of Worship*, p. 367.

[102]Reed, *The Lutheran Liturgy*, pp. 428,429.

[103]Hippolytus of Rome, *The Treatise on the Apostolic Tradition of St. Hippolytus of Rome, Bishop and Martyr*, pp. 50,51.

[104]Pfatteicher, *Commentary on the Lutheran Book of Worship*, p. 353.

[105]Pfatteicher, *Commentary on the Lutheran Book of Worship*, p. 358.

[106]Pfatteicher, *Commentary on the Lutheran Book of Worship*, p. 363.

[107]Pfatteicher, *Commentary on the Lutheran Book of Worship*, p. 365.

[108]Pfatteicher, *Commentary on the Lutheran Book of Worship*, p. 371.

[109]Pfatteicher, *Commentary on the Lutheran Book of Worship*, pp. 368,370.

[110]*Christian Worship: Hymnal*, pp. 226,246.

[111]Pfatteicher, *Commentary on the Lutheran Book of Worship*, pp. 371,372.

[112]Deiss, *Springtime of the Liturgy*, pp. 221,222.

[113]Pfatteicher, *Commentary on the Lutheran Book of Worship*, p. 372.

[114]Pfatteicher, *Commentary on the Lutheran Book of Worship*, p. 373.

[115]Normand Bonneau, *The Sunday Lectionary*, p. 6.

[116]"The First Apology of Justin," in *The Ante-Nicene Fathers*, p. 186.

[117]Bonneau, *The Sunday Lectionary*, pp. 12,13.

[118]*Luther's Works*, Vol. 53, p. 23,24.

[119]Reed, *The Lutheran Liturgy*, p. 290.

[120]*Christian Worship: Manual*, p. 381.

[121]Lizette Larson-Miller, "Christmas Season," in *The New Dictionary of Sacramental Worship,* edited by Peter E. Fink (Collegeville, Minn.: The Liturgical Press, 1990), p. 209.

[122]Senn, *Introduction to Christian Liturgy* (Minneapolis: Fortress Press, 2012), p. 109.

[123]Senn, *Christian Liturgy,* p. 162.

[124]Larson-Miller, "Christmas Season," p. 209.

[125]Senn, *Introduction to Christian Liturgy,* p. 110.

[126]Senn, *Christian Liturgy,* p. 190.

[127]Robert Webber, 176, "The Advent Wreath," in *The Services of the Christian Year,* Vol. 5 of The Complete Library of Christian Worship (Nashville: Star Song Publishing Group, 1994), p. 131.

[128]Translation from "Great O Antiphons of Advent" in *Christian Worship: Altar Book* (Milwaukee: Northwestern Publishing House, 1999), p. 175.

[129]Larson-Miller, "Christmas Season," p. 206.

[130]Senn, *Introduction to Christian Liturgy,* pp. 113,114.

[131]Larson-Miller, "Christmas Season," p. 205.

[132]Larson-Miller, "Christmas Season," p. 207.

[133]Senn, *Christian Liturgy,* p. 161.

[134]Senn, *Introduction to Christian Liturgy,* pp. 116,117.

[135]Reed, *The Lutheran Liturgy,* pp. 479,480.

[136]Larson-Miller, "Christmas Season," p. 207.

[137]Larson-Miller, "Christmas Season," p. 207.

[138]Senn, *Christian Liturgy,* p. 160.

[139]Larson-Miller, "Christmas Season," p. 208.

[140]Senn, *Christian Liturgy,* p. 161.

[141]Larson-Miller, "Christmas Season," p. 208.

[142]Reed, *The Lutheran Liturgy,* p. 490.

[143]Senn, *Introduction to Christian Liturgy,* p. 123.

[144]Larson-Miller, "Lent," in *The New Dictionary of Sacramental Worship,* p. 681.

[145]Senn, *Introduction to Christian Liturgy,* p. 123.

[146]Larson-Miller, "Lent," pp. 683,684.

[147]*Luther's Works,* Vol. 53, p. 24.

[148]Senn, *Introduction to Christian Liturgy,* p. 125.

[149]Larson-Miller, "Lent," p. 683.

[150]Larson-Miller, "Lent," p. 684. Also Reed, *The Lutheran Liturgy*, p. 498.

[151]Senn, *Introduction to Christian Liturgy*, pp. 135,136.

[152]John F. Baldovin, "Liturgies of Holy Week," in *The New Dictionary of Sacramental Worship*, p. 549.

[153]Neil Alexander, "An Introduction to Worship from Easter to Pentecost," in *The Services of the Christian Year*, p. 373.

[154]Richard N. Fragomeni, "The Easter Season," in *The New Dictionary of Sacramental Worship*, pp. 375,378.

[155]Fragomeni, "The Easter Season," pp. 376-378.

[156]*Sermon Studies on the Epistles, ILCW Series A*, edited by Ernst H. Wendland and John A. Trapp (Milwaukee: Northwestern Publishing House, 1986), pp. 215,216.

[157]Reed, *The Lutheran Liturgy*, p. 519.

[158]Bonneau, *The Sunday Lectionary*, p. 162.

[159]Senn, *Introduction to Christian Liturgy*, p. 154.

[160]Reed, *The Lutheran Liturgy*, p. 569.

[161]Senn, *Introduction to Christian Liturgy*, p. 152.

[162]Senn, *Introduction to Christian Liturgy*, pp. 154,155.

[163]Reed, *The Lutheran Liturgy*, p. 566.

[164]Reed, *The Lutheran Liturgy*, p. 561.

[165]Portions of this chapter are based on two previously published articles by the author: "Proclaiming the Gospel in Worship," *Wisconsin Lutheran Quarterly*, Vol. 105, No. 4 (Fall 2008), pp. 248-284, and "Worship and the Right Brain," *Worship the Lord* (a bimonthly newsletter for pastors from the WELS Commission on Worship), No. 79 (July 2016).

[166]William F. Arndt, Wilbur Gingrich, Frederick W. Danker, and Walter Bauer, *A Greek-English Lexicon of the New Testament and Other Early Christian Literature: A Translation and Adaption of the Fourth Revised and Augmented Edition of Walter Bauer's Griechisch-Deutsches Worterbuch Zu Den Schrift En Des Neuen Testaments Und Der Ubrigen Urchristlichen Literatur* (Chicago: University of Chicago Press, 1979), p. 777.

[167]Bessel van der Kolk, *The Body Keeps the Score: Brain, Mind, and Body in the Healing of Trauma* (New York: Penguin Books, 2014), p. 44.

[168]David P. Kuske, "Exegesis of 1 Corinthians 11:3-16," *Wisconsin Lutheran Quarterly*, Vol. 78, No. 2 (April 1981), pp. 101,102.

[169]Herbert Norris, *Church Vestments: Their Origin and Development* (New York: E. P. Dutton, 1950), pp. 8,9,17.

[170]Norris, *Church Vestments*, pp. 15-17.

[171]Norris, *Church Vestments*, pp. 88,89.

[172]John D. Laurance, "Liturgical Vestments," in *The New Dictionary of Sacramental Worship*, p. 1306.

[173]Norris, *Church Vestments*, pp. 55-62.

[174]Norris, *Church Vestments*, p. 70.

[175]*Christian Worship: Manual*, p. 101.

[176]Apology of the Augsburg Confession, Article XXIV (XII): 3,4, *Concordia: The Lutheran Confessions*, p. 220.

[177]*Luther's Works*, Vol. 53, pp. 323,324.

[178]*Luther's Works*, Vol. 34, p. 205.

[179]*Luther's Works*, Vol. 49, p. 68.

[180]*Luther's Works*, Vol. 35, p. 254.

[181]Anna B. Warner (1827–1915).

[182]The first five questions in this list are adapted slightly from *Text, Music, Context: A Resource for Reviewing Worship Materials* (St. Louis: Commission on Worship, The Lutheran Church—Missouri Synod, 2004), pp. 6,7.

[183]Much of the information that follows is based on T. David Gordon, *Why Johnny Can't Sing Hymns: How Pop Culture Rewrote the Hymnal* (Phillipsburg, N.J.: P & R Publishing, 2010), pp. 79-93.

[184]James Tiefel, "The Formation and Flow of Worship Attitudes in the Wisconsin Evangelical Lutheran Synod," *Not Unto Us: A Celebration of the Ministry of Kurt J. Eggert* (Milwaukee: Northwestern Publishing House, 2001), p. 154.

[185]Paul Westermeyer, *Te Deum: The Church and Music* (Minneapolis: Augsburg Fortress, 1998), p. 120.

[186]Paul S. Jones, *Singing and Making Music: Issues in Church Music Today* (Phillipsburg, N.J.: P & R Publishing Company, 2006), p. 173.

[187]Tiefel, "The Devil's Tavern Tunes," *Wisconsin Lutheran Quarterly*, Vol. 97, No. 2 (Spring 2000), p. 147.

[188]Joseph Herl, *Worship Wars in Early Lutheranism: Choir, Congrega-*

tion, *and Three Centuries of Conflict* (New York: Oxford, 2004), p. 21.

[189]*Luther's Works,* Vol. 53, p. 289.

[190]Jones, *Singing and Making Music,* p. 172.

[191]*Luther's Works,* Vol. 53, p. 316.

[192]Augsburg Confession, Article XXIV: 1,34, *Concordia: The Lutheran Confessions,* pp. 47,49.

[193]Apology of the Augsburg Confession, Article XXIV (XII): 1, *Concordia: The Lutheran Confessions,* p. 220.

[194]*Christian Worship: Manual,* pp. 30-32.

[195]*Christian Worship: Manual,* p. 32.

[196]Tiefel, "The Formation and Flow of Worship Attitudes," pp. 145-151.

[197]Philip Schaff and David Schley Schaff, *History of the Christian Church,* Vol. 2 (New York: Charles Scribner's Sons, 1910), pp. 272,273.

[198]Schaff and Schley Schaff, *History of the Christian Church,* Vol. 2, p. 271.

[199]Schaff and Schley Schaff, *History of the Christian Church,* Vol. 7 (New York: Charles Scribner's Sons, 1910), pp. 379-382.

[200]Schaff and Schley Schaff, *History of the Christian Church,* Vol. 7, pp. 382-384.

[201]Schaff and Schley Schaff, *History of the Christian Church,* Vol. 7, p. 382.

[202]The Small Catechism, Morning Prayer, Evening Prayer, *Concordia: The Lutheran Confessions,* p. 344.

[203]*Luther's Works,* Vol. 14, p. 61.

[204]*Luther's Works,* Vol. 22, p. 122.

[205]*Luther's Works,* Vol. 53, p. 102.

[206]Strey, "Proclaiming the Gospel in Worship," p. 263.

[207]Strey, "Proclaiming the Gospel in Worship," pp. 264,265.

[208]Senn, *Christian Liturgy,* pp. 586-589.

[209]Senn, *Christian Liturgy,* p. 588.

[210]Harry G. Archer and Luther D. Reed, editors, *The Chorale Service Book* (Philadelphia: General Council Publication Board, 1901).

[211]Luther Reed (*The Lutheran Liturgy,* p. 176, footnote 9) and Frank Senn (*Christian Liturgy,* p. 591, footnote 76) both indicate that

the 1906 edition of *Evangelical Lutheran Hymn-Book* uses the 1901 musical setting of the Common Service from *The Chorale Service Book* without any citation.

[212]James Brauer, "Trusty Steed or Trojan Horse? The Common Service in the *Evangelical Lutheran Hymn-Book*," Logia: A Journal of Lutheran Theology, Vol. XIV, No. 3 (Holy Trinity, 2005), pp. 26-29.

[213]Tiefel, "The Formation and Flow of Worship Attitudes," pp. 152,153. This article states that the musical setting of the Common Service in the Wisconsin Synod's 1917 *Book of Hymns* is the setting from the 1901 *Chorale Service Book*. However, the setting in *Book of Hymns* is the same as that from the 1912 edition of the *Evangelical Lutheran Hymn-Book*. This error likely derives from the fact that the 1906 edition of the *Evangelical Lutheran Hymn-Book* uses the music from the *Chorale Service Book*, but the 1912 edition used the primarily German music setting which later appeared in the Wisconsin Synod's *Book of Hymns* and then again in *The Lutheran Hymnal* of 1941. The lack of proper citations in the various editions of *Evangelical Lutheran Hymn-Book* likely contributed to this confusion.

[214]This information is gleaned from a note written by Gervasius W. Fischer (1895–1958), a WELS pastor who served as the secretary of the Subcommittee on Liturgics for *The Lutheran Hymnal*. Fischer wrote this note inside the cover of the souvenir copy of *The Lutheran Hymnal* that he received as a gift for his work on the committee. James Tiefel, professor of worship at Wisconsin Lutheran Seminary from 1985 to 2020, has a copy of this handwritten note in his possession, given to him by Fischer's family members. After listing the members of the subcommittee, Fischer wrote, "The music of Liturgy herein is not that which we recommended. Committee favored Gregorian tones to English chants, also that the music be not printed with the Liturgy to allow for greater variety of melodies to be used. Music for liturgy was to be printed in a special section of book. Committee favored some form of Eucharistic Prayer."

[215]Erwin L. Lueker, editor, *Lutheran Cyclopedia* (St. Louis: Concordia, 1975), pp. 120,121.

[216]Paul Grime, "*The Lutheran Hymnal* after Seventy-Five Years: Its Role in the Shaping of *Lutheran Service Book*," *Concordia Theological Quarterly*, Vol. 79, No. 3-4 (July/October 2015), p. 205.

[217]Bryan Gerlach, "Variety: Stewardship for Gospel Impact," *Worship the Lord*, No. 39 (November 2009), p. 2.

[218]Senn, *Christian Liturgy*, p. 588.

[219]*Luther's Catechism: The Small Catechism of Martin Luther*, p. 14.

[220]Daniel Leyrer, "Worship as Evangelism: A Guru Changes Her Tune," *Wisconsin Lutheran Quarterly*, Vol. 104, No. 4 (Fall 2007), pp. 301,302.

[221]Thom Rainer, *Surprising Insights from the Unchurched* (Grand Rapids: Zondervan, 2001), p. 21.

[222]WELS Leadership Forum, November 16-18, 2008.

[223]http://www.pewresearch.org/fact-tank/2018/03/01/defining-generations-where-millennials-end-and-post-millennials-begin/, accessed July 2, 2018.

[224]https://thomrainer.com/2014/04/worship-style-attracts-millennials/, accessed July 2, 2018.

[225]Trinity Sunday, June 15, 2014. A podcast of these services is available at https://complinepodcast.org/.

[226]Michael Horton, *A Better Way: Rediscovering the Drama of God-Centered Worship* (Grand Rapids: Baker, 2002), p. 187.

[227]This anecdote comes from Pastor Jonathan Hein, who served Beautiful Savior Lutheran Church in Summerville, South Carolina, from 1999 to 2017. Since 2017, Pastor Hein has served full-time as the director of the WELS Commission on Congregational Counseling.

[228]Webber, *Worship Is a Verb: Eight Principles for Transforming Worship* (Peabody, Mass.: Hendrickson, 1992), p. 34.

[229]Barry Liesch, *The New Worship: Straight Talk on Music and the Church* (Grand Rapids: Baker Books, 1996), p. 10. Emphasis added. Quoted by Bryan Gerlach in "The Role of Music in Worship: An Evaluation of Two Twentieth-Century Developments," *Logia: A Journal of Lutheran Theology*, Vol. 14, No. 3 (Holy Trinity, 2005), p. 55.

[230]The "Glossary of Liturgical Terms" from Senn's *Introduction to Christian Liturgy*, pp. 223-230, was used as a starting point for the development of this book's glossary.

[231] Apology of the Augsburg Confession, Article XXIV (XII): 72, *Concordia: The Lutheran Confessions*, p. 231.

[232] Apology of the Augsburg Confession, Article IV (II): 60, *Concordia: The Lutheran Confessions*, p. 90. Emphasis added.

[233] Apology of the Augsburg Confession, Article V (III): 33 (154), *Concordia: The Lutheran Confessions*, p. 106. Emphasis added.

Scripture Index

Subject Index